the Innovation Handbook

The world is changing rapidly.
Businesses which apply innovative ideas
and technologies can benefit from new
markets and drive economic growth.
How can we help? By operating as a
catalyst. By providing leadership.
By connecting partners and investing
in new ideas. Our vision: a world where
the UK is an innovation leader and a
magnet for innovative businesses.
Join us in meeting the challenge.

Technology Strategy Board
Driving Innovation

www.innovateuk.org

the Innovation Handbook

How to develop, manage and protect your most profitable ideas

Consultant editor: Adam Jolly

KOGAN
PAGE

London and Philadelphia

Publisher's note

Every possible effort has been made to ensure that the information contained in this book is accurate at the time of going to press, and the publishers and authors cannot accept responsibility for any errors or omissions, however caused. No responsibility for loss or damage occasioned to any person acting, or refraining from action, as a result of the material in this publication can be accepted by the editor, the publisher or any of the authors.

First published in Great Britain and the United States in 2008 by Kogan Page Limited

120 Pentonville Road
London N1 9JN
United Kingdom
www.koganpage.com

525 South 4th Street, #241
Philadelphia PA 19147
USA

ISBN 978 0 7494 5318 3

British Library Cataloguing-in-Publication Data

A CIP record for this book is available from the British Library.

Library of Congress Cataloging-in-Publication Data

Jolly, Adam.
   The innovation handbook : how to develop, manage, and protect your most valuable ideas / Adam Jolly.
      p. cm.
   ISBN 978-0-7494-5318-3
   1. Creative ability in business—Management. 2. Technological innovations—Management.
3. Industrial property—Management. I. Title.
   HD53.J65 2008
   658.4'063—dc22
                                                              2008020778

Typeset by JS Typesetting Ltd, Porthcawl, Mid Glamorgan
Printed and bound in Great Britain by Bell & Bain Ltd, Glasgow

The intellectual property specialists

Consult

Global offices

Australia (liaison)
China
Hong Kong
Indonesia
India
Philippines
Thailand
United Arab Emirates
UK
USA (liaison)
Vietnam

Protect

Commercialise

+44 (0)20 7536 4100

+44 (0)1865 318 400

enquiries@iprights.com

www.iprights.com

Enforce

 rouse & co. international

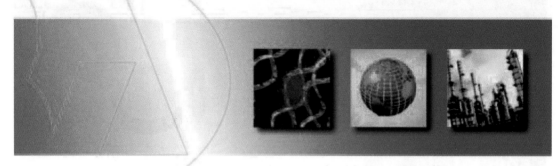

**Patents – Trade marks – Designs – Copyright
UK and European Patent Attorneys**

Bawden and Associates is a firm of patent and trade mark attorneys and provides professional legal services and management consultancy on the identification, development, valuation and defence of Intellectual Property (IP) portfolios for our clients on a UK, European and global basis.

Our attorneys have many years' experience managing the offensive and defensive aspects of IP in industry and practice across the chemical and petrochemical industries, life sciences including pharmaceuticals, biotechnology and medical devices and the mechanical, energy, process engineering and high technology sectors.

Our philosophy is to work as partners with our clients to provide a high quality and timely service at attractive rates to create and utilise business-relevant IP.

The Company:

- High professional quality
- Productivity and timeliness
- Business understanding and focus
- Personal tailored approach
- Attractive and transparent fees

The Philosophy:

- IP with real value
- Maximum utilisation of attorney time giving high quality expertise at highly competitive professional rates
- Speed of service delivery
- Ready integration with client
- High quality administrative staff with high levels of productivity and commitment

Peter Bawden:
4 The Gatehouse, 2 High Street, Harpenden, Hertfordshire, AL5 2TH, UK
Telephone: +44 (0)1582 466700
Facsimile: +44 (0)1582 466709
Email: pb@bawden.co.uk

Stephen Geary:
Noneley Hall, Noneley, Wem, Shropshire, SY4 5SL, UK
Telephone: +44 (0)1939 238820
Email: stepheng@bawden.co.uk

Website: www.bawden.co.uk

bawden
and associates

Contents

changing
the way
forward
in diabetes

There are many ways a company can help fight the growing worldwide diabetes epidemic. Novo Nordisk was a founding member of the Oxford Health Alliance to raise awareness and promote health care and prevention of diabetes around the world. We also support the World Diabetes Foundation in helping to provide essential care and treatment for people everywhere, especially in developing countries.

But to be a leader in the fight against diabetes also means living up to high ideals as we go about our business. In the way we base decisions and actions on their impact to society and the environment as much as to the welfare of our own people and to growth and profitability. And in our commitment to continue investing not only in the development of new therapies, but in helping to find a cure. Because we think the best way to lead is by example. As a model of the difference one company can make, we can change the way forward in diabetes.

novo nordisk®

Microsoft

Imagine ERP and CRM software that your people can actually use.

Microsoft Dynamics™ is business software that works like Microsoft® Office.

Find out more at **www.everyonegetsit.co.uk**

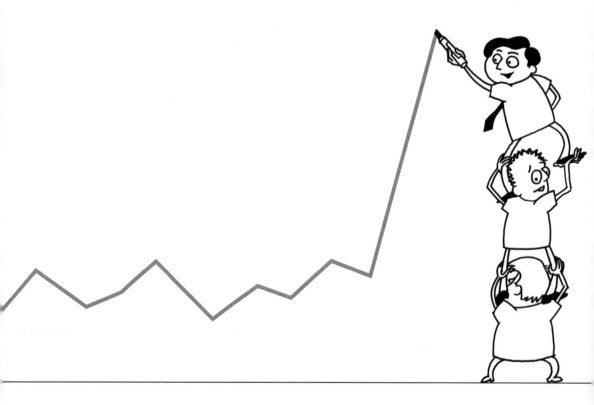

Microsoft Dynamics™

ALBA
innovation
CENTRE

Alba Innovation Centre - the premier incubation facility for the next generation of high growth potential, innovative, start-up technology companies.

One of the leading business incubators for innovative technology businesses in Scotland, the Centre provides a unique combination of specialist business innovation support and flexible incubation space, with critical connections to people who can make a real difference.

Tailored incubation solutions include:

Innovation Advisory Support – delivered by the Centre's in-house team of experienced advisors and complemented by a network of external specialists and entrepreneurs, our specialist advice is tailored to help young technology businesses **launch** and **grow their business**

Accommodation – offering **high quality,** modern, office accommodation, on **flexible** terms under a single monthly licence fee. **Virtual Office Packages** are also available.

Facilities and Services – state-of-the-art facilities and services including high speed internet access, a wireless network, full reception services (including a 9am-5pm manned telephone answering service) and conference and meeting room facilities.

Alba Innovation Centre is operated by Innovation Centres Scotland Ltd.
For further details contact:
Alba Innovation Centre,
Alba Campus, Livingston EH54 7GA
Tel: 01506 592 100
Email: alba@innovationcentre.org
Web: www.innovationcentre.org/alba

Alba Innovation Centre is part of

Edinburgh Science Triangle
www.edinburghsciencetriangle.com

LOCATION, LOCATION, LOCATION
By Barry Shafe, Project director, Edinburgh Science Triangle

LOCATION, location, location. Where you base your business could be more critical than you think to its long-term survival and success.

From the first 'Eureka' moment in the lab, workshop or garage (where Google, Microsoft and Hewlett-Packard all started life), many companies will naturally take root initially in their founder's home town.

But before long, the owners must decide whether this is the best location to access the infrastructure, resources and relationships they will need to grow and develop the business to its full potential.

Staying innovative

Most technology-based businesses are born from a specific innovation that is new to the market at that time. But to stay ahead of the competition and to be able to enter new markets, they must continue innovating and advancing their products and services.

To do this, the company's research and development team will usually benefit from collaborating with an appropriate university department or research institute, perhaps on a short-term consultancy or even a longer-term research project, or often just for access to specialised – and generally very expensive – scientific equipment.

Location is crucial here because being close to the university or institute, or even on the campus itself, will help to build the best relationship possible, both in terms of breeding fresh, innovative thinking and providing convenient access to specialist facilities.

Finding and keeping the best people

A growing business will require an increasing number of qualified and experienced staff. The choice of location will have a major bearing on the company's access to an appropriate talent pool and its ability to retain staff.

The best supply of talent for any specialism in terms of both quality and quantity is generally available where universities have a renowned track record and where a corresponding cluster of large and small companies has developed leading to the creation of a sector hotspot.

This ensures a continued supply of fresh graduates and postgraduates. Critical mass in the industry also provides real career development opportunities, which are vital to retaining the best talent in the area.

Lifestyle considerations are as important in location choice as academic reputation and commercial requirements. The most attractive locations will offer a pleasant working environment and proximity to both rural and urban areas, giving employees a choice of lifestyle. If a city is a popular destination for arts, culture and entertainment, it is also likely to be a more desirable place to live and work.

Gaining competitive advantage through relationships

For practical and cost reasons, being near to market, or supply of raw materials, used to be the primary factor in determining the optimum business location.

Today, for knowledge-based companies, competitive advantage is less about cost and more about gaining technology, market and customer insight before the competition. Being the first to market with new features and benefits may be critical for business growth and sustainability.

To achieve this, most successful companies thrive on formal and informal collaborative partnerships with complementary businesses that provide strong links to the target market or underlying technologies.

Whilst we work increasingly online and in virtual groups, time has proven that there is no substitute for real contact with people when relationships are important, and hence co-location with the company's first choice of partners is highly desirable.

All the infrastructure you need

Back to basics: every business needs suitable transport links to reach partners, suppliers and customers, so the ideal location should provide good road, rail, sea and air network linking it nationally and overseas.

As the world continues to shrink, a well-connected international airport is especially important for any business looking beyond its domestic shores.

The level and scope of business support on offer in a chosen location can also have an important influence on company prospects. Business advice and capacity-building initiatives from local and national economic development agencies can make a big difference to "time on project" – the proportion of working time that core staff are able have to spend on core work.

By providing vital help with essential but distracting tasks and functions such as finding facilities, people and partners, these initiatives release key members of the team to focus the business development priorities of innovation and commercialisation in the market. However there can be a wide variation in the range and quality of business support offered from one location to the next, so it pays to do some research first.

The same is true of finance. Funding in the form of grants and soft loans is often available to support business starts and growth initiatives, and especially innovation projects. Some funds are available anywhere, while often others are location specific. Being close to a financial services centre and investor community is a valuable advantage to be considered for the future.

The availability of professional services including legal, accountancy and corporate finance is another important consideration in location choice. As the business grows, it is likely to demand professional support at a higher level and some cities offer more choice than others of firms with the requisite skills and sector experience.

Freedom to grow

A growing business often requires the freedom to move into bigger premises at relatively frequent intervals. This can be hampered by restrictive terms, and if a move is over any significant distance, then there may be serious staff consequences - for individuals and for the whole business.

If growth is envisaged, it is important to know what options will be available in the future, as well as to meet the immediate requirements of the company.

Science parks

Science parks offer a unique combination of factors making them a first-choice for innovative, growing businesses.

- Flexible accommodation: a range of properties with flexible terms to facilitate moves include managed space; multi-occupancy buildings designed to support both laboratories and offices; dedicated buildings for single occupancy companies or plots for bespoke design and build
- Use of shared facilities: saving time and cost. Access is also often available for science park tenants to university resources that may be otherwise restricted
- Business support and advisory services: these can include the best possible incubation support for young businesses with great innovations but who need help to plan and implement the first steps to market.

Sustainability...and the right image

In short, the right location can influence how effectively, efficiently and quickly your business succeeds. Choosing wisely will not only help you deliver maximum impact in your market, but will set the foundations for sustainable future growth.

Finally, the right address on your letterhead will speak volumes about the quality and reputation of your business. Get this right and you will automatically inspire confidence in your customers, partners and shareholders, now and in the future.

About the author

Barry Shafe is Project Director of the Edinburgh Science Triangle.
Email: *barry.shafe@edinburghsciencetriangle.com*

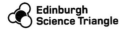

The **Edinburgh Science Triangle partnership** is a collaborative project that brings together the economic development and knowledge exchange agendas of universities and research institutes, science parks including commercial developers, the local government authorities of Edinburgh and the Lothians, and Scottish Enterprise. The twin objectives of the initiative are to attract new mobile investment to the Edinburgh Science Triangle area, and to build a scientific community with unparalleled levels of collaboration between academic research and industry.

PROFILE: Edinburgh Science Triangle

The **Edinburgh Science Triangle** area is one of Europe's leading science and technology locations and a thriving centre of excellence for technology transfer and knowledge exchange. The University of Edinburgh is ranked in Europe's top six alongside Cambridge, Oxford and London and with other universities and world-renowned research institutes makes Edinburgh a world-influencer in life sciences, informatics, micro- and opto-electronics, energy and many specialist disciplines. It is especially well-positioned to exploit the 21st century trend towards technology convergence.

Edinburgh Science Triangle is home to a "super-campus" of multiple science parks and incubation centres designed to accommodate and support innovative companies at every life stage. All the sites are within 30 minutes of each other, the vibrant city centre and the well-connected international airport, and their combined space places **Edinburgh Science Triangle Parks** amongst the 20 largest in the world.

Edinburgh has won many tourism and cultural accolades as one of the world's favourite cities. The whole city centre is a World Heritage site and hosts the world's largest cultural festival every August. The highly-qualified workforce enjoys an enviable quality of life and easy access to Scotland's great outdoors – in 2007 Edinburgh was named the best place to live in the UK. The city has the most prosperous economy and more FTSE-100 companies than any other area outside London and is the sixth most important financial centre in Europe and second in the UK.

In 2008 the authoritative Financial Times' *FDI Magazine* ranked Edinburgh the leading European Small City of the Future. It is, of course, the inspiring capital of Scotland, also ranked by *FDI Magazine* as the Best European Region for investment. Edinburgh is consistently voted "Favourite UK city" and "One of the World's Top Ten Cities" by the global travel industry.

Significant public investment for the future is underway across the Edinburgh City Region, including the creation of Edinburgh BioQuarter, a landmark £600m life science real estate development next to Edinburgh Royal Infirmary; the Easter Bush Research Consortium (EBRC), one of the largest groups focussed on the biology and health of companion and production animals in the world; and a new £42m purpose-built Informatics Forum at The University of Edinburgh. A new tram network offering fast, reliable, accessible and environmentally-friendly transport is being implemented in the city and the development of Edinburgh's Waterfront is the second largest regeneration programme in Europe.

Universities & Research Institutes
1. University of Edinburgh (UofE) Central Area
2. Kings Buildings (UofE)
3. Medical School (UofE)
4. Queen's Medical Research Institute (UofE)
5. Scottish Centre for Regenerative Medicine (UofE)
6. Royal (Dick) School of Veterinary Studies (UofE)
7. The Roslin Institute (UofE)
8. Heriot-Watt University
9. Napier University
10. Queen Margaret University
11. Moredun Research Institute
12. Scottish Agricultural College
13. Heriot-Watt School of Textiles & Design

Teaching/Research Hospitals
a. Edinburgh Royal Infirmary
b. Royal Hospital for Sick Children ('Sick Kids')
c. Royal Hospital for Sick Children ('Sick Kids') - relocation
d. Western General Hospital
e. Easter Bush Veterinary Centre (Animal hospitals)

Science Parks & Incubators
A. Edinburgh BioQuarter life science park
B. Edinburgh Technopole
C. Pentlands Science Park
D. Roslin BioCentre
E. BioCampus
F. Heriot-Watt Research Park
G. Alba Campus
H. Alba Innovation Centre
I. Institute for Systems Level Integration
J. Innotek Centre
K. Elvingston Science Centre
L. Edinburgh Technology Transfer Centre (ETTC)
M. ETTC BioSpace
N. Scottish Microelectronics Centre
O. ProspeKT Centre (Informatics)

advertisement feature

Creating markets for scientific enterprise and the role of UK Science Parks

By Robin Daniels

The UK excels in basic research. British academics are responsible for around 11% of all published papers globally each year and, up until the Second World War, were recipients of around 20% of all Nobel Prizes. Many of the great scientific and technological strides made in the last hundred years are due, in large part, to British innovation.

Take a look at the last fifty years and the picture is not so rosy. Today barely 8% of Nobel Prizes come our way and countless surveys point out that businesses in the UK are not spending enough time or money on innovation. In the 21st century, the UK's inventive capability does not translate into the effective commercial exploitation of science. The perennial comparison of productivity and levels of innovation with the US never makes comfortable reading for politicians, business or academia. That said, macro measures of economic output do, of course, often mask significant individual success stories. The rise and market dominance of technology businesses like chip designer ARM or software company Autonomy are rightly cited as evidence that, here in the UK, we have all the ingredients necessary to take new technologies to global markets. - just not enough of them.

Scale is one obvious advantage that the US has over most other countries. American technology businesses have a huge domestic market, including the world's largest national defence budget. More importantly, though, they have been consciously innovating for a long time. Silicon Valley, for example, is remarkable for its very strong social and operational networks coupled with access to a well informed and vigorous venture capital community. When, some time ago, I asked a senior Stanford academic what was the secret of their success, I was told simply; "we started thirty years ago".

So it takes time, but we have the raw materials – strong science, bright people, access to markets and London, Europe's financial centre. What we must do now is to bring these strengths into alignment. We must make a market.

Define the supply side

Successive government policies have too often been designed to support "Science and Technology", or "Research and Development", treating these as if they all mean the same thing; as if they are exclusive and automatic sources of innovation. The result is that "innovation support" usually consists of making substantial amounts of funding available for research and that, by comparison, very little is done to promote or facilitate the actual process of commercialising new ideas. The reality, the art, of innovation is more complex and more varied than this. The quality of UK science is the foundation stone, on which our economic success depends. The translation of that into commercial reality must be given equal weighting.

Build markets and bolster market access

What makes innovation profitable is having customers who demand innovative products, services, processes.

What makes innovation possible is having access to innovative suppliers, staff, and universities. This is about making a market which supports the transfer of innovation between "players" – universities and businesses, SMEs and global companies, suppliers and clients.

This market does not generally operate well in UK and the failure to recognize and address this is a major failure in the prevailing political mindset of the last thirty years. Cambridge is perhaps an exception to this given the social, co-investment, supply-chain and related networks that have been developed since the early 1980's.

Develop the skills for innovation

A developing market for innovation means that the market for relevant skills also develops. Of great importance is the provision of innovation and entrepreneurship training for researchers – in both universities and companies. Whilst much emphasis is placed on providing such training in schools and for undergraduates, it is unlikely that many recipients will be in a position to put any of this learning into practice immediately. Training post-doctoral researchers or PhD students, by comparison, means that innovation and industrial relevance is applied at the sharp end.

Align research with the market

The Research Assessment Exercise, or RAE, measures the performance of academics and universities according to the number of 'peer reviewed' publications produced. The higher the RAE rating, the more public money goes to the university next time around. This is a pretty powerful incentive to publish. Little wonder that the UK delivers such a disproportionately high percentage of research papers every year. Since we don't measure the practical applicability of that research in the same way, we don't always get it. A revision of the RAE cannot mean any move away from explicit support for the best quality basic research – simply that innovation and enterprise should feature too. It's worth noting that the most commercially successful academics also produce the highest quality research.

Put new technology to work

The demand side of the innovation market is the ultimate judge of new science and technology. The establishment, development and growth of sustainable businesses that will provide increasing numbers of high value jobs, is the most robust measure of both research relevance and market effectiveness. Given the changing shape of manufacturing in the UK and the necessary shift up the value chain, it is crucial to our long term competitiveness that robust technology is pulled through into the market as effectively as possible.

The UK Government has a crucial role to play in accelerating the exploitation of emerging technologies.

US Government departments with significant R&D spend are mandated to put a small proportion of this the way of American SME's. The 'Small Business Innovation Research' (SBIR) program consequently injects between $1.5 and $2 billion each year into the R&D base. In the UK such a model would provide a powerful incentive for SMEs to innovate and introduce a crucial 'pull through factor' to the market.

Hot-house market development - the Science Park

Over the last twenty years the number of UK science and research parks has increased to the point where, by 2004, there were over seventy established parks with a further eleven under development. These parks are now home to around 2,600 tenant companies, turning over £5.5 billion annually and employing almost 70,000 people (UKSPA, 2004). While the origin and development of each park is shaped by the local scientific and economic environment, there are a number of common features. Typically, a science park will:

- Include, or have as a partner, a local university
- Provide a link between academic and commercial activity
- Be principally focused on the provision of business 'incubation' space and larger premises for more established companies.
- Provide services appropriate to the needs of young, technology-based, businesses.

Underpinning the operation of almost all UK science parks is a business plan based on real estate. What usually makes a science park profitable and, therefore, sustainable is maximising the space available for tenant companies and then attracting and retaining those tenants.

The economic benefits of improving the efficiency and effectiveness of technology transfer and commercialisation is now well documented. What is less clear is the extent to which a business plan focused predominantly on real estate can deliver the economic growth required. Those parks with a particularly intimate relationship with the local university have begun to emerge as particularly effective means of establishing an ecosystem, which directly supports translational research and commercial interaction. One such park is in Manchester.

In his report 'Third Generation Science Parks' Professor John Allen, Chairman of

Manchester Science Park, describes six factors as being "common and critical" to the future evolution of science parks:

- A global player, but with local roots.
- A part of the community, with care for people and the environment.
- A healthy business and an opportunity for investment.
- An essential element of university activity.
- Part of a multiplicity of networks.
- Focused on the needs of its tenants.

It is clearly well beyond the capability of the average estate agent to deliver such facets alone. Well run real estate is, therefore, necessary but not sufficient.

Creating a market for scientific enterprise

Science parks are uniquely positioned to engineer and develop the conditions and the market for the commercial development of scientific invention and innovation. By linking supply and demand – and providing both with appropriate accommodation and connectivity – the science park provides the opportunity to create a micro-cluster which, with care, delivers real economic impact for the locality, the region and the country.

Accelerated evolution

John Allen's summary of what the science park of the future should be is a challenging vision. However, it helps to define a real opportunity, taken up by only a handful of science parks so far, to become real hubs of innovation; to connect up the supply and demand sides of the market, to move beyond being exercises in real-estate to create hot-houses for technology entrepreneurship and corporate engagement. Those locations that include a good university, strong research institutes, business incubation facilities and links to established firms have all the component parts necessary to bring about a transformation in the UK's exploitation of science and technology. Science parks provide a physical proximity for players in the market; they can form the basis of a growing sense of community – of a commonwealth of complementary capabilities. Above all, with strong leadership, they have the opportunity to catalyse a new industrial revolution for the UK – one that will ensure that we can continue to pay for the world-class research that underpins the whole endeavour.

Dr Robin Daniels is CEO of the Norwich Research Park – Europe's largest single-site life science cluster and the UK's largest science park.

NORTHERN IRELAND
SCIENCE PARK

Transforming dreams into commercial reality

Patents and the Start-Up Entrepreneur

Introduction

Patents are complex things. Fraught with difficult language and concepts, patents are an attempt to strike the right balance between two competing interests -

- the wider societal need to spread economic change quickly
- and the individual's instinct for secrecy and reward for invention/risk-taking.

Inventors in the corporate world or in universities will have ready access to professional help. But for the lone inventor/entrepreneur, they may be forgiven for mistaking their situation as one of splendid isolation.

This article aims to help the new single entrepreneur think his/her way through the process and to point the way to local resources willing to help.

Visualise

To help visualise the thought processes, imagine building a house. Before acquiring the land, you must consider its aspect and geography. You also need to be sure that you can build what you want on it. Is this to be your own dream house or one you will build for others? If the latter, how might they use it? Will you sell title for a lump sum or rent it out? Or will you retain title for a long period?

Similarly, it's the same for IP. Such myriad considerations will influence your thinking and that of your lawyer. That's why communication between the two of you is paramount to a good project outcome.

As a start-up, you are likely to be rich with ideas and knowledge but poor in cash. You are not likely to have much personal capital. You are not likely to be a good bet for a High Street bank. You might be entitled to some government grants... but if you take them now, you might be ineligible in the future for tax breaks.

So while money may come from friends and family, you are likely to be seeking cash from a Business Angel or an early venture capital fund. Good IP is the collateral of these key early stage investors. So how do you build up the IP without going bankrupt?

The beginning

Early decisions will impact your choices for the life of the project. You need to get it as right as you can.

First and foremost, keep a good, dated and confidential record of all your ideas and tests. There is nothing to beat dated entries in a laboratory-style notebook. It's even better if key ideas and results are notarised by a patent lawyer so that the dialogue can begin early as to the protection and exploitation strategy. Keep it safe!

As the idea forms, check for originality. Do this yourself! It is very straightforward in principle, especially with the internet, but there is still a significant skill required. Remember this is different from intellectual originality. IP is written for those "skilled in the art" and can be deliberately obfuscating. Likewise the concept of "obviousness" is different from common usage. It is worth checking your data base and your skill by trying to find patents and other IP you know exists, before relying on your ability for real in an unknown search.

Even if you find similar work, don't despair. The patents will give you some good ideas and connections to follow up. Your idea might still have business value and the patents can help guide you.

Once you're sure the idea is new and that there is business merit, check out your local development agency. Often there are grants to help prove a concept or to produce and file a patent or to produce a prototype. 'Additionality' means you can't get the money after you've done it, so check first.

Another source of early support comes from business plan competitions. Well run competitions will not prejudice your IP and will give lots of mentoring and other non-threatening support.

For example, the CONNECT movement, spawned in San Diego but now global, formalises the altruistic streak in the high tech business community of a region and your local team will be a good source of help.

Prepared for patent?
Now you have your idea and some notion of the business space into which you wish to go. How do you get some protection?

Copyrights, design rights and trade marks are much cheaper and long lasting than are patents but not as powerful, nor as valued by the investor community. However, even when a patent is to be involved, associating the invention with a trade mark or logo can be very effective – witness Dolby or DVD etc.

Patents are not to be entered into lightly. If you need a patent, then think it all through again. They are expensive and complicated. They offer valuable rights but also contain onerous obligations. They will be made public globally and will bring your work to the attention of others, who may have more resources.

The new entrepreneur should work closely with a skilled patent agent if at all possible.

Patent basics

The patent must contain sufficient descriptions of the invention, its construction and uses to cover all the possible ways in which it might be brought to market or provide economical improvement. It must have no errors of fact or science, yet it can contain reasonable extrapolations not necessarily demonstrated. During the work with your patent lawyer, be prepared to go back to the bench to check a point or to add some additional scope or claim. The world of invention and business is full of patent successes and failures all based on getting this part right.

The Wright Brothers couldn't patent flight - principally due to the existence of birds and Leonardo Da Vinci. They were, however, the first to recognise that powered flight needed control of the wing's aerofoil shape but they only patented their method of providing it (wing warping).

As is obvious today, this method was soon superseded by flaps and ailerons. So the Wrights' patent was not nearly as powerful as their achievement.

Putting a price on IP

If you are an expert in the field of the patent, you might well have a good idea how much it's worth but, if not, how can you tell?

It can be helpful to look at similar patents around the world. Search the internet for the inventors and their organisations and addresses. Look them up in learned journals.

Try to see behind the words and, especially, try to determine who is funding their work. A picture may emerge which allows you to infer the value and to suggest a plan of action.

Remember, the business value may not be a product or service directly for sale to the public. Sometimes the technology of a new process may be just as important. Some years ago the main supporters of computer generated holography were the big car companies hoping to cut months or even years from new car design to showroom times.

You will be in a 'Dragon's Den' situation without the cameras and not for sport. The more you know about the impact of what you've done and what you're proposing, the better off you will be.

When patent is filed... the clock is ticking!

You have only the time it takes to examine and a further year before big decisions are needed and the costs rise steeply.

This is the Patent Cooperation Treaty (PCT) stage and you will need to decide in which countries you wish to file. There is a cost per country (in the region of a few hundred pounds per patent office and per year) and more importantly potential challenges in each country.

Each national and supranational examiner comes fresh to challenge the patent and even if granting was successful in the home country, success at PCT is not automatic. Also to drop a patent just because you can't fund it at this stage can be worse than not ever filing because some international companies are constantly on the alert for dropped filings as the technology becomes free.

A business strategy for a patent is needed from the outset and here follows some thoughts to guide you.

Patents: benefits to the start-up entrepreneur

A good patent describes a business space from which you may exclude all others in order for you to manufacture or charge them for the privilege of use. It obviously has a value to you as the budding entrepreneur. It may also have a value to others in the business space as an adjunct to their patents and it may have value to those under infringement attack as defence.

This value represents your (only) collateral and at this early stage will secure any funds you might get from Business Angels or from Venture Funds.

Patents: manufacturing

The classical exploitation of a patent's monopoly is by manufacture – the making of an embodiment of the invention. This can be less straightforward than it sounds because the patent does not convey an automatic right of manufacture. The product, you want to make, may need access to someone else's IP. It is well worth another search to make sure that you are in clear blue water.

Do bear in mind that in today's world of software driven machine tools and assembly processes that the best way to manufacture may be to pay someone else to make the elements while you control or arrange distribution and sales.

If you go down this route, make sure that you establish your IP rights from the start with your manufacturer and that you don't inadvertently pass them over in the trade.

Patents: assignment & licensing

An equally valid business model to exploit a patent is by assignment or by licence. The first is where you will sell the idea outright, for all markets and for uses, for cash, equity or some other consideration. Most employees do this explicitly in return for their salary.

You might want to become an employee or a consultant to the assignee. You certainly will want to make sure they will do all they can to make the invention available in the market. Sometimes of course they don't – they may want to bury it so it doesn't compete in a market. This can be a tricky situation with regard to the international laws of patenting. Take advice! Remember you can negotiate return of the IP, if agreed targets are not met.

Licensing is similar but you keep control and responsibility for the patent. You should define the segmentation of the market and whether you're allowing manufacture and/or sale. You will agree with your licensee the exact nature of the royalty bearing item and the percentage of cost or price due to you. With most companies, they will demand that the royalty bearing item was described in a claim. If not, you will be forced back down the value chain.

Licensing can be exclusive or non-exclusive. The former is to be avoided as you're adding capital to a company you don't control. In many countries such a deal must be published and once agreed you may be committed for ever.

Better to agree, if you must, no further licences for a period and always make it dependent on your licensee reaching some agreed milestones or targets.

Sometimes your idea will concern some improvement in the way an item is made and you will need rights of access to check. It might be worth having some forensic tricks up your sleeve so you can check for yourself. An example might be some inactive impurity that arises from your method but which reveals that it was made your way.

In any case, you will need rights of access to your licensee's accounts to ensure all is as it seems.

Finally, don't get too disheartened when, as you begin a license negotiation, your IP gets challenged again for validity and usefulness... it's just part of the game!

Conclusion

The best advice is don't start without a business model to exploit your IP; it may need to be as creative again as was the invention!

_____

Dr Norman Apsley is Chief Executive of Northern Ireland Science Park.

Introduction

The North West is a hotbed of science, technology and innovation and home to a multitude of technology-based companies ranging from entrepreneurial start-ups through to blue chips.

One thriving location in particular is Daresbury Science & Innovation Campus (Daresbury SIC). The Campus, which specialises in advanced engineering, IT and biomedical science is home to 70 exciting hi-tech businesses.

Daresbury SIC was formed from the shared vision of six stakeholders including the Northwest Regional Development Agency, The Science & Technology Facilities Council (STFC), Halton Borough Council and the Universities of Lancaster, Liverpool and Manchester. The aim was to develop an internationally recognised community of scientific, innovation and entrepreneurial excellence.

Daresbury has long been associated with science and technology since the establishment of the Daresbury Laboratory, home to the world's first purpose built synchrotron radiation source (a particle accelerator used for fundamental and applied research). Also residing on Campus is the Cockcroft Institute (the UK Centre for Accelerator Science).

Daresbury SIC is a new model for the sharing of knowledge between large scale scientific facilities and the business community. It brings together "best in class" expertise and capabilities in science, innovation, business & entrepreneurship. It is one of two government backed Science & Innovation Campuses in the UK, the other being at Harwell in Oxfordshire.

Benefits

One of the key benefits to tenant organisations is membership of a unique community of like-minded individuals. The secret to this success goes beyond the stakeholder contribution at Daresbury SIC boardroom level; a bigger picture emerges when you look to the wider Daresbury SIC network, hailed as the 'best network in the North West', it is a carefully developed community of hi-tech businesses, specialist suppliers and business support organisations. Members of this thousand-strong community, which is currently doubling in size each year, understand that success is not just about the flow of ideas, but the means to quickly convert those ideas into deliverables, and at Daresbury SIC it's about delivery. Campus businesses and members of the wider network get together at monthly business breakfast networking events where they share information, discuss business, research and new technology and work on collaborations.

The Campus has a number of factors to thank for its phenomenal success to date. Set in rural Cheshire countryside, it is ideally located just off the M56 and is within 30 minutes drive of both Liverpool John Lennon and Manchester International Airports.

Another major attraction of Daresbury SIC is its unique combination of shared resources. Companies can access the world-class facilities of Daresbury Laboratory for research and development, as well as utilising substantial business support, conference and catering facilities.

Business support facilities are provided by a dedicated team to all resident companies. This includes identifying highly specific technical and business expertise to resolve business-critical issues such as core technology, routes to market, corporate financing and grant funding.

Campus News

Daresbury SIC has had its fair share of attention in 2008 including a number of high profile visits.

Earlier in the year, in a visit hosted by the NWDA, The Chief Executive of the Technology Strategy Board, Iain Gray, visited the Campus to discuss the importance of technology and innovation to the region. During his visit he met Daresbury SIC tenant companies and regional scientific and technology businesses to seek their input into the Technology Strategy Board's future strategy and priorities.

Recently, the Minister for Science and Innovation, Ian Pearson, visited Daresbury SIC to announce a £25m agreement that will realise the development of the crucial next phase of the Campus.

The Minister said: "The Government is committed to Daresbury expanding as an internationally renowned centre of science and innovation. Today's announcement demonstrates that the future for the site is an exciting one. The North West Development Agency and its partners are to be congratulated for this next stage of development at Daresbury. Their vision for the site is strongly shared by the Government."

Funding and support

Through Daresbury SIC, the NWDA, UK Trade & Investment (UKTI) and Business Link channel a number of business finance solutions designed to help businesses start up and grow. 10 Daresbury SIC companies have been awarded a total of £1m in grants for research and development (GRAND awards) since the Campus opened. The GRAND awards are aimed at encouraging businesses to carry out strategic research and development projects that they would not otherwise undertake and assist them in levering in finance from the private sector.

The £1m in GRAND awards is fantastic news for both Daresbury SIC and the North West as it confirms the region as a centre of scientific and entrepreneurial excellence with confidence in its hi-tech sector and innovative incubator organisations.

Among the successful companies at Daresbury is Structure Vision, which was awarded a £354k award early in 2008. The company is set to develop a digital modelling tool for use in the nuclear industry which will contribute significantly to the deployment of a world-class nuclear clean-up programme.

Behind some of the successful activity has been an international trade pilot project led by Daresbury SIC with funding from UKTI, which helped the research and development intensive SMEs in the Daresbury Innovation Centre explore the factors constraining international market development. The project was initiated by the launch of the UKTI's new five-year strategy in 2006, which has increased the focus on R&D from both an inward investment and an export perspective.

One of the Campus companies to benefit has been Calon Associates Ltd which has used the funding to take its temperature and lighting control systems into the European marketplace. Using the funding to attend emerging technology conferences in the Netherlands, Denmark and Austria, Calon has been able to experience, first hand, the market characteristics of a range of European regions.

Mike Eccleshall, Deputy International Trade Director, UKTI said: "UK Trade & Investment has been delighted to work with Daresbury SIC on this pilot programme. It is only the start of what we expect to be a mutually beneficial partnership not just for our two organisations but more importantly for the increasing number of companies based at the facility that we are now working with on a regular basis. UKTI's aim is to help the region's businesses improve their international capabilities and our partnership with Daresbury is a positive step forward in helping to do so."

The Future

The future is promising for Daresbury as a scientific, commercial and residential location. The £25m development agreement between NWDA and St Modwen, the UK's leading regeneration specialist, will continue the development of the Campus leading to the creation of around 1,200 jobs. The first step will take the form of a new 37,000 sq ft facility providing office and laboratory/workshop accommodation in units of between 1,000 sq ft and 7,700 sq ft on flexible terms. It will provide a home for the larger companies in the Daresbury Innovation Centre to move onto, as well as attracting other science and technology businesses from across the region. This first phase of development will be ready for occupation in early 2009.

But this is only part of the exciting cocktail of developments on Campus: there will be further integration of public sector science with industry including the development of three technology gateway centres - real-world hubs of scientific and industrial collaboration in areas such as computational science and detector systems technology.

And looking further ahead, Daresbury SIC, STFC, Halton Borough Council and the NWDA along with a host of other agencies, are working on an exciting 25-year masterplan which will develop the site into a major 250 acre location for business, science, residential and commercial land-use, providing a home, in many cases literally, to some 10,000-15,000 people. Already being called a "Technology Village", the area will have at its centre a commercial 'heart' providing a concentration of facilities and amenities, supported by better transport infrastructure, and drawing together the various assets of the larger site in one communal area. Not only does the sheer scale and ambition for the site provide cause for excitement amongst the stakeholders and the local communities, it bodes equally well for British science and innovation.

Companies and case studies

Advanced Engineering
Instrument Design Technology **www.idtnet.co.uk**
IDT provides the world's synchrotron community with a design and project management resource in state-of-the-art mechanical precision instrumentation.

The company has utilised UK Trade & Investment support and funding provided through Daresbury SIC to develop its international presence, with one successful outcome being a deal secured with the Australian Synchrotron Project. IDT is one of only a few companies worldwide operating in the niche of precision instrumentation for synchrotron beamlines. It has also recently been awarded a GRAND R&D Award and has also struck a deal worth around £1m to supply systems to the STFC's Diamond Light Source synchrotron at Harwell, Oxfordshire.

Biomedical
Bioeden Ltd **www.bioeden.co.uk**
Specialty tooth stem cell processing company Bioeden has developed a truly international presence since locating at Daresbury SIC. Bioeden harvests stem cells from children's deciduous teeth after natural tooth loss, and stores the cells for potential use in the treatment of any future disease or illness that the child may develop. Bioeden has progressed, with the help of the UK Trade & Investment presence at Daresbury SIC, to explore markets in the Middle East and Australia.

Creative/Digital ICT/Telecoms
Inventya **www.inventya.com**
Inventya provide specialised market research services to SMEs with new technology based offerings, helping clients leverage knowledge, ideas and innovation. Inventya has developed powerful software for the validation of new business concepts, and has forged a partnership with Microsoft UK to provide software tools and advice for people thinking of starting a business.

For further details about all the companies listed, visit
www.daresburysic.co.uk/locating/tenants

For enquiries, please contact
Mark Blackburn
Marketing Manager
Daresbury Science & Innovation Campus Ltd,
Daresbury Innovation Centre,
Keckwick Lane,
Daresbury, Cheshire WA4 4FS
Tel: **01925 607012** Fax: **01925 607398**
E-mail: **mark.blackburn_dsic@nwda.co.uk**
Website: **www.daresburysic.co.uk**

Daresbury
Science &
Innovation
Campus

giraffe

Giraffe was listed by *The Guardian* newspaper business section as one of the top brightest independent UK green businesses.

Giraffe is a unique form of environmental management consultancy giving advice on:

- Carbon Management
- Carbon footprinting
- Carbon Offsetting –
  One Planet Economy
  www.oneplaneteconomy.com
- Ecological footprinting
- Eco-design
- Environmental Legislation & Policy
- Environmental Management Systems
- Innovation Management
- Broadcasting
  **(www.channel4.com/lifestyle/
  green/chat-win/rob-holdway-blog)**

Contact:
Robert Holdway
info@giraffeinnovation.com
www.giraffeinnovation.com
t. **+44(0)1273 422099**

(Giraffe has run two major public installations:
www.weeeman.org pictured and
www.rsachanginghabbits.org)

Design for a One Planet Economy

Rob Holdway and David Walker – Giraffe Innovation Limited

www.giraffeinnovation.com

One Planet Design

Densely populated mature nations of the West are consuming the bulk of world finite resources and energy. Increasingly China, India amongst others are growing massively and increasing the strain on these resources. If current trends continue, by 2050 humanity we will need a 2nd planet in order to satisfy our demands for energy, commodities and water. Design for a One Planet Economy requires companies to align themselves to macro economic objectives and design their businesses to deliver an **80 per cent cut by 2050 in climate changing emissions (CO_2)** from direct and indirect sources. The UK government's move towards a 'One Planet Economy' as part of the new UK Sustainable Development Framework, emphasises that 'a successful business is consonant with and operates within an economy that grows within the capacity of the planet's resources'.

Design for a One Planet Economy requires **delivering new products and services with lower environmental impacts** throughout the entire lifecycle. It also requires the **delivery of innovative and competitive new business models** and products with new design solutions. This program requires nothing short of major cultural and behavioural shifts-changes in our belief system. This, of course, is massively ambitious and has an evangelical tone. So be it.

A regulatory drive in reporting on carbon emissions will impact all companies across all sectors, not just direct emitters. Measuring the carbon footprint of a business provides a strong benchmark indicator across sectors, but is also instructive for setting goals within the innovation process.

Analysing carbon will demonstrate that companies with stronger environmental strategies have overall higher quality management teams. Estimates have shown significant downstream potential liabilities if companies are required to offset their emissions. Certain sectors could literally face costs mounting into billions of Euros. Leading companies are setting carbon reduction programmes across all operations yet many are still far behind. For companies where most of the tonnes of carbon dioxide (tCO_2e) emitted are from indirect sources there is an opportunity to reduce emissions through increasing energy efficiency and eco-design practices.

Giraffe's focus is on a design-led carbon reduction programme. All companies have a carbon footprint which is *the emissions caused directly and indirectly by an organisation, individual, event, product or service*. A majority of emissions come directly from heat and transport and indirectly from utilities, manufacturing and using products and services throughout the lifecycle.

The process starts by establishing a baseline carbon figure. This accounts for the energy, water and waste associated with running the business. A number of approaches are taken to reducing this figure. The learning's from this analysis are factored into on-going company planning and future projects within the live design cycle. The success of innovation projects is measured against their consonance with the company's year on year carbon reduction targets, along with the typical commercial objectives. Where reduction is not possible Giraffe advises and manages companies on an appropriate offsetting mechanism. This is managed through Giraffe's One Planet Economy service. **www.oneplaneteconomy.com**

Resource reduction is clearly the way forward. By this we mean that it much better to reduce the amount of materials, energy and associated emissions required in the first place rather than dealing with them at end of life or mitigating any responsibility by offsetting. This is clearly the best strategy for the environment, for business and for the bottom line.

Small changes can have a significant commercial and environmental benefits when aggregated across a business or entire sector. Recent carbon reduction projects by Giraffe have identified over £20 million in cost savings and over 50,000 (tCO_2e) along with a number of potential new business opportunities. The benefits of considering embodied CO_2 emissions associated with products and packaging are clear. One carbon-led redesign project undertaken by Giraffe looked at the company's packaging. The proposed redesign identified savings equivalent to offsetting the client's entire UK and Ireland retailing operations across 163 large stores.

This work leads to a significant change in processes and the culture of the businesses we work with which results in specific pledges such as:

- Implementing an environmental management system
- Developing systems of internal reporting to help monitor environmental performance
- Embedding environmental concerns when developing and changing business

activities, processes, products and services

- Engaging suppliers to implement environmental processes, policies and procedures in place
- Lifecycle assessment on innovation projects
- Setting annual CO_2 reduction targets across all business activities.

Innovation Techniques – Eco Dice™

Many scientists, policy makers and politicians, are, out of necessity, developing a better grasp of the environmental and ecological problems. Dr P.R. White of Proctor & Gamble stated that "Sustainable innovation means finding new ways to do new things, as well as new ways to do old things." However, in order to achieve this we need innovation techniques that lead towards a new creative synthesis of innovation within the context of sustainability. The generic innovation process is well established. It can be seen as focussed converging activity. It underpins the activities of most professional sub groups. However, there seems to be something missing from the early parts of the innovation process. Where are the clear outcomes which are desirable, tangible and specific? Where are the visions and prototypes? We need clarity of perspectives and visions of a better future which are so clearly and convincingly rendered that everyone can make informed choices.

There are new forces and demands being brought to bear upon that generic process. The green imperative means that this well established process continues but there are now new criteria, new activities and new tools placed alongside.

In order to facilitate sustainable innovation we need experiential, visual, tactile design led techniques for exploring plausible ideas. Giraffe's Eco-dice™ technique acknowledges the 'distributed' nature of innovation between 'actors' across the entire business, including external sources such as University research laboratories and users.

There is a tendency to stick to the same old solutions and to what you know – for the obvious reason it is hard to stick to what you don't know. Creativity tools act as a catalyst to new combinations and connections. The Eco-dice™ is a generative technique facilitated in workshop sessions and has been used to great effect internationally with innovation teams in companies across all sectors.

The technique acknowledges two fundamental principles of creativity – constraints and randomness. Too often the environmental agenda is neglected within the innovation management process. This technique incorporates sustainability criteria with mainstream considerations such as cost, market, user and time and so on. The target is a proposal, an idea, a diagram, a programme, for a design for a sustainable business, product or service which matches the dice parameters. All ideas generated by the Eco-Dice technique are assessed according to their 'sustainability credentials' which include resources, energy, water, waste, social ethical and product service systems (PSS).

Summary

Companies of all sizes have a lot of power to influence change. We mustn't be victims of our own narrowness and knowledge. We have to take some form of structural understanding of ecology and sustainability. The way forward to not to make us all ersatz scientists, but to give companies grounding in the basics of sustainability. This must be based on reasoned argument and sound science.

We realise that from a business perspective, there is little point making environmentally sensitive products and services if they are not commercially viable. Yet there are commercial benefits in being ahead of the game. For example, the ethical stance a company takes inevitably contributes to its brand. For some it is key to differentiating their offering. For these companies making a profit and philanthropy and not mutually exclusive. For others it is about improving efficiency.

New attitudes will pervade all strata of society. Businesses will operate according to new models. This is a simple choice because the alternative is that we slide, not with a bang but a whimper, into a morass of waste and toxicity. *More than that, in the long term, economic, ethical and environmental targets do coincide – because no company no matter how adroit, can make money out of a poisoned population and a dead planet.*

Giraffe Innovation Limited **www.giraffeinnovation.com**
Giraffe was listed by *The Guardian* as one of the 10 brightest independent UK green businesses.
Contact: **info@giraffeinnovation.com**   **+44 (0)1273 422099**

NHS Innovations

Turning **Great Healthcare Ideas** into **Real Products and Services**

The services we offer NHS Trusts and Staff include:

- Initial Advice & Idea Assessment.
- Guidance on Intellectual Property Protection.
- Market Research Assessing Unmet Clinical Needs.
- Technical Feasability & Business Plans.
- Regulatory Guidance.
- Prototyping.
- Financial Appraisal.
- Identify Commercialising Partners.
- Structuring Legal Agreements.
- License & Spin Out Technology.

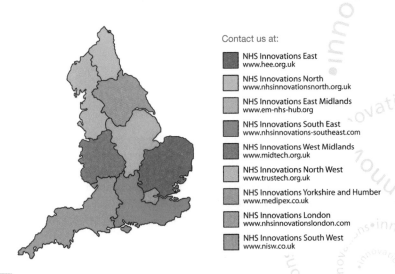

Contact us at:

NHS Innovations East
www.hee.org.uk

NHS Innovations North
www.nhsinnovationsnorth.org.uk

NHS Innovations East Midlands
www.em-nhs-hub.org

NHS Innovations South East
www.nhsinnovations-southeast.com

NHS Innovations West Midlands
www.midtech.org.uk

NHS Innovations North West
www.trustech.org.uk

NHS Innovations Yorkshire and Humber
www.medipex.co.uk

NHS Innovations London
www.nhsinnovationslondon.com

NHS Innovations South West
www.nisw.co.uk

Unlocking Innovation within the NHS

Over the last five years a network of NHS Innovation Hubs have been established with the prime aim of unleashing the huge creative potential of one of the world's largest employers.

By working with a wide range of staff throughout the NHS including clinical practitioners, such as doctors and nurses, as well as staff in support and managerial roles, the Innovation Hubs' role is to provide expert guidance and support through the process of turning a great idea into commercial reality.

Supported by the Department of Health, the Department of Innovation, Universities and Skills (DIUS) as well as regional government, twelve Innovation Hubs have been set up through out the UK. The network consists of nine Hubs in England, and three Hubs covering each of the devolved administrations of Scotland, Wales and Northern Ireland.

Although each of the Innovation Hubs is a separate organisation, their primary aims are the same and they work as a close network to achieve the following goals:
- Improved patient care
- Increase NHS efficiency
- Reduce costs for the NHS
- Generate a revenue stream for the NHS

This means that the Innovation Hubs work on a wide and diverse range of projects. The types of innovation that the Innovation Hubs are involved with cover innovations such as medical diagnostics and laboratory equipment, ICT and software, publications, therapeutics and drug delivery, and medical devices. Although the focus is mainly on product innovation the Innovation Hubs also assist with the development of service improvement concepts that can have a real impact within the NHS Trusts.

The NHS Innovation Hubs are in a unique position of strength in that the innovators they are working with are often the end user of the products and services that are being developed. For this reason, the NHS staff bring a depth of knowledge and understanding to the projects which is extremely valuable and not widely available to industry.

The Innovation Hubs are staffed by experienced, commercially astute, managers whose role it is to guide the inventors through the innovation process. This consists of helping to evaluate the new idea by establishing market need, finding development funding and resources, setting out the most appropriate route for commercialisation and leading the negotiations with potential commercial partners. Central to this assistance is a clear understanding of the strength of the intellectual property inherent in the idea. The Innovation Hubs provide guidance and IP advice to NHS staff and work closely with patent attorneys to ensure that the appropriate protection is in place before an idea is taken to market. This can range from copyright for training materials, design rights for unique devices, trade marks for ideas with a commercial potential and patents for technical concepts that are truly unique and novel.

To assist the Innovation Hubs in their role and to allow the effective development of a strong pipeline of ideas to be realised, best practice project management tools and a robust stage gated innovation process have been put in place. In addition, the development of a large network of collaborators and partners has been built up to facilitate the development of the best ideas in the most effective manner. The Innovation Hubs have partners in academia and business as well as access to the wealth of talent and expertise within the NHS itself.

This approach is showing great results: The Innovation Hubs have now dealt with over 1000 ideas, carried out more than 140 deals and spun out in excess of 10 new companies.

The following examples of the types of projects the NHS Innovation Hubs are involved in highlight the strength of this new initiative and the importance of IP protection when reaching a commercial agreement.

A novel tracheal tube designed by a Consultant Anaesthetist at Papworth Hospital NHS Foundation Trust which is capable of being inserted up to ten times faster than current devices. It will be particularly useful when emergency lung isolation is needed, such as in field situations, as well as in general and thoracic surgery. Potential savings are impressive. For elective procedures, treatment costs will be halved whilst for trauma situations there is nothing comparable on the market. IP protection is extensive and is in place in the UK, US, EU, China, India and Japan. The idea made a big impression on P3-Medical Limited when introduced to the idea by NHS Innovations East. As a result, P3- Medical has signed a nine-month option to negotiate an exclusive license and to help with IP-related costs during clinical trials. Simon Talbot, the company's managing director, said, "The opportunity to deal directly with professionals experienced in technology transfer is a great example of how the NHS and the private sector can co-operate to facilitate innovation in patient care."

HDA medium is a test for antibiotic resistant strains of MRSA and other micro-organisms, invented by the Operational Services Manager at Newcastle's Freeman Hospital. Halving the standard diagnosis time, the HDA medium now has a patent pending in the UK and internationally. Six overseas diagnostics companies are interested in manufacturing it and a deal is awaited.

A Derby hand surgeon came up with the idea of a plastic sleeve that allows a patient's arm to be sterilised before he or she goes into the operating theatre.

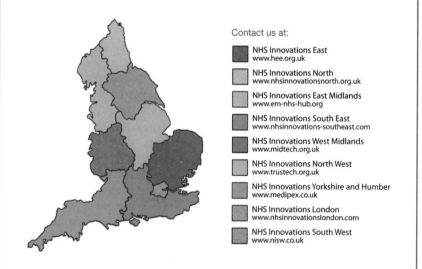

NHS Innovations

Harwell Science and Innovation Campus

Oxfordshire
UK

www.harwell.org.uk

Harwell Science and Innovation Campus

A world-leading centre for science, technology and innovation...
Building on over 60 years of excellence in science, research and development, the Harwell Science and Innovation Campus is now being developed as a world-leading centre for science, technology and innovation. The fundamental strengths of the Campus are well established:

- The integral role which it is expected to play in the delivery of the UK Government's Science and Innovation policy

- World-leading facilities. Investment in recent and current large facilities is of the order of £500 million. The Campus is a candidate location for yet more. Existing facilities and major science and technology programmes include:

  o Diamond, the largest science facility to be built in the UK for more than 30 years

  o ISIS, the world's leading pulsed neutron and muon source

  o Central Laser Facility including Vulcan, the world's highest intensity focussed laser, and the new Astra Gemini dual beam laser

  o Europe's largest space science and technology department

  o Substantial core capability in high technology instrumentation and engineering including prototype design, manufacturing and leading metrology resources for mechanical, electronic and microelectronic engineering

  o Key Medical Research Council (MRC) facilities including the Mary Lyon Centre for mouse genome research

  o The Health Protection Agency (HPA) Centre for Radiation, Chemical and Environmental Hazards

- World-class science and technology programmes, employing highly qualified scientists and engineers. The activities of the Science and Technology Facilities Council (STFC) at the Campus, together with those of the other Research Councils and public agencies will ensure a robust long term science and innovation environment at the Campus, making it an attractive location for the international R&D sector and a rich source of innovation opportunity

- The wide range of science carried out on the Campus from nanotechnology to e-science and space science, with the potential for exciting new cross-disciplinary collaboration

- A growing community of commercial science and technology organisations
- Significant space for innovation
- The knowledge transfer programmes already in place and being developed at the Campus. STFC has developed a formal Knowledge Transfer Delivery Plan and has a wholly owned technology exploitation company (CLIK). MRC also has a vehicle (MRC Technology) that it uses to translate research into products and technologies
- The role the Campus plays in the development of scientists and the training of technicians
- A 300 hectare (741 acre) site with extensive development potential to support significant growth of both public and private sector science and innovation activity, related infrastructure and housing
- The world-renowned Harwell and Rutherford Appleton Laboratory (RAL) "brands" based on 60 years in the vanguard of science and technology development
- Proximity to world-class universities
- An attractive location with good access to major transport infrastructure.
- Amenities and facilities to support resident organisations and their staff

Over 60 years of science, research and development...

The Campus started life as RAF Harwell with the site playing a significant role in the Second World War.

In 1946 with its established infrastructure, attractive location and proximity to the key academic centre in Oxford, Harwell was chosen as the UK's centre for nuclear research, a role for which it quickly gained an international reputation. The RAL (now part of STFC) was set up at the Campus in 1957. The National Radiological Protection Board (now part of the HPA) was established to give advice and conduct research in radiation protection.

In the 1960s Harwell's role was widened with an increasing range of research being directed towards helping industry. This led, amongst other things, to the spinning out of Amersham International (now part of GE Healthcare) and, in 1996, to the privatisation of AEA Technology, a company providing technical, safety and environmental solutions worldwide. A range of other private sector companies have chosen to locate at Harwell.

The research programmes into civil nuclear fission were concluded in the early 1990's signalling the start of a process of decommissioning of nuclear facilities at the Campus. As a result substantial areas of land have been prepared for new uses.

The Campus today...

Today the Campus is a focus for significant public sector research led principally by STFC at the RAL where work includes multidisciplinary research and technology programmes including materials, bioscience, aerospace, particle physics, engineering and instrumentation. In addition there are a number of other significant research/administration facilities occupied by the MRC and the HPA. The MRC has recently constructed the Mary Lyon Centre to support mouse genome research.

The Campus was recently chosen as the location for the £350 million Diamond Synchrotron. Diamond, the largest UK-funded scientific facility to be built for over 30 years, commenced operations early in 2007. Government is also investing £100M in major enhancements to STFC's ISIS facility. Further major investments in scientific facilities at the Campus are underway, including new research laboratories adjacent to Diamond and a major new computing facility, and more are planned.

Today there are approaching 100 different organisations at the Campus, all technology-based or providing services. There are more than 80 private sector companies, ranging from start-ups to major corporates. Overall, approximately 4,500 staff currently work at the Campus and significant employment growth is planned consistent with economic development and spatial planning policy.

An environment for living and working...

The Harwell Science and Innovation Campus, which covers some 300 hectares (740 acres), lies in the North Wessex Downs Area of Outstanding Natural Beauty in south Oxfordshire close to the ancient Ridgeway. The Campus has good road (A34/M4) and rail (Didcot Parkway) access and is within easy reach of London and its airports and the key regional centres of Oxford, Reading and Newbury. It is linked to the National Cycle Network and is serviced by a number of bus routes.

Resident organisations and their employees enjoy a range of amenities including retail, leisure, medical, childcare, catering and conferencing. Construction of a major new hotel on the Campus is due to start later in 2008.

The Campus represents a significant component of the major science, technology and education cluster that exists in south central Oxfordshire, the growth of which is afforded priority in the emerging South East Plan – the regional spatial strategy. The Campus is also specifically identified in the South East Regional Economic Strategy.

Space for innovation and business...

New companies are being generated in Oxfordshire at a high rate. They need a choice of supportive locations, access to networks and flexible premises. The Harwell Campus offers an increasingly attractive proposition. The Harwell Innovation Centre, run by Oxford Innovation, already provides about 45 small and start-up companies with premises and support services (see www.oxin.co.uk/centre/harwell). Increasing the innovation capacity of the site, the new START ELECTRON centre, run by START International, opened in July 2007 (see www.start-international.co.uk/locations/harwell/index.html).

The range of premises and land at the Campus, together with the support of private sector development partners, means that Harwell is able to offer property solutions to most organisations. A range of development sites is available for B1, B2 and related use schemes.

A Public-Private Partnership for the future......

In 2008, the UKAEA and STFC will be setting up a joint venture with an investing private sector partner to accelerate the development of the Campus as a world-leading centre for science and innovation.

Steven Moss
Head, UKAEA Property Development Unit,
The Library, Eighth Street
Harwell Science and Innovation Campus
Didcot
Oxfordshire OX11 0RL
Tel: **01235 431650** Fax: **01235 431670**
Email: **steve.moss@ukaea.org.uk**
Website: **www.harwell.org.uk**

Gillhams
// Solicitors

INTELLECTUAL PROPERTY
INFORMATION TECHNOLOGY
REGULATORY COMPLIANCE
PROCUREMENT
DISPUTES & LITIGATION
CONTRACT ADVICE

Gillhams Solicitors specialise in providing legal advice on technology and intellectual property protection.

Our solicitors include qualified and experienced software engineers. As members of the British Computer Society, we understand technology and focus on legal issues. We believe that obtaining legal advice should not require training your solicitors on the subject matter upon which they are required to advise.

We advise large national companies on intellectual property rights and their nexus in commercial transactions and disputes.

Specialist technology legal advice at cost-effective rates in the United Kingdom and Europe.

Lexcel Accredited.
Quality Assured Legal Services.

Gillhams
// Solicitors

Second Floor
47 Fleet Street
London EC4Y 1BJ

T +44 (0) 20 7353 2732
F +44 (0) 20 7490 2733
www.gillhams.com
solicitors@gillhams.com

Director's Duties and
Ownership of Intellectual Property Rights

Introduction

When a company engages the services of directors to perform services in the absence of written contractual arrangements, difficulties are caused in determining the ownership and rights to use intellectual property services. Unless or until disputes arise, this does not present a problem; the company trades and the directors continue with a common approach to promote the interests of the company. Indeed, the directors may also be shareholders. Should directors or shareholders fall out, solicitors are frequently instructed to assist determining the ownership of intellectual property rights.

Properly drafted contracts of engagement between a company and either directors or external consultants clearly set out the intended owners of intellectual property rights where they are created during the course of an engagement. Ownership of intellectual property rights of employees presents fewer difficulties, as the Copyright, Designs and Patents Act (the 'Act') and similar statutes makes the employer the default owner of intellectual property rights. This is not the case for external consultants and directors.

Background to Ownership of IP Rights

As an example of the rules of ownership of intellectual property rights, the general rule is that first owner of copyright of literary works (such as software, for instance) is the author of the work. The author is the person who created the work. Where a director does not have a contract of employment and is not engaged by way of a directors' service agreement dealing with the ownership of intellectual property rights, it will probably be the case that the director is the owner of the legal title to copyright. This however is not the end of the matter in respect to ownership of intellectual property rights. As with other types of property, the legal title and beneficial title (otherwise known as the equitable ownership) may become separated in respect to the property. The effect of this is that the beneficial owner is entitled to call upon the legal owner to transfer their legal title to them.

Company directors owe fiduciary duties to the companies in which they hold office. The same duties also apply to de facto directors of companies. It is these duties that may cause the legal title and beneficial title in intellectual property to split as that the director owns the legal title and the company the beneficial title.

Fiduciary Duties: General Principles

Fiduciary duties imposed on directors require them to act in the best interests of the company. When directors take office, they take control of property not owned by them; that is, the property of the company. When these assets are placed in their hands, directors are regarded as trustees and are bound to use them in the best interests of the company. They will not be permitted to deal with the property of the company where they have, or may have a conflicting personal interest or interest that may conflict with the interests of the company. This is known as the 'no conflict rule'.

Similarly, directors who use their fiduciary position to make a personal profit that is properly the company's profit are liable to account for that profit to the company. Thus, a fiduciary is required to account for any benefit obtained or received by reason of their fiduciary office, or from an opportunity or knowledge resulting from it. This is the 'no profit rule'.

The no profit rule and no conflict rule are applied flexibly. Courts have held that it is enough in appropriate circumstances that the duties will be breached where they find a real possibility of conflict. Further to this, it has been held that it is not necessary to show that a fiduciary duty has been breached, but simply that a non-fiduciary obligation which has the tendency to interfere with the fiduciary duties in the future has been breached. Thus the tests take as their measure the consideration of risk, rather than actual breach. Evidence showing that the transaction was fair; that the fiduciary acted honestly at all times; that the principal has the opportunity to enter into the transaction themselves is not relevant to the question of whether the fiduciary duties have been breached, or whether the person must account to their principal.

The articles of association of a company may have an effect on the ownership of intellectual property rights created by directors. Article 85 of Table A of the provisions of Companies (Table A to F) Regulations state the fiduciary duty and the no profit rule apply only where the 'company is interested', read: *"Subject to the provisions of the [Companies] Act, and provided that he has disclosed to the directors the nature and extent of any material interest of his, a director notwithstanding his office (a) may be a party to, or otherwise interested in, any transaction or arrangement ... in which the company is ... interested, ... and (c) shall not by reason of his office, be accountable to the company for any benefit which he derives from and such ... transaction or arrangement"*;

The UK case of *Ultraframe (UK) Limited v Fielding* involved the ownership of intellectual property rights in designs, where a director and shareholder of a company made the designs. The director used writing materials provided by the company to create the designs. For the most part he created them during company time. The drawings were reviewed by company employees whose remuneration was paid by the company. For these reasons, the designs were treated as the assets of the company, as the Court found that the director was engaged by the company and performing work for and on its behalf. The Court of Appeal held that, as the beneficial title to the designs was owned by the company, the company was entitled to call upon the director to assign the legal title to it at any time.

In a contrasting decision, *Wilden Pump & Engineering & Anor v Fusfield*, was concerned with a managing director who created drawings during his directorship. The managing director was found not to be an employee of the company, and so the issue of ownership fell to whether the fiduciary relationship operated to create a beneficial interest to the intellectual property rights in the company. In the course of judgment, Whitford J found that a managing director does not necessarily hold any copyright interest in trust for the company. Regard must be had for the surrounding circumstances of the particular engagement. If the intention of the parties was not consistent with an intention that the company should own the intellectual property rights, then the result may be that someone other than the company may be held to be the owner.

Analysis

So, where a director uses materials, information and assets of their company to create works, they may be required to account to the company for the intellectual property rights arising as a result of their office. Should this be the case, the director will be the trustee for company of those rights. The duty to account will not be enforced where the director acts with the fully informed consent of the company, which may be exercised in a general meeting, and less frequently where an informal arrangement has been reached amongst the shareholders. This however cannot be done *ultra vires* the powers of the company, Whether or not such action will be *ultra vires* the company would be determined by reference to the articles of association. Also, shareholders in a general meeting may discharge a director from liability after the event provided that they do not act *ultra vires* the company and do not commit a fraud over the creditors.

Drawing from these authorities, it is clear that it is the factual matrix that will determine the ownership of intellectual property rights that have been created by a director during the term of their office with company.

Conclusion

In the event that these matters are not addressed and resolved expressly at the outset of the service of the director, the resolution of disputes may easily become protracted and divert the company's resources from trading activities in an effort to preserve rights that it assumed that it was entitled to at the outset. Thus the risk of disputes arising later may be mitigated easily and conveniently at the outset of the engagement of directors by dealing with their engagement in writing. Properly drafted contractual terms create a high degree of certainty as to the ownership and use of the rights created during the course of the term of office of a director. Accordingly, disputes are often avoided or otherwise the scope of the dispute is narrowed to specific issues.

Universities UK
Celebrating 90 years
1918–2008

Diana Warwick, Chief Executive, Universities UK

Universities play a key role in the UK economy. The 168 higher education institutions (HEIs) in the UK have an income of some £21.2 billion per annum, and generate £45bn of output per year, a figure larger than the output of either the UK pharmaceutical or aircraft industry.

Universities also bring far wider benefits to the UK. As employers and providers of skilled graduates and a source of research and knowledge for business, universities contribute to their local economies. Two thirds of universities provide distance learning for businesses, with more than 80% providing short courses on business premises. In addition, they work with employers to develop business-focused degrees, tailoring some of their courses to the needs of businesses, and enhancing graduate employability. Their social and cultural impact is also felt through their provision of sports facilities, art galleries, cinemas and theatres.

World-class research

The UK has a remarkable record for producing world-class research, where it continues to punch well above its weight. The UK accounts for 4.5% of the world's spend on science, but produces 8.8% of the world's scientific papers (US 33%, Germany 8.1%, France 5.8%) and has strengthened its share of the world's most influential papers, from 12.9% to 13.2%. Furthermore, UK research is strong across the full range of scientific disciplines from engineering and physical sciences, through to the arts and humanities.

This strong performance by the UK has been achieved with relatively lower investment than its international competitors. While public investment has increased significantly under this Government – particularly with the 10-year Science and Innovation Strategy – we still lag behind all other major industrialised nations. We're very aware that, for example, China's R&D spending as a percentage of GDP has more than doubled from 0.6% of GDP in 1995 to 1.23% in 2004. In the US it's 2.68% and 3.13% in Japan – while the UK's spending on R&D as a percentage of GDP is 1.88%.

Spin-out companies

The UK remains ahead of its competitors in terms of commercialisation activity, with more spin-out companies created per £ of research income in the UK than in the US. The latest University Companies Association (UNICO) survey shows, in addition, that 30 UK university spin-out companies have floated on the stock market in the last four years with a combined value of £1.7bn.

In 2005-6, graduates in the UK formed 1,172 new businesses, with an annual turnover of around £85 million. Universities are also getting even better at exploiting intellectual property (IP). IP income shows that higher education institutions are active on a global scale, with £7.8m income from overseas in 2005-06, around a fifth of all HEIs' income from intellectual property rights. There are also currently 9,000 active patents held by UK higher education institutions.

All of this underlines the importance of continuing to foster a culture of entrepreneurialism within the UK's HEIs, and the need to ensure that there are as few bureaucratic and intellectual property hurdles as possible. HEIs want to foster the climate, conditions and impetus for enterprise and entrepreneurship – but to do this, and to create a culture in which this thrives, we need to be autonomous and have control of our policies and resources. I also suggest we need a lighter burden of regulation than we currently face in UK higher education (HE).

Many universities have made excellent progress in developing and exploiting links with small and medium enterprises (SMEs) and public and voluntary organisations, starting with the employment of graduates and moving towards increased engagement in R&D activity. However, because SMEs often have little money to invest in research and innovation, further support is needed if they are to progress along the 'innovation escalator' through their increased interaction with universities.

Skills and employability

Universities produce around 300,000 graduates a year and equip them with the skills they need to perform successfully in an increasingly competitive workplace. This includes not only specific skills, but generic transferable skills such as creative thinking, problem solving and the ability to analyse complex information.

Lord Leitch's review of skills in 2006 showed that the UK faces an increasingly competitive international challenge and that we need to address higher-level skills shortages if we are to meet that challenge. As such, universities are working increasingly closely with employers to design and deliver courses that equip students with the skills these employers need. For instance, nine out of ten HEIs now offer flexible, tailor-made courses for business at their campuses, and over three quarters of HEIs report that employers are actively engaged in the development of curricula. So, clearly, universities are increasingly working with employers to deliver the skills they need and value.

Universities UK is currently responding to the Government higher-level skills consultation, which will set out a strategy for the future (beyond Leitch) to deliver the skills the UK economy needs. We hope that the HE sector is recognised for the huge progress that has been made and is provided with appropriate support to continue in this vein.

Unique Partnership

The Government needs to support Higher Education and Business in their attempts to build better understanding and communication, for instance in research, graduate skills and HE-business partnerships. Universities UK and the Confederation of British Industry (CBI) are working together in a unique partnership in order to do just this. The programme will encourage greater mutual understanding between business and HE; address the strategic issues and challenges for HE and business in working together to meet identified skills needs; and contribute towards the removal of existing barriers to partnership working. The partnership will also raise awareness of existing good practice in the collaborative development of provision by HEIs and employers. We also aim to produce publications on partnership and employability, which will provide universities and employers with a resource to draw upon when rethinking their approaches to supporting the development of higher-level skills in the workforce.

The Government is currently undertaking work on many of these key areas, as is the review prompted by John Denham MP, Secretary of State for Innovation, Universities and Skills. These are big policy issues and it is vital that all the relevant stakeholders engage fully with these agendas for the sake of the UK's national and international competitiveness.

www.universitiesuk.ac.uk   tel. 0207 4195424

Help for Individuals and SMEs

Affordable Product Design for Developing New Ideas

Innovate is a product design agency that helps small businesses and individuals turn their ideas into viable, marketable products. With a complete understanding of the invention process and a thorough knowledge of how to develop an idea on a tight budget; Innovate's expert advice will prove invaluable.

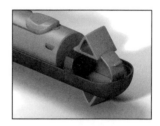

Benefits of using Innovate's design service:
- Specialising in design on a tight budget.
- Service specifically orientated to individuals and SMEs.
- Advice on exploiting intellectual property.
- Working with CIPA patent agents for cost effective IP protection.

Benefits of product design when developing new ideas
Product design is a vital stage in the invention development process. The benefits are wide ranging and depend on the individual idea. Below is a summary of the benefits of product designs:
- Computer aided design (CAD) produces photorealistic images of the product for presentation purposes.
- Product design inspires confidence in the idea from investors and industry.
- The design process resolves issues not necessarily spotted by the inventor.
- Design can develop the idea to avoid infringing existing patents.
- Materials, manufacturing and production costs are fully considered.
- Electronics and/or mechanics will be developed and resolved.
- Product design can create additional intellectual property for the inventor.

Benefits for Patent Agents
Innovate helps the clients of patent agents to further develop their intellectual property and commercialise their ideas. The design development of the idea often produces further intellectual property and Innovate refers clients to suitable patent agents.

Reducing Prototyping Costs
Prototypes are recommended when it is necessary to prove that a unique part of the idea actually works. The graphic presentation is often enough to demonstrate the feasibility of the idea and therefore avoid the expense of prototyping.

There are three different types of prototype to consider:

1. Proof of principle: A prototype that simply proves that a particularly new system or mechanism works. Often it is just part of the overall idea and it does not need to look like the final product.

2. Aesthetic model: A prototype that looks like the final product but is not fully functional.

3. Pre-production prototype: A pre-production prototype looks, feels and works like the final product. This type of prototype can be produced to mimic how the product would actually be manufactured and to check that everything will fit together correctly.

Case Study

Cone Champ and was invented by Gary Shepherd. It is a device for picking up sports marker cones and it makes clearing up after sports practice much quicker and easier.

Gary already had a patent on his idea but he needed someone to design and develop the mechanism for picking up cones. Innovate Design resolved the mechanism and built a virtual prototype of the final design. The design was sent back to his patent agent to amend the patent application based on the new mechanism. The virtual prototype was used to produce presentation boards and a working prototype followed. These were used to secure a partnership with an investor.

The engineering design stage involved further developing the product. Economic manufacturing and assembly were considered and the design was simplified where possible. The handle was redesigned to be more comfortable and the mechanism developed from the lessons learnt through the extensive testing of the first prototype. Two further prototypes were built using rapid prototyping technology to ensure the design was correct.

The CAD files were then forwarded to a company in Germany for tooling. The tools were machined and the injection moulding of the components began early in 2008. Shortly afterwards the packaging was finalised and Cone Champ is now on the market throughout Europe.

Product design is invaluable when developing a new idea or invention. Innovate are experts at providing affordable product design to individuals or SMEs.

www.innovate-design.co.uk
020 7354 5640
info@innovate-design.co.uk

Foreword

Unique features, distinctive capabilities and exclusive know-how are the surest way to stay ahead of the market for any length of time. But the way in which these assets are created and commercialized is changing.

In fast-moving markets, no organization can expect to find and keep the best ideas by working in isolation. Innovation is increasingly running on an open model with input from many different disciplines and sources. Transformative ideas can come from anywhere and everywhere: specialists, employees, suppliers and, in particular, users. This is equally true for a large corporation looking for its next blockbuster, as for a smaller company wanting to adapt its line for the next season.

The difficulty for most organizations is not in generating ideas, but in pursuing the right one at the right speed on the right scale. Alongside flashes of brilliance, innovation depends on combining strategic insight, inspired leadership, suitable funding, adept marketing, motivated teams and appropriate intellectual property in the right business model. Innovation is just as likely to lie in changing a business process or improving the experience for customers as in anything more tangible. Pursuing open innovation effectively is likely to involve managing the many activities that cut across the standard functions of an organization. Ideas are easily lost and decisions are delayed. For small enterprises, the risk often lies in deciding in which direction to take an innovation and in what time frame to expect a return. For example, by using their intellectual property (IP) assets, organizations can buy and sell the commercial rights in an innovation, allowing them greater scope to specialize in what they know best and add on any extra improvements from outside. Attracting investment is also a key factor. Without a clear commercial application combined with an effective development and exploitation strategy a new innovation is unlikely to excite the venture capital community.

This book is designed as a practical guide to the effective management of ideas and knowledge for leaders of organizations who want to move ahead of their competitors and offer new sources of value to their customers. Drawing on a wide range of experience and expertise in strategy, technology, brands, intellectual property, finance, marketing and management, it discusses how best to identify winners throughout the innovation chain.

It makes interesting reading for anyone who is in the business of developing and commercializing innovations. I hope you enjoy it.

Robin Webb
UK-IPO Director of Innovation

Innovation - From The Ground Up

At C4Ci we deliver *ground up innovation*™, not just blue sky thinking.

As experts in the building and construction sector, we know that every idea has to work in practice, on site. That's why our consultants are equally at home on a muddy site as in a boardroom or a design research centre.

Of course, every innovation starts with an idea, just as every structure is first built in the architect's imagination, but ideas alone do not create sales growth or sustainable profit streams. Ideas need to be researched, tested, benchmarked, analysed, funded, priced, market trialled and delivered.

And that's where C4Ci has the skills and experience to support you every step of the way. From inspired concept to full commercial launch, C4Ci's unique *ground up innovation*™ process delivers proven results.

The construction industry faces eye-watering targets for energy and carbon reduction, fierce regulatory and technical burdens, and a rapidly changing economy. *Ground up innovation*™ that delivers tangible commercial benefits in a realistic timeframe is the only answer.

To discuss how C4Ci can help your innovation programme get its boots dirty, contact James Sweet today at james.sweet@c4ci.eu

The innovation premium

Move from ideas to business advantage

Is your business Ready to: compete?
grow?
succeed?

And to ask for help?

LONDON
DEVELOPMENT
AGENCY

www.lda.gov.uk

Innovation through the growth cycle

Innovation is becoming critical to each of the four main stages of growth, says Dr Max Broadhurst, Head of Innovation, London Development Agency.

As the global economy gathers pace, the marketplace becomes increasingly competitive. The pace of change is accelerated by technological developments, competition and consumers' demands. Developing an organization that can adapt quickly to change and turn challenge into commercial opportunities is now critical to both survival and success.

To succeed businesses need to be able to answer three important questions:

1. How can I grow my business in a competitive world?
2. What can I do to maintain innovation as we grow?
3. Where can I get advice to turn new ideas to a business advantage?

'Innovation' provides the answers. Innovation is no longer just reserved for 'men in white coats carrying out R&D on new products'. Now entrepreneurs and growing businesses also see how innovation in processes and services leads to business advantage.

Google, Facebook, Dell and eBay have not only demonstrated pioneering technologies but also adopted new innovative business models. These businesses have created market leadership through understanding that innovative products and services require innovative business processes to underpin them. Moving ownership of innovation from a departmentalized view to one that transcends all functions is the first step in embedding it in the culture of the organization.

Innovation management priorities

Although innovation belongs to all business functions, priorities will depend on the specific internal and external characteristics of the business. External factors impact the type and speed required for the innovation to be successful, while internal factors can either inhibit or encourage the organization's ability to be creative and ultimately innovate (ie, implement the creative ideas).

External factors include:

■ the rate of product/service obsolescence within the sector;
■ the availability of finance and resources to invest;
■ the intensity of competition.

Internal factors include:

■ the ambition of senior management and plans for growth;
■ the size of the business;
■ the culture of the business, eg attitude to risk and failure.

The successful management of innovation is therefore very specific to the nature of the business and the current business climate in which it operates. It cannot be duplicated from business to business or even within the same business at different development phases.

From starting up to becoming an established business, needs change and as a business grows, management should adapt to encourage and optimize this. The next section describes the common innovation needs relating to four stages of growth, shown in Figure 1.1.1.

Stage 1. Starting up

Starting up a business is challenging and upfront research and planning is essential. If innovation is built into the heart of a business, it has a better chance of surviving.

Intellectual Property advice is important to establish the distinctiveness of your product or service and to identify potential competition. This will determine the potential value of your business for investors and help you understand how to sell the advantages of your offer to consumers.

> *Brendan O'Neil was at university when he invented KryoMedic – a portable cooler that allows aid workers to safely drop medical supplies in disaster zones. A 1-2-1 advice session with the in-house patent expert at the British Library Business and IP Centre helped Brendon find out how to make a patent*

*application. Brendan is now looking at developing a prototype of KryoMedic.
(www.bl.uk/bipc)*

Business planning is more than just an operational plan; it is a chance to communicate the uniqueness of your idea, of your product or service and the business model behind delivering this at a profit, even in light of competition.

Access to finance is critical to getting any business off the ground; to fund setting up equipment, office space, prototypes, production, logistics and salaries if you are able to pay them. Too few business ideas have the funds to initialize the business or a clear enough investment case to secure financial backing.

After initial success Trampoline hit serious competition. G2I helped the organization to look at the company from an investor's perspective and question some deep-seated assumptions. Today Trampoline has refocused 90 per cent of its development on to analysis, developing a new product, and has now secured funding; Trampoline has signed up the likes of Channel 4 and the Foreign Office as customers and is looking to the US for rapid growth. (www.g2i.org)

Stage 2. Getting going

Getting going once you have finance in place and are moving from business plan to commercial transactions is the ultimate test. To deliver, innovation requires the right skills, knowledge and processes.

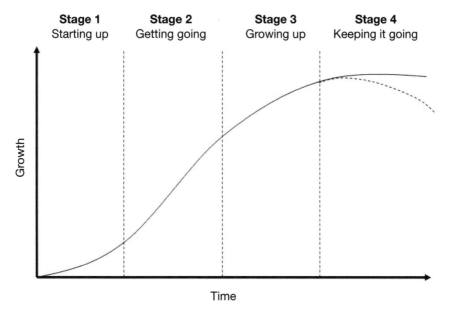

Figure 1.1.1   Innovation needs and growth

Recruitment strategies ensure that you find the right skills and the best fit with the rest of the team. There are many different approaches and ways to identify talent once you have a clear idea of what you need and what type of team you are trying to create.

Expertise networks are especially important when your team is small. Trade organizations, businesses networks and local universities are a good way to access expertise, research and specialized equipment you do not have.

> *Jenny Runnacles, studying Geography at The University of Bristol, was placed with Ming Foods to develop a new product. The company owners required a solution for how to use the waste pancake dough that was a by-product of their automated process. Ming Foods estimate that they will increase their profits by £230,000 in the next three years due to this project, which not only re-used the waste dough but turned it into a premium snack product. (www. stepenterprise.co.uk)*

Design and marketing are both crucial to developing the right product or service and communicating it convincingly to your target market. Creative skills will help differentiate your offer from the competition by better understanding the needs of your customers and users.

Stage 3. Growing up

Growing up requires scaling up operations; recruiting more staff, moving to larger premises and refining internal processes that will increase the overall capacity of the business.

New product and service development processes must also be refined as a business gets larger. A more sophisticated approach is required to be more efficient and to deliver on bigger and more complex orders.

> *Contactum, a leading producer of electrical accessories, originally contacted London MAS when it was about to launch a new range of slimline switches. It needed to accommodate production and storage of the new products without increasing resources or space at existing facilities. In addition to re-organizing production processes and the layout of the factory, using 'lean' manufacturing principles MAS, also applied the principles internally to deliver additional productivity gains. It is estimated that productivity has improved by 30 per cent, turnover increased by 22 per cent and on time delivery has increased to 95 per cent. (www.mas.co.uk)*

Brand development has benefits internally as well as externally. In addition to building brand loyalty by developing a memorable identity that connects with the values of the customer or supplier, a brand can also galvanize employees and create a sense of pride.

Challs International began manufacturing cleaning products in the early 1990s. Sales were satisfactory, but it was becoming much more difficult to be stocked by supermarkets due to competition. The Designing Demand team helped Challs focus on their core products and clarify the brand's personality and positioning to improve on-shelf stand-out. Although Challs is a small business up against blue chip rivals, the Buster range is now sold in virtually all national chains. Following the launch of the newly branded range and new sales presentation kit, sales grew by 35 per cent in 2005 – and in 2006 they are on course to rise by a further 25 per cent year on year. (www. designingdemand.org.uk)

Mentoring and coaching can be a useful way to get an external strategic perspective when often much of senior management's time is spent 'in' the business rather than 'on' the business. Coaching can help to develop new skills and make time to reflect on the overall strategy and direction of the company.

Stage 4. Keeping it going

Keeping it going can be a satisfying yet challenging time. Reaching your goals and the ambitions for the company is worth celebrating but is not the time to become complacent.

R&D that includes traditional technology-led research alongside market research, user research and trend analysis, is how leading companies keep ahead of the competition. Investing in research will prevent your offer from becoming obsolete and help exploit new opportunities in the marketplace.

PPU is a company pioneering applications of 'Pay Per Use Software', enabling software to be offered as a service, rather than hosted directly on clients' computers. They used Proof of Concept grant to accelerate development and tap into specialist research expertise. The scheme involves 30 HEIs in London and has an overall value of £11.8m. (www.poc.co.uk)

Business collaborations are an excellent way to bolster research, maximize expansion opportunities or share the risks of new developments. Collaboration can stimulate innovation and bring ideas and skills that are new to your business.

London Technology Network opens up opportunities for business across world class academic research centres. Through this network, Archer Trice, an advanced engineering company and developer of specialized rotary engine, was matched with Dutch high-tech group ICCU Holdings and Crycle Cryogenic Development N.V. – the first company to license a NASA patent. They have since signed an agreement that will lead to a multi-million investment. (www.london-irc.org.uk)

Retaining talent helps to keep valuable corporate knowledge and learning within the company, and stability within the team can help form shared goals that can sustain innovation.

'Unlocking London's knowledge assets to secure economic growth for all its businesses' is the mission of the London Development Agency (LDA). Our role is to catalyze, facilitate and broker the unique partnerships required to enable businesses realize their full potential through harnessing the benefits of innovation.

The UK, and particularly London, cannot compete in the modern marketplace on the basis of a low-cost, low-skills workforce. If we are to modernize our economy and create products and processes to gain sustained competitive advantage, we need to capitalize and expand on the creativity and scientific excellence of our world-class higher education institutions, our people and our businesses.

The challenge for the LDA is to formulate the environment to support the long-term growth and competitiveness of London's economy by embedding innovation, design and creativity practices into businesses.

Getting your business to innovate is only half the battle, as you can see from stage 4 of the growth curve. 'Keeping it going' is critical and below is a simple checklist to help monitor how innovative your business is.

Top 10 actions for sustaining an innovative culture in your business

1. Turn dissatisfaction or frustration from customers and employees with an existing product, process or service into a new idea – *this approach will stimulate employees' curiosity and get them developing new ideas.*
2. Ask your customers or potential customers through market research what they want and don't want – *customer feedback is critical to keeping your business ahead of the rest.*
3. Create ambition and challenge employees to be outward looking and question the status quo – *management needs to be supportive of this way of thinking.*
4. Do not let exploration of ideas end prematurely, especially from those who 'know' why your idea will not work – *they are experts in doing things the way they have always been done.*
5. Capitalize on your employees by giving them the opportunity to think without constraints. Don't limit their potential by job roles, and share knowledge – *it's surprising where new innovations may come from.*
6. Management need to be passionate and have faith in new developments, even if there is no demonstrable track record or experience – *confidence breeds success.*

7. Let competitive threats to your business drive your innovation – *convert fear of a competitive product or service into an idea for a new, superior product or service of your own.*

8. Take advantage of experts outside of your organization – *look beyond customers and suppliers and use the knowledge available in universities and research institutions to help you innovate.*

9. Utilize business networks to exchange ideas with other businesses and find potential partners – *collaboration can lead to winning solutions for both parties.*

10. Don't pay innovation lip service and do it once in the business. Embed innovation into mission statements, employee appraisal systems, resource allocation programmes, and customer and business partner interactions – *this will reinforce innovation throughout the organization as a 24/7 activity.*

For more information on the London Development Agency and its current projects, visit www.lda.gov.uk/innovation.

Innovation in a knowledge-based economy

The race for the best ideas now extends far beyond the boundaries of even the largest organization, says Dr Treve Willis at Oxford Innovation, so enterprises are now having to learn how to operate in supply chains of knowledge.

The process and opportunities for companies and organizations to innovate are changing. The list of reasons is long and includes globalization; the spreading of education (especially higher education); the world wide web; the creation of online knowledge marketplaces and communities, such as Yet2, Innocentive and YourEncore; the rapid rise in venture capital and corporate venturing leading to a 100-fold increase in technologically advanced start-ups and small companies; the increasing proportion of R&D being carried out by small companies relative to large ones; increasingly rapid technology development and obsolescence (making the shelf-life of internally generated IP much shorter than it was); rapidly increasing technological complexity; the relative decline of corporate R&D (in the 20th century great labs such as AT&T's Bell labs used monopolistic cash flows to develop ideas such as transistors as essentially 'gifts to the world'). These have all dramatically expanded the inventive and innovative capacity of the world, taking it far outside the boundaries of even the biggest organizations.

One of the key responses to these new challenges and opportunities is 'open innovation'. Open Innovation is a powerful concept that in recent years has come to the forefront of the management of innovation. The Innovation Advisory Service in the South East of England has become the leading exponent and facilitator of the idea in the region, having worked on open innovation projects with hundreds of companies of all sizes. While different names are used to describe it – for instance P&G, the highest profile users of the idea, call their programme 'Connect and Develop' – Henry Chesbrough coined the term in his seminal book, *Open Innovation* published in 2003. Chesbrough's innovation was to create and publish a common language for people and companies to describe to the world and each other what they do. This common vocabulary has enabled people to examine and implement ideas much more quickly and coherently than was the case before Chesbrough wrote up his observations. It is undoubtedly true that most companies will have been doing some aspects of open innovation long before 2003 but the world has truly changed over the last few years, making open innovation both easier to undertake and more essential.

Closed innovation, which pertained for most of the 20th century, is where ideas are dreamed up and developed within corporate R&D labs and sold to a grateful marketplace. In principle, closed innovation follows a linear path from idea to market within a vertically integrated single entity.

In public policy terms the 'linear model' of innovation has held sway for a long time; in this model ideas are generated in specific silos (such as corporate R&D labs or universities) that are then developed and marketed by a company through a series of discrete steps. In the 21st century in many sectors this is no longer true, with ideas coming from a variety of sources. Indeed, in IBM's 2006 Global CEO study, academia and internal R&D came at the bottom of a list of 11 key sources for innovation, with employees, business partners and customers topping the list.

In the same way as the vertically integrated manufacturers in the physical world have moved to a tiered supply chain model, the virtual world of knowledge has inexorably moved towards a 'knowledge supply chain' model, for many of the same reasons.

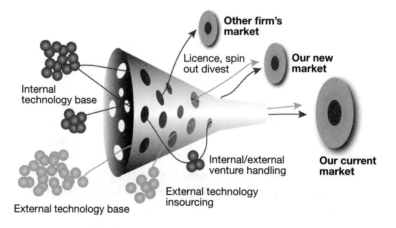

Figure 1.2.1 Open innovation

The concept of Open Innovation is that by looking outside their own boundaries, companies can gain better access to ideas, knowledge, technology and markets than would be the case if they relied solely on their own resources. This is shown schematically in Figure 1.2.1. It is a relatively uncomplicated concept, which makes many people dismiss it as too simple or that it merely describes what they have been doing for years. To many people the individual elements of Open Innovation are not new concepts and indeed most organizations will have employed some of them in their business for many years. Equally, many companies will not have recognized internally or externally what they, their suppliers, customers and competitors are doing and, by providing a common language, Chesbrough has enabled companies to efficiently coordinate and develop their Open Innovation activities.

Open Innovation is an umbrella concept covering specific ideas such as consumer-led innovation (eg, Lego's development of robot building sets), which is distinct from the 'open source' movement (eg, Linux development) where the intellectual property (IP) is essentially a common good with no one owning it. Currently in Open Innovation IP ownership needs to be distinct and clear, mainly so that companies and investors will realize a return on their investment using current business models. This may change as IP becomes more commonly available, giving multiple routes to answers.

Some people see Open Innovation as a way of outsourcing their entire internal R&D activity, essentially as a cost cutting exercise. This is a big mistake. To be able to find and profit from external ideas companies need to have the in-house expertise to know a good idea when they see one. It is also extremely unlikely that the idea will be fully formed and ready for market exactly as required, so some internal work will be needed. Without effective internal technical and innovation skills this will not happen.

Open Innovation involves culture change; looking outside intelligently for ideas; changes in staff incentivization; different leadership styles; all the while retaining the internal capacity to both know a good idea when ones comes through the door and to be able to develop it for the market. Open Innovation is not an excuse to close down all internal R&D – it is essential to retain the expertise that it brings, just to deploy it differently and perhaps to grow it more slowly relative to the size of the company's overall growth.

Leading thinkers on innovation have observed that to thrive in this open environment companies and organizations need to have simple and efficient interfaces for people outside the company to interact with them. Once in contact they then need to move quickly, especially if the external partner is a small company without the financial resources to survive a protracted courtship; decisions and negotiations need to be undertaken speedily. It is easy for a large organization to accidentally break a small one by carelessness or poor communication; it is also easy for small companies to wildly overestimate the chances of forging a successful relationship with a larger one. Both of these can lead to the small company's failure.

Once relationships are formed they will need to be nurtured as ultimate success is far from inevitable. It is all too easy for culture clashes to arise, as well as slow contracting or bill payment causing small companies severe, sometimes terminal, cash

Inspired science

Edinburgh Science Triangle is one of Europe's top 10 research locations and a thriving centre of excellence for technology transfer and knowledge exchange. Edinburgh is a world influencer in the 21st century in life sciences, informatics, micro and opto-electronics and energy. That's on top of being a global destination city for culture and heritage.

Edinburgh has the most prosperous economy and more FTSE-100 companies than any other area outside London. The highly talented workforce enjoys an enviable quality of life. Seven science parks lie within 30 mins of the airport, the city centre and the renowned universities and research institutes. Be inspired in Edinburgh.

www.edinburghsciencetriangle.com

Enlightened business

Edinburgh Science Triangle
www.edinburghsciencetriangle.com

EDINBURGH
INSPIRING CAPITAL

Incubators increase probability of business success

Entrepreneurs starting out in business have lots of things to consider – what's their innovation, which market will they target, how will they create their product/service, how will they fund their business, where will they locate their business? One consideration for these entrepreneurs is to think about establishing their business in a business incubator or innovation centre where they will get full support to establish and grow their business alongside like-minded entrepreneurs.

According to the UK Business Incubation association (the best practice body for the industry) business incubation provides a nurturing, instructive and supportive environment for entrepreneurs during the critical stages of starting up a new business. The goal of an incubator is to increase the chance that a start-up will succeed, and shorten the time and reduce the cost of establishing and growing its business.

Currently, there are approximately 300 incubators in the UK, supporting in excess of 20,000 dynamic, creative and innovative businesses – a significant proportion of the UK's new business start-ups!
Business Incubators have an important role to play in supporting local and regional businesses, but you may ask whether they actually work. Over the last 9 years, UK Business Incubation has measured the impact that incubators have on the local economy and workforce. The research proves that an incubator's client businesses provided an average of 167 jobs (full time equivalents) per incubator and are home to an average of 30 client businesses. Most (60%) incubators also operate "outreach" services, helping and advising companies outside the incubator. Those operating outreach activities support an average of 150 additional businesses. Across the sample, an average of 75% of client companies' turnover up to £500,000, but only 1.5% had a turnover of > £5 million.

Most importantly, business incubators have an *average success rate of 98% of businesses succeeding whilst in the incubator* (compared to a national average of less than 50% of all small and medium sized companies registered) and 87% surviving after 5 years of starting.

Alba Innovation Centre, located in the Edinburgh Science Triangle area in Scotland, is one of the premier providers of business incubation services in the UK. With a current tenant base of 20 companies, the Centre is already 65% occupied and the tenant companies employ 77 staff. Since its' inception at the end of 2006 there have already been 5 successful graduations (that is, companies growing-up successfully and moving out of the centre), including Elonics, a semiconductor company specialising in radio-frequency wireless silicon devices; Oligon which integrates microphones into silicon chips, was incubated at the Alba Innovation Centre and then acquired by Wolfson Microelectronics, one of Scotland's and UK's leading electronics companies and Catalise which developed a joint venture with SMG to create Smartycars.

Modeled on the highly successful, award winning Hillington Park Innovation Centre, the Alba Innovation Centre is much more than a managed property facility. The Centre provides an enabling environment within which businesses receive in-house intensive growth support, the opportunity for creative development and networking with other businesses, and access to a network of successful entrepreneurs and specialist expert knowledge.

The Centre's aim is to make a significant difference to ambitious, innovative technology businesses, through a structured and tested process of innovation advisory support. This involves examining all aspects of the business, challenging where appropriate, but ultimately aiming to deliver exceptional support which will remove barriers and facilitate growth.

The Innovation Advisory support team provides top-class advisory services to companies and entrepreneurs to help ensure their great ideas become successful businesses.

This is delivered through our Innovation Programme, offering a full range of products including:

- Products and Technology
- Finance and Funding
- Legal and Intellectual Property
- Market Opportunities
- Sales Strategy
- People and Management

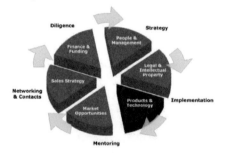

The secret behind the success of Alba Innovation Centre is a combination of factors, the selection of companies selected to become tenants, the network of innovation contacts and a targeted market focus, which together all aid the success and growth of the client tenants businesses. Their idea has to be innovative, the management team has to have entrepreneurial flair and the technology has to be right for market. Alba Innovation Centre targets companies that are developing new technologies for which both they and the Centre's advisors think there might be good sustainable market opportunities and a sustainable commercialization package. The innovation doesn't necessarily have to be ground breaking as long as it's the application of technology or the merging of technologies that's being cleverly applied in the marketplace which ultimately makes the company innovative.

Companies in the Centre work across all areas of ICT – most tend to be software orientated but there is also a range of companies working in the mobile and wireless sector, digital media sector as well as web applications. Most of the companies are at start-up/early stage which enables the Innovation Advisory support team to help in all areas of getting the business off the ground from finding the right funding package, through to sorting IP and legal implications and then identifying routes to market for the companies' technology.

Companies who are looking to locate their business in an innovation centre need to consider a number of factors

- Is the market focus of the innovation centre the same as your business model?
- Have they got good in-house advisory support?
- Does the advisory support programme match your company's requirements?
- Will they offer a good network of experts and contacts?
- Do they have flexible accommodation to enable your business to grow?
- Are there all the facilities you require to run your business efficiently
- Is the innovation centre itself 'innovative'?

Incubation is an important factor for both the Scottish and UK economy, but it is the innovators in incubation that really make a difference. Alba Innovation Centre is not just about delivering innovation services but about developing and innovating ideas within the technology market.

The impact the Alba Innovation Centre has on the wider community is quite significant – a number of celebrated entrepreneurs who have visited the Centre and all of whom are blown away by the shear success of the Alba Innovation Centre and the companies who have located there.

Alba Innovation Centre is a partner of the Edinburgh Science Triangle. This alliance of universities and research institutes, science parks, councils and the economic development agency for Scotland, Scottish Enterprise, aims to attract international investment in the science and technology sector to Edinburgh and the surrounding Lothians area, and help build an interactive community between business and academia leading to more ideas and innovations. Alba Innovation Centre plays a number of important roles within Edinburgh Science Triangle including nurturing young technology businesses, providing a landing stage for new investors into the region, and taking the lead with a number of highly effective collaboration initiatives including Wireless Innovation, Scotland's national initiative for wireless and mobile technologies and the Open Doors events which connect small companies with the global technology corporate giants.

By working as part of the forward-thinking Edinburgh Science Triangle alliance, Alba Innovation Centre can promote its' services and successes to a global market, which enables the Innovation Centre to compete globally with other, more established Science Parks and incubators.

One of the key benefits Alba Innovation Centre receives as being part of the Edinburgh Science Triangle is the share of knowledge across the seven science parks and various rapidly-changing sectors including life sciences, energy, electronic markets and enabling technologies. Client tenants of the Alba Innovation Centre can tap into the knowledge of other like-minded companies across all the parks and share information and experience gained within their own and other sectors.

Alba Innovation Centre is managed by Innovation Centres Scotland Ltd (who also run the award winning Hillington Park Innovation Centre) and is strongly supported by Scottish Enterprise and West Lothian Council.

Written by Anna-Marie Taylor, Marketing Manager, Innovation Centres Scotland Ltd.

For more information on initiatives mentioned in this article please contact
Tom Ogilvie, CEO, Innovation Centres Scotland Ltd

For further details on the Alba Innovation Centre, contact Peter Andrew,
Centre Manager, Alba Innovation Centre on **peter.andrew@innovationcentre.org**
or **01506 592100**

For further details about the Edinburgh Science Triangle, see the website at
www.edinburghsciencetriangle.com or contact Barry Shafe, Project Director,
on **barry.shafe@edinburghsciencetriangle.com** or **+44 (0)131 200 6303**
Wallace Building, Roslin BioCentre, Roslin, Midlothian, EH25 9PP, Scotland

For further details on Open Doors, contact Tom Ogilvie, CEO, Innovation Centres
Scotland Ltd on **tom.ogilvie@innovationcentre.org** or **0141 585 6300**

For further details on Wireless Innovation, contact Alisdair Gunn on
alisdair.gunn@innovationcentre.org or **0141 585 6300**

flow problems. Additionally, if the business is there to be had it is too tempting for the smaller partner to take on more work than it can sensibly fund or is reasonable for a balanced customer portfolio – thus threatening its long-term viability.

To thrive in an Open Innovation world companies need to gain status as preferred partners; sellers or purchasers; to be good corporate citizens. In an open environment knowledge of slow or indecisive decision making, or outright dishonesty, will spread quickly. Most small companies and individuals are very concerned about trusting their ideas to larger organizations – they have been fed a diet of invective against large company practices and they in turn generally believe that large companies will not treat them well, despite most large companies in fact being pretty paranoid about avoiding the charge. In fact, so paranoid are they that in many cases they deliberately avoid external ideas so that they cannot be accused of stealing them. This, however, is not a strategy that will work in an Open Innovation world.

The trust (or lack of it) issue is epitomized by the NDA (non-disclosure agreement) conundrum. Nearly all sellers will have been told not to say anything substantial to a potential purchaser of their IP without an NDA being in place first. Most purchasers are large companies and very few of them are in a position to sign an NDA as they have wide-ranging expertise across the globe and it is simply too time-consuming to trawl their internal portfolio of knowledge before signing an NDA without knowing whether it is worth doing. The result – a stand-off. What can be done to break the impasse?

One solution is to use a trusted intermediary. An independent organization that both parties trust can objectively assess whether the IP on offer is genuinely interesting to the potential purchaser without exposing the seller to the perceived threat from the buyer. If they decide that it is, then it is worth both parties investing in working out how to trust one another, meanwhile using the intermediary as needed.

Indeed it is the arrival of these intermediaries, such as Oxford Innovation (www. oxin.co.uk), that make it possible for Open Innovation to thrive without vast and inefficient investment by companies. Online services such as Yet2, Innocentive, YourEncore and NineSigma have sprung up to efficiently support the global exchange of solutions to problems. Further intermediaries will scout for opportunities amongst the plethora of small companies around the world providing a steady stream of high-quality, qualified offers to potential purchasers of their IP.

In the South East of England the Innovation Advisory Service (www.iasse.co.uk) helps to enable the required regional environment within which open innovation may flourish as well as offering specific help with Open Innovation programme implementation and intermediary services, such as scouting for ideas and organizing open innovation events for specific companies. The Innovation Advisory Service has found a surprisingly great willingness of large companies to engage with open innovation thinking. It seems that even the world's largest companies cannot risk being left behind in the race for the best new ideas.

Reference

Chesbrough, H (2003) *Open Innovation*, Harvard Business School Press, Boston, MA

About the author

Dr Treve Willis is Project Director at Innovation Advisory Service South East – the leading exponent and facilitator of Open Innovation in the region – and a Director of Oxford Innovation Limited. Oxford Innovation provides services to entrepreneurs, growing innovative companies, and to government bodies that promote enterprise. The company operates 13 Innovation Centres that provide flexible office and laboratory space to over 350 technology, knowledge-based and creative companies. Oxford Innovation also manages three highly successful Investment Networks that link investors with entrepreneurs seeking funding from £20,000 to £2 million. During the last five years, the investment networks have helped over 90 companies raise £19.5 million. For further information: www.oxin.co.uk or e-mail enquiries@oxin.co.uk.

The technology challenge

The Technology Strategy Board has £1 billion to invest over the next three years to accelerate business innovation in the UK. Director of Strategy, Allyson Reed, gives an insight into the course that she is going to be steering.

In the last decade innovation has become pervasive. It has broken free from being a discipline for specialists and is becoming a core activity for the organization as a whole. Where we might once have talked about innovation becoming more open and happening more quickly, it is now turning to reality.

Take the universities. Ten years ago, there was a total of 50 spin-outs. Now, there are 600, which have raised a total of £2 billion between them. Behind this surge in activity lies a genuine commitment to engaging with business. Most universities have appointed a vice-chancellor for enterprise and nearly all run an office for knowledge transfer.

Equally, in a digital economy, the pressure is on business to pick up the best ideas from wherever they can and to act on them quickly. Companies realize they have to find partners and link together in value chains if they are going to have a chance of meeting their customers' expectations.

In a recent survey by IBM, two out of three chief executives said they were expecting to effect fundamental change in their organization through innovation. Perhaps that explains why demand is taking off for chief innovation officers, who understand both a technology and its market.

In the UK, we are already starting to see results. Recently, we were re-admitted to the elite group of world innovators. It is an encouraging sign, but not a conclusive one. The scale and scope of innovation itself is changing too rapidly. You cannot afford to judge your level of performance on technical measures alone.

Do not get me wrong. In the UK, we want to build on our first-class research base and I am as committed as anyone to in-house, science-based manufacturing. After all, it is an area where I spent 10 years of my life, leading a start-up venture at Oxford Instruments and forming spin-outs at Qinetiq. When these innovations take off, you really can achieve a long-term source of value.

But innovation is moving well beyond science and engineering. A technology might work, but innovation only really starts when you take it to market. Will it work commercially? Is it at the right price point? Is the market ready? You have to be really focused on how you are going to compete. That can often mean wrapping a service around a product and developing a new business model. You have to see the technology in context.

It is tough trying to find the right application. In voicing the market need, you have to stay open to a different range of solutions and realize you might have to bring in technologies from outside. Do not be fooled into thinking that your ideas are closer to market than they really are.

To my mind, these are questions for any enterprise that is pursuing high growth. By definition, they are almost certain to be technology-enabled in defining their business model, in configuring their data or in approaching their market.

At the Technology Strategy Board, our remit is to invest in projects that accelerate business innovation. Large and small; product and service; established and emerging technology. We work from automotive and life sciences through to financial services and the creative industries. Our job is to make things happen.

Our activities break down into three main themes. First, we are aiming to coordinate the response to major national challenges, such as network security and low-carbon vehicles. Second, we want to build a pipeline of high-quality technologies that will apply to a number of different markets in future. Third, we are going to stimulate the climate for innovation in the UK, encouraging contributions from all points of the value chain – researchers, investors, managers and entrepreneurs.

Any resulting projects from these activities will typically be run on a collaborative basis. We will match any funding from our partners, but will not take any IP in any innovative outcome. That is down to the consortium to develop. Our interest lies in creating another strand in the UK's reputation for technological excellence.

Where these projects can go wrong is when the partners try to ring fence their intellectual property. There has to be a clear understanding right from the beginning about what everyone is trying to achieve. You have to be realistic about how close an idea is to market, as the benefits of radical technologies can take a long time to realize. Ideally, each of the parties should have interests at different points in the value chain. So, of course you must protect your IP, but find ways of using it flexibly.

The principle of networks and exchanges cuts right through the TSB's work. After all, it is at the interfaces that unexpected connections are usually made. Ideas crossing over from one market to another is one of the most lucrative sources of business advantage. So in 24 key areas, such as digital communications and mathematics, we are running knowledge networks encouraging a broad level of participation from anyone who is interested. We will also be expanding our scheme to transfer knowledge from universities to companies by seconding researchers for up to two years.

Our goal is to be needs driven and to keep as close to the market as possible. That is the way innovation now happens. So in meeting a major challenge such as assisted living for the elderly, we will bring together government ministries, researchers, corporates and enterprises in 'a sandpit'. We will spend a week identifying the truly important questions and looking at where we could really make a difference. How can we use technology to allow people to live longer in their homes? Unless we can find a way of changing, the social costs are going to be daunting. It is also potentially a big market in its own right. Once we have thought through these ideas, we will run a competition looking for collaborative partners, whose funding we can match.

As an organization that sits at the crux of government, research and business, we have a good view across the technological landscape and want to join up all the different connections that can be made in finding a solution. As an innovation is developed, you should be able to find a logical progression of different levels of advice and support. We want to be in a position to help wrap enough innovation around a project to make sure that is more than a one-hit wonder, and has enough momentum to spin out second and third waves. That is when we can start to see technologies operating on a globally competitive scale.

The Technology Strategy Board's key underpinning technologies

■ high-value manufacturing;
■ advanced materials;
■ biosciences;
■ electronics, photonics and electrical systems;
■ information and communication technologies;
■ nanotechnology.

The TSB's key application areas

■ environmental sustainability;
■ energy generation and supply;
■ healthcare;
■ transport;
■ creative industries;
■ high-value services;
■ built environment.

About the author

The Technology Strategy Board was established in July 2007 and launched its strategy in May 2008. It is an executive non-departmental body, operating at arm's length from government. Its mission is to promote and support the research, development and exploitation of science, technology and new ideas for the benefit of business in order to increase sustainable economic growth and to improve the quality of life. For further details see: www.innovateuk.org.

IP as an intellectual asset

Use intellectual property strategically to prevent any erosion in your competitive position and lock in future value, says Ben Goodger of Rouse & Co.

Ask yourself where the *true* value of your business lies: what differentiates your business from those of your competitors? Is it the brand name and associated goodwill and reputation? Is it your leading-edge innovations or designs? Is it the skills and talents of your people? Is it clever pricing or other business techniques? Delivering your products faster, better and/or cheaper? Is it a combination of all or any of the above? If so, then a huge part, perhaps most, of the value of your business lies in its intangible or intellectual assets. Like any other assets these need to be carefully nurtured. One of the fastest-growing areas of business management thinking is intellectual asset management (IAM). 'Intellectual Property' is merely the legally protectable part of a business's overall intellectual assets. This chapter sets out some of the key principles of IAM, and the benefits.

Getting it right from creation

Every business should be built on secure foundations. In a technology business, managers should ensure that there are effective systems in place to capture innovations or potential patentable inventions as they are created, and that these are evaluated for patentability. Records should be kept of when the inventions are made as this can be vital to ensure enforcement down the track. Even if it is decided that an invention is not strategically worth patenting, records should be kept of the invention. This may be handy for invalidating a competitor's patent over functionally identical technology, at a later date.

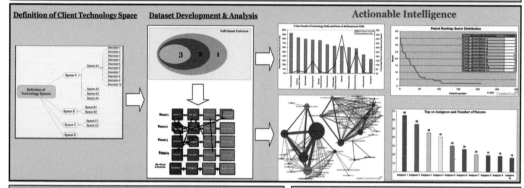

Ilian Iliev (CEO, CambridgeIP)
Quentin Tannock (Chairman, CambridgeIP)

Toward Phase 2 in the Evolution of IP Intelligence Use

If you ask most young technology companies, and many mature ones, about how they use patent information most would answer that they primarily use it for assessing their Freedom to Operate (FTO) in a particular technology area, the patentability of a new product or process, or monitoring specific infringement threats. And rightly so: such uses are after all the mainstay of developing and maintaining an IP strategy. Let us call this type of analysis **Phase 1** in the evolution of IP Intelligence services. Providers of Phase 1 IP intelligence are widespread: almost every Patent Agent or IP lawyer can help you in this regard, and there are many free and paid-for patent searching services. Every time you file a patent application, the patent examiners will conduct a similar analysis to determine whether you should be granted a patent or not.

However, with increasing volumes and availability of patent data and with increasing integration of a firm's IP management into the broader strategy of the firm, other uses of IP data have emerged that go beyond the Phase 1 uses. This is illustrated in the outcomes of a CambridgeIP survey of Corporate R&D and IP Managers conducted in early 2008. As expected, all respondents use patent data for FTO analysis. But the uses of patent data are multiplying. Competitor identification and monitoring, pro-active identification of out-licensing and in-licensing opportunities, collaboration due diligence, identification of new markets, short listing of acquisition targets, building of an investment case to internal and external investors: these are all important strategic applications of IP-based intelligence by survey respondents, uses that go to the core of a company's growth strategy.

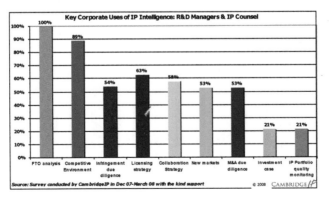

Let us call this **Phase 2** in the evolution of IP-based intelligence. CambridgeIP is at the forefront of developing Phase 2 applications, in addition to streamlining and harmonising traditional Phase 1 uses.

To understand the attractiveness of using patent data for such advanced analyses, consider its advantages: patents as data are structured, objective, comparable, and information rich. That allows research companies such as CambridgeIP to conduct complex analysis using an enormous amount of data, and to extract meaningful analytics that can form the basis of actionable IP intelligence. Moreover, it can be done more efficiently than using many traditional sources of strategic information. That in turn allows our clients to become educated about a field rapidly, and then to decide whether they need further in-depth research using the traditional market and competitive research tools. Let us consider a few examples.

Many technology-intensive companies operate in a complex field of multiple technology solutions, multiple standards and multiple scientific approaches to solving needs. Operating in a complex industry translates into a complex strategic monitoring challenge: to understand adequately all dimensions in your competitive space you would need to monitor not only developments in your own technology field, but in that of substitutes. That is a very complex task that requires a significant allocation of resources. Or is it? We have helped clients setup a monitoring campaign across several fields, enabling the cost-effective monitoring of developments across several fields. Consider the IP map of the biosensors field below: each technology field represents a patent search algorithm that we have developed. The left Y-axis represents the age of the field: how many patents as % of the total were filed in the last 5 years. The right Y-axis represents 'market share': what is the proportion from all the patents accounted for by each field. Simultaneous monitoring and comparison of participants across these fields allowed us to identify companies that are simultaneously entering several technology fields; as well as to identify new (and unexpected)

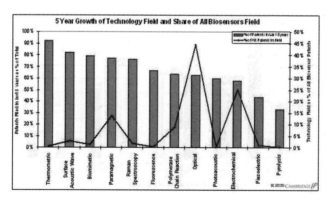

entrants in the most novel fields. Depending on the field, clients may identify convergence opportunities, and decide to diversify or modify their R&D strategy. Or they may identify non-competitive out-licensing opportunities.

Another strategically important use of IP intelligence is the analysis of inventor networks of competitors or collaborators. Once your patent landscape has been defined, it is possible to develop intuitively simple (if information-rich) visualisations of inventor networks. The Inventor Network analysis shown is based on information contained in patents: who has co-invented with whom (blue bubbles), and who owns the patents (red bubbles). Aggregating this information in an IP Landscape allows us to analyse and visualise literally thousands of potential linkages specific to an industry space. We were surprised by the variety of uses our clients found for this form of analysis. Some used it for developing a licensing strategy: "these are the people in this field who can give us introductions to the major players". Others used it to shortlist hiring opportunities: "Prof.Johnson is the CSO of our key competitor. I want to hire former PhDs and post-docs of Prof. Johnson". Clients selling a technology into a field use it to identify key influencers and the most networked individuals in order to develop a market entry strategy. And so on.

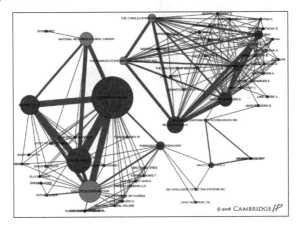

What about IP valuation? Most companies that have engaged in licensing or investment round negotiations have had to face the treacherous waters of IP valuation. We have not found a silver bullet (yet!), but again adopting the broader IP Landscape approach can help you get the right facts before you decide what valuation technique to use. Within each technology field we can identify the most influential patents (as measured by number of forward citations). With the help of the client we identify the most appropriate benchmarks (measured by technology or market application); that then provides you with a set of benchmarks which you can look for market comparables to get a financial value. Or you can use the IP Landscape to identify stock market listed companies heavily reliant on IP licensing, and use the information to develop market comparables. There are other approaches that may be appropriate, depending on your industry space.

So far the discussion has focused on patents as a source of IP-based intelligence. However, increasingly other high-quality sources of data are being integrated with patent-based analytics. For instance, combining journal article and patent data can help University Tech Transfer Offices to identify not only which departments are most prolific patenters, but also locations with high levels of technology outputs (measured by journal articles in high-grade journals), but lower levels of patent productivity. Such information may help large organisations (and not only Universities) to better target business development resources, and identify exploitable gaps between technological and scientific capability and commercialisation.

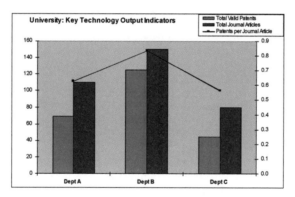

For some of the readers, the prospect of developing the various levels of business intelligence outlined here may seem daunting. For others, it may seem no substitute for in-house deep expertise. In a way both are right. The approach we advocate is user friendly and is no substitute for in-house expertise: often it is a way of capturing and exploiting the in-house expertise, by developing a set of communicable findings that can be disseminated throughout the firm. It can also be a very valuable first step in identifying the most important trends and risks toward which in-house resources should be allocated.

Finally, a key barrier to adoption of the Phase 2 of IP Intelligence we have encountered is related to a silo-thinking in larger organisations: a failure to appreciate the wider applicability and importance of the knowledge captured by a firm's IP department or specialists. Moving to Phase 2 of IP Intelligence use is about increasing, and not undermining, the importance of IP Management to the firm as a whole.

Choosing a brand name is also critical. However compelling your marketing department might think a name that is highly descriptive of a product is, it will be an uphill struggle to gain any kind of legal protection over a very descriptive mark. This means you cannot secure the right to exclude others from using the same name, which a trade mark registration confers. There are many stories of companies that have wasted enormous amounts of money on expensive re-branding after launch of a product, because of poor decision making at the time of choosing the brand.

In other areas of business, the key intellectual property right is copyright. This is particularly true where software code is being created, or packaging or graphic designs are being created. Frequently the writing of software code, or the creation of artwork, is outsourced to third parties. Businesses will not, even if they commission this work, own it unless it is transferred ('assigned') to them *in writing*. Do not be like the well-known pharmaceutical company that discovered, after one of its leading over-the-counter (OTC) drugs had been on the market for 20 years, that it had failed to get ownership of the copyright in its distinctive packaging. When, at this late stage, it went back to the original design company it was asked to pay in excess of £50,000 for an assignment.

Knowing what you've got

It is surprisingly common for businesses to have an incomplete grasp of their intellectual property assets. At a very basic level, any business should have at its finger tips a full list of its *registered* IP rights such as patents, trade marks and registered designs. There are numerous database products on the market to manage and supply this information. But there is far more to IP than merely registered rights: copyright (as noted above), business methods, trade secrets and confidential information, domain names, etc. It is best practice to try to maintain an inventory of the most important IP assets. If assets have to be enforced, or if they are to form part of a transaction, eg disposal or licence, asset lists that are well organized and readily available save enormous amounts of time.

Manage your portfolio efficiently

Many businesses take a reactive and 'defensive-only' approach to their IP portfolios, often based on the assumption that IP is nothing but a required cost and not much more. The problem with this is that a 'bare minimum' approach can often lead to inefficiencies such as the continued maintenance of trade marks or patents that have ceased to have any commercial value, and (more important) the failure to spend the time to consider what new protections need to be added as the business grows, develops and changes.

A key question is: should this management be done wholly using internal resources, or should it be outsourced? If internal, what level of seniority and experience should the people running your IP have? How big should the department be? If outsourced, what danger is there of key information ending up with people who are not part of the business? Many external firms are only too pleased to sit on key information as this gives them leverage with their clients, keeping them dependent.

Other areas to be considered in terms of efficient portfolio management are: is the ownership structure of IP as efficient as it could be? There are many different views on whether a single IP-owning vehicle is the way to go, or whether IP should be owned and managed by the individual divisions/business units concerned. Should all the IP be located offshore? What about transfer pricing issues on internal licensing of IP within a multinational group? These are complex issues and there is no 'one size fits all' answer. However, with intelligent analysis, using a combination of tax, marketing, accounting and legal expertise, the optimum structure, balancing all the various competing interests, can usually be arrived at, delivering considerable financial benefits. One thing is clear: there should be consistent policies on the management of the IP assets within the group, even if the actual ownership and decision making in relation to those assets is devolved. It is for senior management to ensure that there is consistency of approach, whether through enforced IP management policies and training, or through locating the key decision making in a central committee.

Finally, under the heading of 'efficient portfolio management', the smart business should be constantly looking for synergies from within its IP portfolio: especially after an acquisition, it may be that there are new assets such as patents or brands that can be combined with existing assets in innovative ways. As we shall see below, this does not mean that vast internal resources need to be diverted towards developing and launching new product lines: intelligently bundled rights can simply be licensed to willing parties thereby securing royalty income streams.

Keeping your portfolio aligned with your business strategy

Time and again our IAM team at Rouse reports seeing clients in severe difficulties because they have not taken a proactive and strategic approach to the management of their IP. A classic example is companies that have failed to protect patents, designs or trade marks in emerging economies such as China. Many businesses still take the view that they will only protect IP in markets where they are selling. They need to realize that they should also protect their IP in markets where they are likely to be copied. It takes someone in a senior management position – we would argue board level – to ensure the IP strategy is aligned with the business strategy.

Leverage your IP to generate revenue

In today's highly competitive and fast moving business world, it is simply no longer an option to carry on doing today what worked yesterday. Businesses need to be alive to potential sources of revenue from leveraging assets that they have, or can acquire, in order to make sure that if mainstream sources of revenue decline or are threatened, they have other sources to fall back on, or future avenues for growth. Thus, a business that has built up a famous brand in one particular area, eg Caterpillar, in relation to earth moving vehicles, can very successfully open up a rich seam of alternative revenue through licensing the trade mark for completely different goods, such as clothing.

Similarly, film, TV and book producers now derive a great deal of extra revenue from merchandising their 'properties', eg on toys, home accessories and clothing. This is done through the medium of licensing, an art that needs to be practised carefully. Sometimes (eg, Thomas the Tank Engine), the licensee can end up making more money than the original owner, because of poor licensing control and lack of strategic thinking by copyright owners. The beauty of licensing is that it can, with minimal effort and cost to the original IP owner, generate revenue from business areas where the IP owner is simply not active. Every IP owner should be looking for licensing opportunities. In the pharmaceutical field, for example, a producer of a drug that is aimed at hospital pharmaceuticals may have a spin-off product that uses the same patented technology applicable in the OTC market. Thus a relatively small company that focuses on the hospital market may be able to derive considerable additional revenue from licensing to a player in the OTC market.

Many deals can be done with intellectual property assets, often involving the cross-licensing of different assets. This is particularly true again in the technology field. Sometimes this is in the context of you being attacked by another patent holder. The best form of defence in such a situation is to counter-attack by showing that the party attacking you itself infringes key patents that you own. You cannot make this argument unless you have built up a strategic portfolio. With such an armoury, a cross-licensing deal can then be negotiated that can be highly beneficial for both parties. Indeed, there are some businesses that are built on the income that can be derived from licences entered into by parties as an alternative to being sued. The US 'patent trolls' are an extreme case of this. As is well known, RIM, the maker of the Blackberry hand-held device, recently had to pay US$612,500,000 to NTP by way of settlement of a patent dispute. It preferred to do this than to fight the case all the way to the court and risk having an injunction granted against it, preventing it from trading altogether.

A good IP portfolio can have a value in an M&A context. If the business is going to move in a different direction, it may make sense to dispose of the related patent/ trade mark portfolio to a party that would pay good money for it. Many companies, if they are moving out of a particular sector, simply allow their registered intellectual property rights to lapse. This is a terrible waste of a potential selling opportunity. Indeed there are specialist deal brokers who can find opportunities for the sale or disposal of IP portfolios.

Finally, do not ignore the fact that since your IP may well be your single most valuable asset, it can be used as security for raising finance. The practice of creating security interests over IP assets, and indeed over the financial receivables from the commercial exploitation of IP assets (ie royalties), is another growing field. As with any set of security interests, it is vital to preserve enough freedom for the ordinary business to carry on, and to ensure that once loans are paid back, or replaced, the register of charges is kept up to date.

Be prepared to enforce – intelligently

Intellectual property rights prevent other people from doing things or copying things. The commercial value is in either blocking the progress of your competitors, or by getting them to pay you to grant a (limited) relaxation of those absolute restrictions, ie licences. All litigation is therefore essentially commercial.

If you are the type of business that gains intellectual property rights but never enforces them, you are very likely to be eroding the value of your company over the long term. If competitors copy your valuable assets and you do not stop them doing so, you will lose your uniqueness in the marketplace. Well-advised IP owners budget for a certain amount of intellectual property enforcement in any year. The key is to decide which matters are so mission-critical that they must be defended at all costs, which may be worth fighting and, importantly, which should be ignored. Some companies pursue litigation or opposition in a manner that delivers little commercially to the business and wastes a lot in legal costs. Once again, a thought-through policy is the answer. As with all intellectual property management, having your house in order and your records in good shape will significantly reduce the cost of litigation and increase the chance of quick success.

Early warning of potential dangers is vital. For relatively low fees, 'watching services' for trade marks, patents and competitive products can be organized. These enable you to take action quickly. Enforcement of your IP rights sends a message to the marketplace: 'Keep off our grass'. This may be enough to send copyists over to your competitors who may be less prepared to stand up for their rights.

Look ahead

We have discussed knowing what IP you have; managing it efficiently; seeking to leverage revenue opportunities from it; and the commercial advantage of enforcing appropriately. Once these lessons have been integrated into the company's operations, it can be seen that IP management is central to the management of the organization. But as with any aspect of business, truly enlightened IAM involves looking ahead. Where is the marketplace going in your particular sector or sectors? What territories that could buy your products are coming on stream or are you looking to expand into? Thinking several years ahead can prompt you to make sure that your IP is protected well in advance. It is a bad idea to enter a market and *then* think about protecting your brands and patents. In the case of patents it may be too late. There is a rigid window of opportunity to extend patents, after first filing. Once closed it is closed forever. Equally, with the threat of cheap Chinese imitations of Western products, often a strong IP position in your home markets will be the only way to prevent the economic erosion of your position in the marketplace. If the Chinese companies cannot sell their products in your key markets or have to pay licence fees in order to do so, this may eliminate their key price advantage. In this sense, IP may be the only way to withstand the threat from cheap Chinese competitors.

siness: Briefing

Working with business is now common-place at the University of Exeter and we recognise that some clients will be working with us for the first time. Therefore, we aim to make our processes as clear, simple and efficient as possible.

Innovation: Do you want to access our knowledge and expertise to produce a new product or service?

Talent: Do you want to take on a high calibre, employable student or graduate to manage an important project?

Professionals: Do you want to work with us to develop you and your staff?

Facilities: Do you want to hire state-of-the-art facilities and equipment?

Networks: Do you want to make fresh contacts, explore new ideas or contact us?

If so, contact us. We will treat your enquiry in an efficient and confidential manner.

Call: 01392 263456
Fax: 01392 263686
Email: innovation@exeter.ac.uk
Visit: www.exeter.ac.uk/RES

ERSITY OF
ETER

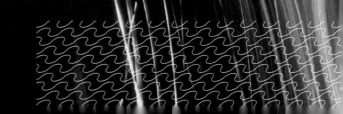

The Lost Property Office

Paul Tiltman, Head of IP and Commercialisation, University of Exeter

A real asset

The innovation process creates many forms of knowledge, providing a platform for the creation of knowledge capital as an intangible asset for business interaction. The value of these assets to the UK economy has increased in importance over the past 25 years – a point made in the Governments' review of Intellectual Property (the Gowers review) in December 2006.

However, the creation, ownership and protection of these assets is often fraught with difficulty and complexity. Many businesses, large and small, as well as UK Universities spend a lot of time, effort and financial resource in establishing a commercial platform for their exploitation. It is expensive to obtain and defend Intellectual Property (IP) rights in the UK and the costs are onerous for all businesses and for SMEs in particular.

Over the past 25 years UK Government has spent a great deal of time trying to create a support system for business to enable us to compete in the global economy, and as can be gleaned from the Gowers review, this has many failings.

The fundamental issue is the fact that proving novelty and ownership is complex and requires expensive legal expertise. Also, the language is very confusing and the processes are not widely understood. The lack of expertise in the small business community and the over-sensitivity to some of these issues by UK Universities has created further issues in that small businesses are forced to get-by, on minimal protection of these rights to establish a short-term exploitation position. UK Universities however, on the whole, tend to over-value their position and find it difficult to engage commercially, when considering the trading of intellectual property. Much of the early effort and costs associated with initial protection of this property is lost due to the lack of effort, costs and lack of commercial awareness to grow these assets.

As a result, a high percentage of IP, mainly in the form of patents, never sees the light of day and becomes 'lost property' residing on the shelves of the UK Intellectual Property Office.

An intellectual situation – to licence or spin-out?

Evidence shows that there is an enormous mountain of untapped intellectual property in this country alone and Government has helped create much of it over recent years.

Many UK Universities are being pushed to grow their research and to collaborate with business, in an attempt to translate research into products. The growth in the Government's Higher Education Innovation Fund (HEIF) over the past 10 years has now established a permanent stream of funding for knowledge transfer activities in UK Higher Education Institutions. With this, there is a growing resource of IP and commercial expertise available from UK Universities, however, although there are some very strong areas, in the main this is still relatively embryonic.

Here lies a further dilemma for the UK University sector.

The current Higher Education sector in the UK is highly competitive and the future of many of the more research-led Universities is heavily reliant on their ability to bring-in external commercial income in the form of financial return relating to IP. In many cases, the University's strategy may be to create a spin-out company to exploit its IP, in which it can take a shareholding and following a series of successful investments, seek to exit via a trade sale in the future.

This way, the expensive upkeep of the IP (usually in the form of patents) is picked-up by the spin-out and is often seen as efficient and effective for the Institution. However, this approach cannot only be expensive to set-up but may offer a poor return, whether the venture is successful or not. Often if it is successful, profits are usually re-invested in the venture and a series of funding rounds dilute the shareholdings of the founder partners – any financial return to the University is usually in the long term.

On the other hand, licensing of IP to third parties can be very effective with a guaranteed return to the University in a variety of forms. This can be as a lump-sum, royalty, revenue share or a mixture of any of these. However, any financial returns can be reduced by the costs of upkeep by the Institution of the IP. However, we are now seeing a range of strategic partnerships with UK Universities that offer creative mechanisms whereby the partner agrees to pick-up the ongoing fees.

Licensing is crucial to trading in IP and the earlier Lambert review of Business-

University collaboration recommended model licensing agreements for use between such parties, which have had a very positive effect.

Andrew Gowers, in his review, goes on to discuss the creation of similar model agreements by Government for use between businesses and suggests that this would greatly assist the small business economy.

Knowledge-based businesses

The structure of the UK economy is such that a very high percentage of business remains in the small business sector. This has both advantages and disadvantages when considering growth, in that small businesses can be more agile and responsive to innovative thinking, whereas larger businesses, which have more structure, often find it difficult to respond to change quickly.

However, the majority of small businesses with high growth potential are often faced with financial constraint, which prohibits their ability to grow fast enough and to invest correctly in their IP. This is compounded even more by the inability of small businesses and indeed, UK Universities, to be able to afford to pay for the correct and appropriate legal advice and to develop a robust IP strategy on which to grow the business activities. Therefore, access to cost-effective and appropriate legal and technical advice is critical.

Government should not only ensure that the small business community has access to expert advice on IP issues but should ensure that the UK business support system, through Business Link, gives accurate and appropriate advice including brokerage to relevant expertise. During the 1990's the UK Government introduced many effective grant support schemes such as the Small Firms Merit Award for Research and Technology (Smart), now delivered through the Regional Development Agencies as Grant for Research and Development, which was highly effective in bringing small businesses into contact with the then UK Patent Office (now UKIPO) by way of official patent searches. The response from many of the applicants, successful or not, was very positive.

Access to accurate and appropriate information for small businesses via Business Link has been very patchy over the past few years and there is a need to ensure a more formal link between the UKIPO and Business Link. Gowers discusses the example undertaken by the French Patent Office in 2005, whereby small businesses were offered a free IP audit, and recommends that this idea should be introduced by the UKIPO via Business Link.

The Gowers review goes on to underline the issue of complexity and basic understanding of the UK IP system, a good example being – Licence of Rights patent.

'Licence of Rights' patent is a means of increasing the use of information contained in patents. Under licence of right provisions the patent proprietor pays only half the patent renewal fees. In exchange, a third party can apply for a licence as a right under terms agreed between the parties – this can increase liquidity in the marketplace. The take up of this approach is still very low, which in part is due to the lack of awareness – following the Gowers review, access to patents issued under 'licence of right' are accessible via the European Patent Offices esp@cenet web database.

So where now?

The UKIPO is a unique business, offering individuals, businesses and others the opportunity to hold a monopoly on an idea for 20 years in the form of a patent. Of course it also offers similar offerings for designs, trade-marks and advice on the ultimate form of IP, that of copyright. This is big business and the costs of maintaining this monopoly position can be prohibitively expensive.

Strategy is all important when considering protection for your IP, and the rush to get formal protection is not always the right one. Patent filing can be relatively cheap, but is best done through a patent agency, as these are legal documents. Timing is also important and the use of confidentiality agreements can be useful in aiding timing, once filed the patent clock starts ticking and at the 12 month stage the costs start to ramp-up, particularly when considering the costs of searches and international filings.

Because of this it is important to plan the introduction of new innovations carefully. 'Patent pending' may well be enough for many businesses to get to the market and be ahead of the competition. But experience has shown me that a relatively small initial financial outlay on professional advice from a patent agent in the first instance is invaluable – do discuss strategy – otherwise, your ideas may very well end up in the 'Lost Property Office'.

In the patenting context, if one can have the vision to see where technology is moving and strategically secure patents at what are called the 'choke points' so that all those in the future who develop technology or products in this territory will need to obtain a licence from you, you can increase the value of your business by a huge multiple. It just takes that ability to look ahead.

Be aware that also on the horizon is a greater compliance burden for companies, especially those quoted on stock markets. Sarbanes–Oxley and Turnbull are examples of this. Increasingly, the accounting system recognizes that IP needs to be identified and valued, eg IFR3. Rather than see these as chores, we suggest that they can be used as a catalyst to promote good IAM within organizations with all the benefits we have tried to point out above. That way the compliance can be done easily and the business can then benefit as a whole.

Finally, in the area of big transactions such as a hostile takeover bid, IPO or stock market flotation, or major acquisition, having your IP house in order and being in a state of 'IP readiness' will enormously increase your bargaining position. It is very easy to chip away at the value of the purchase price for businesses if significant IP holes can be picked out in due diligence.

Conclusion

Good intellectual asset management makes a major contribution to value in a number of different ways: it prevents the erosion, and maintains and increases the value of the business. Understanding of IAM will help to sustain and support the value of the enterprise going forward. Businesses that ignore the importance of good and proactive intellectual asset management risk seeing their businesses decline and wither away, either slowly over a period of time or dramatically, for example if they are successfully sued by stronger IP owners. Western economies rely more and more on the importance of their intangibles. Therefore, a systematic way to manage and extract the most from your intangibles should be high on the agenda of any business manager.

About the author

Ben Goodger is a partner of specialist IP law firm Rouse Legal, and head of Rouse & Co International's IP commercialization group. He has broad experience of IP commercialization, in the UK and elsewhere. He recently spent two years in Shanghai, where he managed the firm's China business and its Asia commercial group. Further details: Rouse Legal, 1st Floor, 228–240 Banbury Road, Oxford OX2 7BY, UK, tel +44 (0)1865 318400, e-mail bgoodger@iprights.com, www.iprights.com.

Low-cost patent
strategies

Patents have many other uses than simply as tools to block rivals from markets. Jeremy Philpott, Innovation Support Manager at the European Patent Academy, explains how alternative patent strategies, not linked to owning and litigating granted patents, can provide competitive advantage at low cost.

Any honest IP adviser will tell you that the patent system is not cheap. Application fees, translation costs and patent attorneys' services can easily reach €50,000 when trying to get patents granted in the major European countries. Add another €15,000 for the United States and Japan. These are just ball-park figures, and vary from one technology to the next. After grant there are the annual renewal fees (typically several hundred Euros per country) to keep the patent in force. And all these costs pale into insignificance next to the costs for litigation, which can run into millions of Euros for those who can afford to go to court.

It is quite understandable, therefore, to hear new companies, start-ups, SMEs and the like say, 'We do not use the patent system because we cannot afford to.' In reality many businesses are operating in areas where patents are not traditionally seen as relevant, so it is not high cost but rather a perceived lack of need that keeps them away from the patent system. Much of the service industry sector and the creative industries (music, film, TV, games, advertising, graphic design, etc) have little use for patents, despite innovating to a very high degree.

Only a minority of businesses are innovating in sectors where patent ownership is relevant, and when those amongst them say they are not using patents, they typically mean they are not filing or owning patents. Good for them. They are saving money that can be better spent on growing their business. But there are so many other ways in which the patent system can be used to create commercial advantage.

Patent information as technical information

A key purpose of the patent system is the dissemination of technical information. This is why applications, even before they are granted, are published and made available to the public, typically via internet databases.

One does not need to be a patent owner to be a user of patent information. Looking through databases to see the results of the research efforts of others could provide valuable insights and short-cuts in your own projects. Time and again research is carried out into technologies that have already been developed, and published, by others. Much of what is published is not published anywhere else, so if researchers are only looking in academic papers and technical journals they may be missing out on the majority of relevant developments in their field.

Many of the patent applications published in the databases are not 'in force'. This means that the technology described therein is free to use (unless it is also covered by some other patent, one which *is* in force). Why might so many patents not be 'in force'? Often they were applications that either failed the examination process or were withdrawn without being granted. Of those that were granted, many were not renewed annually, and hence lapsed. Even those that ran for their full 20-year lifetime would expire.[1] The only patents that could keep you out of a sector or oblige you to buy a licence are those that were granted and stayed in force in the relevant country.

Not only are many patents free to use, over 60 million of them are free to read on the European Patent Office (EPO) patent database, http://ep.espacenet.com. Freely accessible collections of patents can be found on the websites of most national patent offices too. Numerous commercial patent hosts exist that provide more sophisticated search tools and other 'value-added' services.

Patent information as commercial intelligence

Quite apart from the technical information contained in patents, the commercial intelligence they provide can be quite staggering. By isolating those documents that relate to a particular technology, and studying who owns the patent applications in that area, you can learn a lot about the activities of other companies. Some of these could be your next customers, or suppliers, or rivals or partners.

The dominant players in some markets do not have brands you see in the shops; nevertheless, a search in the patent database will soon reveal their influence. For example, you might not know Valeo and Ricardo but they are major providers of parts and technology to the automobile industry. The patent database shows that their technology portfolios are as prolific as any of the major motor manufacturers whose cars are on our streets. So anyone looking for a partner in auto-related technology should be looking more widely than just the recognized vehicle brands; patent searching can lead you to these other suppliers.

Publication – signpost in the market

Filing a single patent application need not be very expensive. Unless withdrawn, a patent application will be published (usually with a search report) typically at 18 months from the earliest filing date (or earlier at the applicant's request). Once published it can be detected by others searching the databases – which could be useful in attracting partners, customers and even investors who are using the database as part of a 'commercial intelligence' search (see above). Even if the patent application itself goes no further – it is not examined or granted – the application will remain in the database as a signpost to the entire market that your company is active in that area, and potentially worth talking to. Compare that with the cost of an advertisement in a trade magazine, and consider the global accessibility of the patent databases, and suddenly the small cost of getting the application filed and published is easy to justify.

Patents as signposts

A graphic designer was once given a job to print advertising material on paper that had to fold in a very special way – from A4 down to the size of a credit card. He approached one supplier of such paper but found their offer rather expensive. The supplier alleged he was the owner of patents on the paper folding technology, and told the graphic designer that he had no option but to buy from him.

Upon advice from a patent expert, the designer checked a free patent database where he discovered that:

∎ the supplier had only a pending application – it was not yet granted;
∎ the pending application had had several documents cited against it by the search examiner that challenged the novelty of many claims and therefore cast doubt on the scope of any future granted patent;
∎ there were many other patent applications for similar products, some of which had not resulted in granted patents or were not otherwise being kept in force.

This patent search therefore led the designer to contact a second supplier. This second supplier confirmed that it still used the technology, and still made the products, even though it had abandoned its patent application before grant. The second supplier was able to provide the designer with what he needed at a reasonable price and on time.

The designer was not a patent owner, nor was the second supplier. But both concluded a profitable deal because the patent database enabled one to find the other.

Publication – a 'spoiler' for rivals

Many SMEs when asked about owning patents say they have no wish to 'control a monopoly' in their market. It would be too much effort. Rather, they are content with their share of the market and are quite happy to compete equally on conventional grounds like product price, product quality, delivery times, after-sales service, accessories, etc. However, the one thing they could not tolerate would be any other player in their market having exclusive patent rights – this is the thing they dread.

In such circumstances a perfectly valid and effective strategy can be to disclose your invention's technical information in such a way as to prevent any rivals obtaining a patent on the same invention at a later date. This is so-called 'prophylactic disclosure' – a disclosure that protects you from being subject to someone else's later patent.

To help any patent examiner find your 'prior art' when considering the applications filed by rivals in the future, it is best to make your disclosure in a patent application. Even if your application is never granted, it will still spoil the later patent ambitions of others.

For those who might read about a competitor's patent application (once published in the database) and who believe that they have evidence that casts doubt on the novelty or inventiveness of said application, there is the option to file evidence against it for free. These are called 'third-party observations', and give the public a chance to add to the stock of evidence an examiner will consider when deciding whether or not to grant a patent. Those who submit such observations do not become involved in the examination process – they just file their evidence and walk away. The EPO provides an online file inspection service so that you can see the fate of the unfolding examination rounds on any published pending application.[2]

Licensing-in

Often businesses are told that owning a patent can generate licensing revenue. This is true. But not so often are businesses advised that they can be spared the hassle of owning a patent, and the hassle of inventing or developing solutions to problems, by licensing-in someone else's technology.

When addressing any new technical problem, try to calculate how much the problem is costing you, and then measure that against the cost of developing your own solution. Often licensing-in makes perfect business sense if it is cheaper, and yet again it gives a chance to form a partnership or strategic alliance with another player in your area. Once you are buying a licence from them they are more likely to treat you with favourable terms in their other dealings with you. Furthermore, if you were to develop an improvement to the product or process you are licensing from them, you might just be able to patent that and license it back to them.

Alternatives to litigation

One day your enterprise might be making enough money to be able to pay for a patent to be granted, and pay for all its associated translation costs[3] and renewal fees. But when your patent is infringed, the litigation costs can be very much more than all the costs already paid for the patent, and there is always a risk that your patent will be found to be invalid (for example because of some prior art not available to the examiner when he or she first granted the patent). Then you would be left with no patent, no exclusivity in the market, no damages, in fact nothing except a very big bill!

When infringement occurs, and that red mist descends, and you want to scream for justice and get your 'day in court' – keep cool. Reflect. Ask yourself: are you in business to win court cases, or in business to make a profit? If you can make more money staying out of court, then consider the alternatives.

Mediation (a negotiation led by an independent facilitator) and arbitration (where an independent expert imposes a decision) are quicker and cheaper than many court cases. They also tend to produce the sort of compromise solutions not seen in black and white court judgements. Best of all, such proceedings are confidential (unlike court cases) so there is less risk of publicity harming your reputation, or of trade secrets (relied upon as evidence in the dispute) being made public.

Ideally you want to turn the infringer into a partner, so try to sell them a licence. If they refuse, offer them the licence on cheaper terms. Selling a cut-price licence is better than making no money at all, or risking losing any litigation. The infringer might have access to larger markets than you could ever reach on your own, so having them as a partner (rather than making an enemy of them in court) could be more profitable in the long run.

An inducement for a reluctant licensee (or a bold infringer) is to offer them a licence in not only the patent but also in any complementary know-how (eg, optimal process conditions, supporting process data or trade secrets). If you have such additional cards up your sleeve, now is the time to play them. It is worth mentioning at this point that when the patent was first drafted the intended commercialization route should have been a factor. If licensing was the purpose of the patent, it should have indicated how it integrates with the systems of potential licensees, so as to encourage licensing.

If the infringer cannot be converted into a licensee, consider these three more radical options (all of which I have seen done):

1. Take the money that would have been spent on litigation and spend it on marketing, thereby recovering more market share faster by simply out-selling the infringer.
2. There is no point suing an infringer who is in financial trouble anyway (bankrupt firms do not pay damages), so buy the infringer's company and bring their equipment and materials into your own premises.
3. Sell or license your patent to the infringer's leading competitor. The infringer knew you could not afford to take them to court, but they will get a shock when the new owner of the patent sends them a writ!

Be aware that in some countries not attempting to enforce a patent within several years of an infringement taking place can lead to the courts saying that the patent has become unenforceable. Your unwillingness to enforce would be taken to be an implicit approval of the infringement, which the rest of the market can then take for granted.

If you do decide to go to court, be very careful about how you make your allegations and to whom. The law provides defences for those who might be aggrieved by the threats of a patentee. For example, if a medium-sized company does not fancy its chances against a larger infringing firm, it might decide to bully the large firm's small retailers instead. It would threaten each of those small retailers with infringement proceedings, just for stocking and selling the alleged infringing products. This would not be allowed – the dispute has to be taken to the manufacturer if at all possible.

Conclusion

There is more to patent strategy than owning, renewing and licensing out granted patents. Commercial advantages can be had just by using patent information. Simply publishing a patent application without seeing it through to grant can attract customers, partners and even investors. For patent owners facing infringement there are alternative and cost-effective ways to recover lost market share, even if they do not result in 'justice' for the offence. Keep calm – dashing into court is rarely wise.

At all times remember that you are in business to make money. Patents are a means to that end, not an end in themselves.

About the author

Jeremy Philpott is Innovation Support Manager at the European Patent Academy, based in the European Patent Office in Munich. He leads on a range of projects to educate industry, business advisers and technology transfer professionals on patent strategy and innovation management. Most recently he has worked in a consortium of 19 European institutions in the development of IP training materials for business, covering commercialization, enforcement and patent searching, as part of the European Commission's 'ip4inno' project.

The European Patent Office is Europe's patent granting authority. It has a mission to support innovation, competitiveness and economic growth for the benefit of the citizens of Europe. The European Patent Academy promotes and supports patent-related IP training activities in Europe.

Further details: jphilpott@epo.org, www.epo.org.

Notes

[1] The active ingredient in medicines, pesticides and herbicides can enjoy additional protection after expiry of the patent if its entry into the market has been delayed by, for example, official safety approval procedures. This is possible using Supplementary Protection Certificates (SPCs), which may last up to five years.

[2] Register Plus service from the EPO: http://www.epoline.org/portal/public/registerplus.

[3] Translation costs in Europe have come down since the implementation in May 2008 of the London agreement. This means that in many countries there is no longer a requirement to file a translation of the full granted patent document in the language of the country in question, but only a translation of the claims. For more information see: http://www.epo.org/topics/issues/london-agreement.html.

2

The creative organization

 STRATEGYN

Strategyn UK
Revolutionize the Innovation Process for Predictable Growth

Strategyn UK helps product and service companies in B2B and B2C sectors create corporate innovation programs that drive product, service, operational and business model innovation.

We enable companies to create a culture of innovation and a systematic, rigorous engine for risk-mitigated organic growth. At the heart of our approach is Outcome-Driven Innovation.

WHAT IS OUTCOME-DRIVEN INNOVATION?

Outcome-Driven Innovation is a proven innovation methodology that helps companies discover more breakthrough product and service opportunities and enjoy fewer abandoned and failed development efforts. Applying the principles of Six Sigma, it transforms innovation from a hit and miss, high-risk, costly activity into a more rigorous, predictable and measurable logic and process.

The ODI method is based on two simple yet compelling principles.

1) Customers use products and services to help them get "jobs" done
2) Customers have a range of measurable "outcomes" they are trying to achieve as they try to get a job done.

By identifying important yet unsatisfied jobs and outcomes, Outcome Driven Innovation reveals precise areas of opportunity for market growth, disruption or the creation of new markets.

Outcome-Driven Innovation has been adopted by several Global 500 companies such as Microsoft, Hewlett Packard, Motorola, Bosch, Johnson & Johnson, AIG, Medtronic and State Farm Insurance. Moreover, it has supplanted QFD, Voice of the Customer and other programmes in firms as a best practice and new standard for innovation.

Strategyn UK clients span the UK and mainland Europe and include Coloplast, Novozymes, AXA Group, Garlock, Hager, ESRI and Freedom 4.

OUTCOME-DRIVEN INNOVATION FEEDS STAGE-GATE®

Many organizations use the outcome-driven innovation approach to feed their Stage-Gate® product development process. In doing so, they achieve higher success rates and faster returns on investment. This is just one of many applications of the method.

WHAT WE DO

Strategyn UK provides outcome-driven innovation project work, education, training, consulting, and mentoring services – everything a company needs to unlock hidden opportunities, devise breakthrough solutions, and gain intellectual and financial backing for its unique and valued ideas. Our programmes are designed to help you overcome inherent organizational barriers to innovation. With Strategyn UK's guidance, companies can adopt the outcome-driven paradigm and surge to the forefront of innovation.

CONTACT STRATEGYN UK

Strategyn UK, Portland House, Bressenden Place, LONDON. United Kingdom. SW1E 5RS
www.strategyn.co.uk   Phone: + 44(0) 845 057 4091   Email: uk@strategyn.com

Stage-Gate® is a trademark of Stage-Gate Corporation

Outcome-Driven Innovation:
Revolutionize the innovation process
by Anthony W. Ulwick, CEO and Founder, Strategyn
and Chris Lawer, MD, Strategyn UK.

Innovation is the key to company growth, yet as a business process, it is poorly understood, its execution is highly inefficient, and its output is unpredictable. Why? Because the innovation process and the development and marketing activities that support it are broken for two very fundamental reasons. First, there is no agreement on precisely what the inputs into the innovation process should be. Second, there is no consensus on how the inputs should be used to make marketing or research and development decisions. It's that simple.

It is time for companies to give the innovation process the same level of scrutiny as other business processes. It is clear that outdated paradigms must be shattered and that new standards are needed. The outcome-driven innovation methodology is the key. By sweeping away outdated thinking and reinventing the front end of innovation, the outcome-driven methodology enables companies to transform innovation from an unstructured process into a predictable, rules-based discipline. With clear insight into what a customer need is, with methods for accurately quantifying which needs are unmet, and with new ways to devise solutions to address those unmet needs, the outcome-driven methodology gets the fundamentals of innovation right. It is being acknowledged by firms across the world as the new global standard for innovation.

The outcome-driven innovation methodology is philosophically different from other approaches to innovation in eight distinct ways. We examine each in turn:

(1) THE INNOVATION PROCESS IS EXECUTED IN A SEQUENCE THAT ENSURES SUCCESS

To execute the innovation process effectively, a company must first identify *all* the customer's needs, then conduct research to determine which are unmet, and only then devise solutions that address those unmet needs. In other words, all unmet needs must be discovered *before* potential solutions are devised. This is the sequence in which the outcome-driven methodology is executed, and although this sounds like a logical sequence, it is in stark contrast to most innovation processes, including the widely accepted Stage-Gate process, which put the generation of ideas first.

Generating ideas first is an inefficient approach to innovation because it is only by chance that a company will devise a solution that successfully addresses a number of unmet needs. After all, how can solutions that address unmet needs be devised in a predictable manner without knowing what those unmet needs are to begin with? Brainstorming solutions and testing them with customers in an iterative fashion is common, but this practice is analogous to guessing at the answer to a simultaneous mathematical equation – the guessing could go on forever, and the equation might never be solved.

By knowing what the customer's unmet needs are up front, the guessing stops, process efficiency improves, and the process output becomes predictable. These improvements combine to bring lower costs, less risk, and high success rates to companies striving for growth through innovation.

STRATEGYN

(2) VALUE CREATION IS BASED ON A SYSTEM OF MEASUREMENT INSTINCTIVE TO CUSTOMERS

Many companies support the theory that customers buy products and services for a specific purpose: to get jobs done. By *job*, we mean the fundamental goals customers are trying to accomplish or problems they are trying to solve in a given situation. (Harvard Business School professor Clayton Christensen backs this thinking in *The Innovator's Solution*). Making the job the unit of analysis is the cornerstone of the outcome-driven innovation philosophy. From the customer's perspective, it is the job that is the stable, long-term focal point around which value creation should be centered because the job's perfect execution reflects the customer's true definition of value.

Accepting the job as the sole unit of analysis has important downstream ramifications. Once accepted, companies must stop capturing requirements on products and services and instead must understand and capture requirements on the jobs those products and services are intended to perform. Figuring out how to help customers get a job done better or helping them get other jobs done becomes the goal of innovation. This is a whole new way of thinking and dictates the type of customer input that is needed to execute the innovation process.

(3) THE PURPOSE, STRUCTURE, CONTENT, AND FORMAT OF A NEED STATEMENT IS STANDARDIZED

Because customers buy products to help get jobs done, in order to improve an existing product or to create a new product, companies must be able to figure out where the customer struggles in the execution of a specific job and then devise new ways to make improvements. To accomplish this task, companies must analyze the job of interest and ascertain from customers what must be measured and controlled to ensure the job is executed with the speed, predictability, and output they desire. The metrics customers use to measure the successful execution of a job are what we call the customers' desired outcomes; they are the customers' fundamental measures of performance associated with getting a job done. So, when trying to help customers get a job done better, the goal is to uncover the customers' unmet desired outcomes first and then to devise solutions to address them. This is where the term "outcome-driven innovation" originates.

(4) THE INPUTS NEEDED TO DISCOVER OPPORTUNITIES FOR NEW MARKET CREATION ARE STANDARIZED

When a company wishes to engage in adjacent market growth or wants to discover opportunities for new market creation, it must discover which jobs customers are having trouble getting done rather than discovering which outcomes in a specific job need improvement. Finding these underserved jobs enables companies to discover new market growth opportunities. Once an underserved job is discovered and becomes a growth target for the company, the job is dissected and the customer's unmet desired outcomes are uncovered for that job.

(5) UNMET CUSTOMER NEEDS ARE DISCOVERED AND PRIORITIZED WITH PRECISION

Which desired outcomes represent the best opportunities for core and new market growth? Which jobs represent the best opportunities for adjacent and new market creation? To answers these questions, companies must be able to figure out which outcomes or jobs are most important and least satisfied. The opportunity algorithm, shown below, is a simple mathematical formula that makes it possible for companies to do just that. Using this algorithm, which has proven effective in hundreds of applications

over the past eight years, companies can uncover hidden opportunities with precision and prioritize the most promising opportunities for growth.

As part of the outcome-driven innovation philosophy, it is assumed that an opportunity for innovation exists when a job or an outcome is important and not well satisfied. The more important the job or outcome is, and the less satisfied customers are, the greater the opportunity is for value creation.

(6) HIDDEN SEGMENTS OF OPPORTUNITY ARE DISCOVERABLE IN EXISTING AND NEW MARKETS

When it comes to segmenting markets for the purpose of innovation, it is well accepted that companies must be able to successfully identify groups of customers that share a unique set of unmet needs. Finding these unique segments of opportunity – if they exist – can transform an entire industry. Companies must use the customer's unmet needs as the bases around which to segment the market, but without an agreed-on definition of a need and an agreed-on method for quantifying the degree to which a need is unmet, needs-based segmentation methods will not work. This explains the volatility in traditional needs-based segmentation methods and their historical lack of success.

When, however, *need* is defined as a desired outcome and *unmet* is defined as important and unsatisfied, needs-based segmentation can finally be put to practical use. Being able to segment markets into groups of customers with different unmet needs not only enables companies to discover hidden segments of opportunity, it informs other strategic decisions as well. For example, companies are able to determine how best to enter a market as a new entrant, detect the presence of overserved segments that are ripe for disruption, determine if certain customers would pay more for advanced solutions, and decide which customers should not be targeted at all.

(7) FOCUSED IDEA GENERATION METHODS REPLACE SCATTERSHOT BRAINSTORMING TECHNIQUES

Many companies tie the success of a brainstorming session to the number of ideas that are generated. It is not uncommon to see hundreds of ideas generated in a seemingly successful session. But then reality sets in: someone must try to determine which of those ideas are worth pursuing. Searching through the clutter of ideas can take months and will involve guesswork unless the company knows what unmet needs the customer has.

In the outcome-driven world, the approach is turned around. With customer needs already identified and prioritized, creative efforts are much more focused: they concentrate solely on devising valued and potentially breakthrough solutions to address high-priority, unmet needs. The goal of this effort is not to generate hundreds of ideas; rather, it is to devise one or two ideas that will dramatically increase the customer's level of satisfaction for each unmet need and do so for little product cost, development effort, or technical risk.

(8) ALL MARKETING AND DEVELOPMENT STRATEGIES ARE ALIGNED WITH MARKET OPPORTUNITIES

In many companies, research and development, marketing, and sales independently capture requirements from customers in an attempt to get the information they need to guide their decisions and strategies. Because their reasons for obtaining these inputs may differ, and because there is no

agreement on what inputs are needed to begin with, each function is likely to end up using different inputs. As a result, their strategies are likely to be misaligned, dividing the company's energies and focus. To overcome this problem, all the functions must use a single set of customer inputs -those derived from the outcome-driven innovation process.

In the outcome-driven organization, a single set of customer inputs drives and aligns strategies for messaging, positioning, purpose branding, and sales, along with strategies for beating the competition, pipeline prioritization, concept creation and evaluation, patent portfolio development, acquisition assessment, research and development, and other related activities. Because it aligns company thinking with the customer's value measurement system, the outcome-driven methodology has far-reaching benefits.

ADOPTING A NEW STANDARD FOR INNOVATION

The secret to success in innovation lies in a company's ability to gain agreement amongst all those responsible for innovation as to what a need is and what unmet means. This is a prerequisite to agreeing on what solutions best address customers' unmet needs. Adopting the outcome-driven philosophy brings resolution to these debilitating problems, as it provides an elegant, integrated system that brings predictability to innovation.

Using this system, companies are able to uncover true customer needs and to determine which are unmet, and how much so. Companies are able to focus their creativity on devising solutions that address opportunities for growth. With the data the outcome-driven methodology provides, companies can make innovation investments, and the big bets, with confidence. And the data are also used to guide many other marketing and development activities – infusing them all with information that revolutionizes and energizes their execution. The outcome-driven philosophy is the master key that unlocks the door to success in innovation.

A whole company approach to innovation

Today, ideas are developed and refined in conjunction with multiple stakeholders – customers, retailers, suppliers and users. Garrick Jones, a partner at Ludic and a research fellow at the London School of Economics, reports.

The collective knowledge in any commercial organization contains a wealth of contextual information – a vital source of ideas for innovation. Nobody knows more about the market, customers, issues, trends and opportunities than those who are working with these realities on a daily basis. The question is how to best get at that knowledge in a way that takes maximum advantage of the opportunities and leads to real innovation in products and services, in a timely manner. We call this the whole company approach to innovation. It is a multi-layered yet simple combination of people management, design events, product research and development, and lean continuous improvement principles that lead to rich, innovative outcomes. Through careful sequencing of multi-disciplinary events throughout the design process, new products and services are informed by the knowledge of those closest to the market. A model for this could be continuous cycles of learning, creating and communicating.

The nature of work is rapidly changing. Most innovation and production is project led, powered by teams that disappear after its goals are achieved. This is becoming as true for aircraft production as it is for the development of new derivative products for banking. Another condition we face is the loss of proximity. Teams may be working on components of a solution across geographic and time boundaries. The time that teams are able to spend together is precious. How can the most be made of those interactions? One response to tapping into the contextual knowledge resources of the workforce is design workshops and lab events. No longer is innovation the domain of the specialist removed from the real world, cooking up new ideas in a distant lab.

For reasons to do with the growth of the knowledge economy, innovation and competitiveness, organizations require new skills, and are under pressure to be 'porous' using networks, strategic alliances and partnerships to achieve their aims. Today, when the economic and competitive pressures on organizations to grow are increasing, it is the means by which organizations innovate that make the difference. The trend is clear – those companies that are shifting toward open, collaborative and multi-disciplinary practices have the advantage.

Innovation is a group sport

Bringing new products and services to market successfully requires the broad co-operation of many very different teams beyond just the ideas merchants. Marketers, product and service designers, programme managers, IP lawyers, distributors, advertisers, supply chain managers, producers and packagers all have to be factored in. In the most successful cases teams are working in parallel, kicking off processes that are vital to successful implementation long before the finished product has been decided. Boeing created the 777 and had it certified on both sides of the Atlantic simultaneously. Apple got the iPod out in time for Christmas.

It is no longer cost-effective to allow isolated design phases and research to hand over an idea in search of a market. Today, ideas are developed and refined in conjunction with multiple stakeholders – customers, retailers, users and sales-people.

Trust and flexibility are vital. Successful organizations create cultures of trust and enable flexible networks that promote mutual understanding, rapid learning and the ability to change course mid-stream. Competitive advantage can be described as the ability to learn, innovate or continuously reposition with respect to the competition.

Complex programme management requires many threads to operate in parallel. Alignment between these parallel processes is enabled by interaction and communication. Successful organizations, whether formally constructed or networks of affiliated companies, need to work hard at enabling both the relationships and the communication required. The best managers actively design opportunities to do so.

As we move to a networked economy the concept of the linear supply chain has transformed into that of the non-linear value web. Successful organizations are able to identify the members of their value web and create opportunities where all these resources are working in harmony and focused on a single goal – getting the products or services to market on time, on budget and desirable to the consumer.

IBM, Sony and Toshiba are working together on new IT products; they have had to work together to stay in the market, and been innovative as a result. The micro-projector (soon to be found in every mobile phone) is a joint production by multiple specialist technology companies. However, open innovation practices are not only limited to extending the traditional boundaries of the organization into its value-web.

Today, everybody within the organization who has a stake in the outcome of a project has a voice. This requires a different way of organizing projects, and very large scale events or design labs are where the work is being done.

Collaboration, both formally and informally arranged, has significantly increased within organizations as a tool for strategic development, innovation, corporate education, and problem-solving purposes. Along side collaborative practices, action research, activity-based systems and participatory media are being employed as organizational processes for enabling active employee engagement. We call such approaches collaborative authored outcomes.

Spaces for innovation

Physical and virtual environments are evolving to support these new requirements for knowledge led innovation. Collaborative learning environments (CLEs) are fully flexible workspaces equipped so that groups of different sizes may actively engage in learning-based decision-support processes. As group-based tools and techniques grow in sophistication, so too do the demands made on the environments in which innovation is taking place. Some of the forms that these environments take range from the informal to the highly structured, the improvised and mobile, the laboratory to the socially integrated, the physically static to the highly ephemeral – these structures are providing opportunities for the combination and recombination of ideas through generative and instrumental mechanisms. Some exist as centres of decision making, others exist only for the period in which the groups come together for a specific purpose.

Spaces for innovation are constructed fundamentally as learning and production environments. These are places where groups from across the disciplines and functions are able to get together to exchange contextually relevant information, and to put it into production. The idea is to put ideas into action there and then.

A physical environment

Imaginative environments for innovation full of toys, puzzles and books have been around for some time now. However, the playful interior often masques a serious infrastructure that means business. These work spaces are designed for creative work – and they often work very hard indeed.

They are essentially theatres for large group work, which also contain smaller spaces to work individually or in teams. It may be possible to draw on the walls, but more significantly, there is ready access to information and focused databases, which enable rapid decision making, There may also exist a team of people who are dedicated to capturing everything you produce and placing it in an easy to access web tool, seconds after you have produced it. These environments contain a matrix of electrical and audio visual sub-systems to permit multiple configurations for group work.

They ensure that when large groups get together the experience is potent, useful and enjoyable. Where film making has pre-production, production and post-production facilities to successfully create in a highly networked creative environment, so too does the innovation industry. The products may differ but the techniques are very similar.

A virtual knowledge environment

The collective knowledge inherent in any commercial context contains a wealth of information. Such a database exists physically, virtually and socially, both within our heads and within groups or teams.

Paying attention to the knowledge environment in which a group is innovating enables more powerful decision making. A support crew captures all the information generated by participants, in every format, documentation, video, sound, handwritten, photographic and the web. Making this generative knowledge base available to participants seconds after its creation allows them to be used as powerful reflexive resources.

The capture and display of information in multiple formats provides instantaneous feedback to large groups. Through ever more increasing cycles of feedback, a group is able to navigate its way through labyrinths of information. Providing documenta- tion and knowledge bases for large groups as they move through cycles of creativity, design and production creates a narrative of the journey of their development, as well as cataloguing both the end goal and the iterations that were needed to achieve it. Beyond a single project, these virtual records become powerful learning tools for the next set of programmes coming after. They also provide context-rich records, which enable those joining the teams later in the cycles to understand what has been going on.

Online tools exist that enable asynchronous development of ideas across geo- graphies and time boundaries. Collaborative authoring tools, participatory media, project management tools and other social software are enabling very large groups to exchange information. Online 'jams' are being held as events across a number of days, to specifically enable vast numbers of employees to focus their ideas on a particular topic or set of prototypes. Video conferencing allows people to exchange ideas at their desktops.

However, despite the sophistication of online tools, nothing can substitute for the assiduous sequencing of events and information that leads to the successful development of an idea from conception through to launch in the market. This is a process that will always require careful design and nurturing.

Prototyping, simulation and play

When a large group is engaged in collaborative decision making, it may be useful to construct all manner of models of conceptual ideas, and to test them. Simulation, the playing of games, the construction of small worlds, testing of hypotheses, questioning, the reordering of information and scenario testing are all tools used for innovation.

A collaborative learning environment provides all the resources required to do so. These may include construction materials for modelling, spreadsheets for financial modelling, large surfaces to write on and iterate ideas, surfaces for moving information around the space, screens for running simulations between groups, areas for role-play, break-out spaces for groups to work in parallel, and video facilities for groups to create scenarios. Networked technology enables parallel work by groups exploring the contextual field as they work through group processes of defining and refining options.

Essentially, whole company innovation is about connecting the right team with information, design resources, processes and documentation in a manner that enables deep understanding of the landscape of information, critical exploration of alternatives and opportunity to prototype ideas – and launch them into the market.

Flexibility and communication in a value web are directly related to the quality of interpersonal relationships – establish multiple opportunities for these to develop.

As a system moves through the cycles from innovation, proof of concept, piloting, testing to production, marketing and distribution – the qualities and skills required of teams change. These phases have their own distinct personalities and qualities and it takes a savvy manager to promote the context, attitude and environment required for each team within each phase to be successful.

During innovation phases teams function best if they are:

■ autonomous;
■ configured with the best members for the task;
■ connected to customers;
■ connected to your value-web;
■ skilled in disciplines associated with innovation;
■ incentivized and measured.

Each phase in the lifecycle requires different skills to take the lead – in principle moving from the unstructured to the structured. Even self-organizing teams need to recognize that the leaders of creative phases are usually different from the leaders of piloting, testing, production and distribution phases. An important thing not to lose sight of though, is that as the baton changes hands, the teams are still checking in with customers and the entire value-web. Rapid iterations and feedback cycles are best at all phases. Empowerment is vital – understand the acknowledged experts in the teams and let them make the decisions. Let packaging experts decide on packaging, let the logistics specialists decide on distribution, let designers make the design decisions. Flatten the hierarchies, and enable decision making.

Check in with your value-web

The opinions of your clients, employees, suppliers, customers and learning networks continue to be vital throughout the inexorable march to market. Encourage osmosis of ideas. In addition to generating ideas, you also begin to mobilize the users of the products, creating the buzz around the new products long before they are launched, and creating an influential user community in the process.

Rapid iterations and feedback cycles

Creating opportunities for rapid iterations and feedback increases the sophistication of the product. IDEO creates project spaces and displays for its products in design that are open for conversation with anyone who is passing. The products are always visible, the teams are always in close proximity to each other. The same holds true for the design of services, process flows, video scenarios and use-case descriptions, which enable the communication of these ideas. Encourage teams to build formal and informal feedback cycles into their processes, throughout the lifecycle of development and production.

Empowerment is vital

Flattened hierarchies only work when roles are clear and everybody knows who takes responsibility for what. Making these roles visible helps. This is not to say that everybody is allowed an opinion on everything. The eureka moment may come from anywhere on a team, but the final decision should rest with the expert on the team.

The serving role of leadership

The role of leadership within fast moving, complex networks is to serve the needs of the team's ultimate objective – through facilitation, arbitration and demonstration. Leaders need to be sensitive to changing moods of the network, to understand what blockages exist and to facilitate the opportunities for teams to solve the problems. Arbitration is vital when differences of opinion exist – to ensure differences are tested and to ensure that decisions are made in order to enable progress. Fundamentally leaders of innovation model the behaviours they desire to encourage within the broader context of the programme.

Acknowledge the programme phase

Sensitivity to the phase of the programme enables a large group to be clear about what needs to be done and who needs to take the lead. Film production is a powerful example of this because it's so visible. Studio time is costly, and everyone is aware of the phases of production – from filming, to editing, to screen testing and distribution. Acknowledge the programme phase and acknowledge the phase leader.

Incentives and measures

Although teams need to be autonomous, it is important that members of the teams feel rewarded for the work they are doing. Most learning takes place in failure and the design process honours failure. High volume, low risk failure! However, business success is also a factor of time and budget – and incentives to meet these targets are vital. Measuring the success of teams against understood criteria, established clearly at the start, provides security. Getting things to market requires clear goals and deadlines. Healthy competition between teams allows the bar to be continuously raised on quality, outcome and sophistication. Teams find a sense of flow when they are challenged and tested in an environment that provides the skills necessary to achieve. All successful innovation, at the end of the day, is about people having fun.

The state-of-the-art collaborative learning environment represents a complex ecology of support systems, environment, tools and technical systems, production systems, learning systems, project management and process support. These represent the infrastructures required to enable a whole company approach to innovation. To paraphrase Einstein, if we wish to get different results, we have to use different tools – and in this case, it's those tools that enable us to harness the collective knowledge of the whole company that leads to successful innovation.

About the author

Garrick Jones is an academic, consultant and musician based in London. He is a partner of the Ludic Group, which produces innovation programmes and advise on the development and operation of collaborative learning environments (CLEs), and design-led innovation. His career includes Director of Ernst & Young's Accelerated Solutions Environment (ASE) and Director of the Innovation Unit – Innovate:UK. His academic research is focused on large scale group work and he is the first 1851 Commission Fellow in Design, where his research is focused on the power of games for educating design thinking in business. He studied at the University of Oxford, is a research fellow at the London School of Economics and Political Science (LSE) and a Senior Lecturer in Industrial Design and Engineering at the Royal College of Art and Design (RCA) and Imperial College. Further details: Garrick Jones, Institute of Social Psychology, London School of Economics and Political Science, Houghton Street, London WC2A 2AE, e-mail G.A.Jones1@lse.ac.uk.

Creativity, design and innovation

Creativity is a natural resource. You just have to find a way of harnessing it, says Lorelei Hunt, Director of Innovation at the South West Regional Development Agency.

Creativity is the generation of new ideas – new ways of looking at existing problems, or seeing new opportunities, exploiting emerging technologies or changes in markets. *Innovation* is the successful exploitation of new ideas. It is the process that carries them through to new products, new services, new ways of running the business or even new ways of doing business. *Design* links creativity and innovation. It shapes ideas to become practical and attractive propositions for users or customers. Design may be described as creativity deployed to a specific end.

The role of creativity in business

Creativity and design are integral to economic growth at a macroeconomic level. The extent to which living standards can increase over time depends on the economy's ability to expand the value of goods and services it produces, relative to the population. Creativity in all its forms is essential to this process. Growing economies depend on the generation of a wide variety of ideas that can be turned into new products, services and ways of working. This ability to generate a diverse set of business options through new ideas is a central feature of innovation in business and, as such, is central to sustained economic growth.

Linking knowledge, innovation and creativity

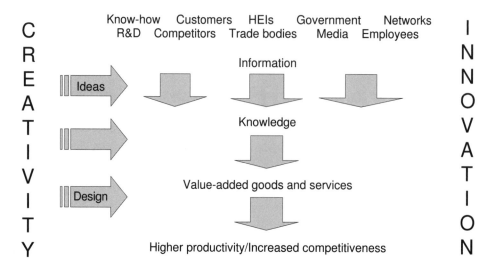

Figure 2.2.1 Linking knowledge, innovation and creativity

Sustained success in business, regardless of sector, increasingly requires the ability to innovate: to exploit new ideas and new opportunities ahead of the competition. Creativity can be thought of as the first stage in innovation – the production of new ideas that are fit for a particular business purpose and have the potential to be turned into successful innovation. The ability to innovate thus depends on the availability and exploitation of creative skills.

Creativity needs to be channelled in the right way – it is a necessary but not sufficient condition for innovation. It has a role in enhancing all aspects of business performance, from the design of new products and services to their production, marketing and distribution. Creativity is often linked to certain industries such as film, music or design, but this is to take a very narrow view of the role and potential of creativity. The challenge is to encourage creativity in all industries in order to promote innovation and growth.

Creativity and design can be used to describe processes within business as well as outputs such as new and improved products and services. There are clear links between creativity, design and research and development (R&D). Design and R&D are both ways of channelling creativity for commercial advantage, and aspects of design form part of R&D. However, design is also an important form of innovation in industries that tend to invest less in R&D. This means that creativity and design may be particularly important for innovation in the service sector.

The diverse nature of creativity and design highlights the significance of different types of design skills using a whole range of knowledge, from the very rational knowledge of engineering design, to the expressive, subjective knowledge of fashion and graphic design. Most goods and services design requires some combination of both subjective, artistic activities and 'hard' objective sciences. The development of novel concepts or approaches is not always dependent upon new technologies and may be developed by non-technical people, including users and customers, who see new solutions or ideas to existing or new problems or opportunities using established technologies.

Creativity and business performance

Models developed in the UK (Swann and Birke, 2005, and the Work Foundation) emphasize the creative workplace or climate in the workplace as an important driver of creativity and firm performance. This captures the idea that successful companies will look not only to R&D or design as creative inputs, but seek to promote creativity in all parts of the organization. It builds upon the notion that creativity is not the province of specialists or gifted individuals but a common human capability. Studies have shown a positive link between creativity and overall company performance across nearly 3,000 UK firms; a survey by the CBI found that creativity and innovation was cited by 37 per cent of businesses as important to organizational competitiveness – the fourth highest of 15 possible factors.

The importance of design

Interest in design has grown as a result of global competition and the growing importance of non-price factors in determining competitiveness. Design underpins a whole variety of product and service characteristics, including style (product design), durability, convenience and quality, waiting times and customization. These characteristics can be more important than price in generating demand.

Design, as a structured creative process, is an important competitive tool for firms in many sectors and there is a variety of evidence to support the role of design in enhancing firm performance. Firms with higher design intensity are more likely to carry out product innovation; and there is a positive link between design expenditure and the productivity growth of a firm.

Surveys suggest that design is distributed across sectors and by firm size – it is a more accessible tool for innovation than R&D. The Community Innovation Survey (CIS) and other UK-based surveys show the extent to which firms report investment in design; or the importance they attach to design within their business. However, of all businesses, nearly 70 per cent report that design is of little or no importance to their business. This might be because there is no official definition of design (as now exists for R&D) and no formal design process used in many businesses.

It can be more difficult to see the impact of design in different industry sectors. Design is easily associated with the specific 'look' of manufactured products, and the role of industrial product design can be understood. It is less easy to understand how service design can affect how customers experience the delivery of a service, or to fully appreciate how elements of design, particularly graphic design, will form part of product, service and company branding and advertising strategy and help to build assets such as market reputation and credibility.

Manufacturers are much more likely than service businesses to claim that design, creativity and innovation played a significant role in their business. It is a cause for concern that design, innovation and creativity are considered of less importance within the service industries when this sector is responsible for such a significant proportion of UK GDP.

Internal factors impacting on creativity and innovation

'Human creativity is the ultimate economic resource. The ability to come up with new ideas and better ways of doing things is ultimately what raises productivity and thus living standards' (Richard Florida, 2002). Creativity is a natural resource, but needs to be harnessed to impact on company performance. The company's ability to use creativity will be affected by the following factors:

■ company culture;
■ skills;
■ management.

Culture

This includes the extent to which the company gets involved in networks. This will influence its ability to collaborate and to be creative, and to benefit from other creative firms through knowledge exchange. This requires the business to be able to absorb and exploit new knowledge by incorporating it into goods and services, or new business processes. The culture of a company also includes the existence of conditions in which employees feel motivated and enabled to use their creativity. Creative businesses are creative throughout.

Skills

This includes the existence of 'creative skills' and the extent to which all of the employees in a business possess these and can use them to support the innovation process. Stereotypes of 'creative' individuals tend to focus on a few characteristics, but the capacity to think creatively is widespread. An effective approach to design at the firm level involves a broad range of people, not just those with specialized training. Turning creative ideas into new ways of thinking and into successful products and services requires a fusion of different skills.

Management

Creativity needs to be skilfully managed. The readiness to consider new ideas must be matched by the ability to recognize and assess their potential, to decide which ones to back and to put them into effect. Key to this is effective managers who understand when to call in external specialists and how to work with them. The way that a business is managed has a significant impact on the extent to which employees can use their creativity to feed the innovation process, and to how design is used to create competitive advantage. Lack of awareness of the role that greater creativity may play in the business has been identified as one of the key barriers to small and medium-sized enterprises making greater use of creative skills, and creativity and design are too often seen as optional extras.

Bibliography

Advanced Institute for Management (AIM) and Imperial College Work Foundation (2005a) *Cracking the Performance Code: How Firms Succeed*

Bessant, J, Whyte, J and Neely, A (2005) *Management of creativity and design within the firm*, DTI 'Think Piece'

Florida, R, *The Rise of the Creative Class*, Basic Books, New York

DTI Economics Paper No 15 (2005) *Design, Creativity and Business Performance*, November

Swann, P and Birke, D (2005) *How do creativity and Design Enhance Business performance? A Framework for interpreting the Evidence*, DTI 'Think Piece', University of Nottingham Business School

Tether, B S (2005) *The Role of Design in Business Performance*, DTI 'Think Piece', Centre for Research on Innovation and Competition (CRIC), University of Manchester

www.research.ibm.com/eclipse/

About the author

Lorelei Hunt is Director of Innovation at South West Regional Development Agency. Her current portfolio includes a wide range of activities aimed at encouraging innovation in regional businesses to build a knowledge-based regional economy. The South West RDA leads the development of a sustainable economy, investing to unlock the region's business potential. Further details: www.southwestrda.org.uk.

Leading for innovation

It is hard to fake belief in innovation. Sincerity and consistency at the top really do matter, says Dr Bettina von Stamm at the Innovation Leadership Forum.

If there is one thing that can make or break the innovation culture in an organization, it is you, the organization's senior management and leadership team. It might sound a little drastic but this chapter is too short to mince words.

My aim with this chapter is twofold: a) to convince you that I am right (about an innovation culture hinging on the organization's leadership) and, b) explain what it actually means to lead for innovation, and hence what is required from you.

The argument

The first time the importance of the modelling role of leadership occurred to me was in 1987 when I was working in an architects' practice of about 30 people. I had been wondering why everyone seemed to be so much in the habit of tearing into whoever was not present in the room, and that no one thought much of it – until I overheard one of the partners encouraging one of the employees to give him the low-down on the other employees: 'So, what is the latest gossip around here?' Telling on colleagues was pretty much requested by 'senior management'; no wonder everyone was busy doing it! In Germany there is a saying, *wie der Herr, so das Gscherr,* which means, like the master so the servants, and I certainly believe that it is very true. Have a look around you and see whether you can observe some of it – in yourself as well as others. Do you notice yourself referencing or quoting your parents? Do you hear your children and think, gosh, that's just what I always say? Imitating and referencing 'the powers that be' starts rather early in life.

Let me share another story. A few years ago I conducted a case study on a smallish creative company (around 35 people). The company had its offices next to Kensington Gardens and the director/owner of the company emphasized how important the location was in as much as it gave employees the opportunity to go out over lunch to clear the head, and get freshly inspired. Agreeing with the importance of having space and the benefit of fresh air and nature, I asked him (for a 'he' it was), how he was spending his lunch time. He looked at me, almost in amazement, and said, 'Of course I am here, in the office, at my desk! I am far too busy to wander about in the park.' When asked whether many of his employees were making use of the park he said, 'No, actually, they don't... peculiar that...'. Do *you* think it is peculiar? Don't you rather think it is quite natural? While the employees *hear* that the boss is emphasizing the benefits of clearing one's head over lunch, they *observe* that he is not doing it. Most of us will follow the example set by the boss rather than 'stick our head above the parapet'.

So it is important to understand that people don't really listen to what we say but observe what we do and draw their conclusions from that. A well-known piece of research by Professor Albert Mehrabian revealed that only 7 per cent of meaning is conveyed through words. That is less that 10 per cent! Thirty-eight per cent of meaning is transmitted through the tone of our voice, and the remaining 55 per cent – over half – through our body language. This is why you can say to a person, 'You are really absolutely terrible' with a laugh, while hugging them, and they will view it as a compliment; or you can say, 'Oh, really well done' in such a tone of voice and expression on your face that there it is quite clear that the person has just made a big mistake.

So it is our actions that matter so much more than our words. This is why sincerity and consistency are such important aspects of innovation – it is hard to fake a belief in innovation. In order to create an innovative organization you have to encourage people to experiment and acknowledge that failure is part of it. If you do not really mean this people will sense your doubts in your tone of voice and spot it in your actions. If you say innovation is important, and then shut down the long-term, speculative project in favour of rescuing next quarter's results, the message will be heard loud and clear. If you say you want innovation, and follow up by saying, but it should fit in with existing operations processes and structures, the message is loud and clear: innovation is nice, but not really that important. And each individual will set their own priorities accordingly.

Consistency is important because creating an innovative organization is about establishing a certain set of behaviours and a certain mindset – and changing behaviours is not easy, nor does it happen quickly. So issuing the message that innovation is important one day, and then changing your mind the next leads to confusion – and keeps people in the status quo. Changing behaviours takes time and effort, and if people believe that it is a passing fashion they will not even try to change, but just wait and lie low until the storm is over.

So, how can you demonstrate that you *are* serious about creating an innovative organization?

What it means to lead for innovation

The first thing you need to do if you want to lead for innovation is to define where the innovation journey is supposed to go – what is the *dream?* What are you trying to achieve? Where is innovation supposed to get you?

> In a recent workshop with senior people working in innovation it was emphasized that it is much more powerful to provide an aspiring vision or dream (opportunity) than using a 'burning platform' (threat) as the starting point for innovation.

It is quite hard for people to innovate against an entirely open brief. If you ask someone, 'Do you have a good idea?' what are they supposed to say? Some guidance is needed to help people assess which idea is a good one and which one is not. The first question should be, does the pursuit of this idea bring us closer to our dream or not? (A possible second question that only slowly moves onto organizations' agendas might be, 'If the idea is not right for us, is there someone else for whom it might be right?')

Part of the guidance you provide should include a description or definition of what kind of innovation you are actually hoping for. Do you really, truly want something outside the business boundaries (and accept all the upheaval and disruption of existing knowledge and structures that goes with it)? Or do you rather seek radical innovation within existing boundaries? Or do you really only want incremental changes to the existing? What do you mean by 'radical' or 'disruptive'? We all seem to have slightly differing views of what radical actually means, and having a shared language for innovation in your organization is essential if you want to avoid confusion and frustration.

Clarifying the boundaries and how much we want of each of the different types of innovation is essential in managing expectations, as well as allocating resources. People are full of ideas – we all have a desire to contribute. Taking the risk and putting an idea forward and getting rejected is tough; but getting rejected and not understanding why is even worse. What has started as an exercise in motivation ends up being the cause for resentment and disengagement.

Once you have created a shared dream you need to ensure that people know how they can contribute to achieving it. Whom do they go to with their idea? Who might be able to help them to develop the idea into a coherent concept? Where are the resources coming from? Putting a different set of processes and structures in place that facilitate this is important. The emphasis is on *different*. The processes and structures you have in place will work well for incremental improvements, but the very aspects that make them so efficient and suited for incremental changes are the ones that would kill off radical changes during the first stages. For radical innovation you need guidance and flexibility, not rules and bureaucracy.

You could wait for ideas to come to you – or you can proactively seek them out and nurture them. You cannot do this by staying in your office. You have to go out and roam the corridors and offices of your organization – and beyond. When you find budding ideas, don't even think about saying: 'We have tried this before', 'That will never work', 'Why has no one else thought of it before' or 'It cannot be done'! What you want to do instead is to check with the originator how the idea might contribute to achieving the dream. If it fits, cut him or her some slack to explore and experiment with the idea. After that you ought to take an active interest in the project's development – go and ask him or her how the project is doing! The 'active interest' includes ensuring that resources are available – which does certainly not mean giving a carte blanche. For radical innovation, leading organizations tend to use staged funding.

Allies for creating an innovative organization

If you are looking for allies in your organization that can help you to shift values and behaviours in the right direction (for innovation is a frame of mind, driven by the prevailing values and behaviours in an organization) you may want to seek out your HR and organizational development people. Bring them on board to make sure that innovation is a stepping stone in people's career – and not an ejector seat. Make sure that behaviours leading to innovation, such as collaborating, networking and taking considered risks are rewarded and recognized rather than punished. Please note that there is increasing evidence that money as a means of motivation and reward has to be considered with the greatest of care. It can even be counterproductive as it undermines the very behaviours that lead to innovation.

During development, check occasionally whether the project is still doing what it set out to do. If it has developed into a different direction, is this for the better of worse? Has it perhaps been curtailed so much that nothing but an incremental change remains? Smith & Nephew put the responsibility for checking the validity of projects to the project teams directly, with quite remarkable results: occasionally the teams themselves would suggest the cessation of a project because they felt it was not really the best use of company resources.

It is your responsibility to ensure that the project is protected from the organization's immune system and not killed in its infancy. Part of this is to take it upon yourself to communicate about the project to your colleagues and to ensure that innovation is on the leadership agenda – and not as the last item either.

One final point: please don't blow your lid when things do not go quite as planned. Failure is part of the innovation game; if you never fail, what you are trying is probably not truly different or new. Embrace and understand the failure, and make sure you learn as much as ever possible from it. Many of our successes are built on the learning to be gained from our failures.

One word of advice

Learning to lead for innovation is essential for the future survival and success of your organization. But do not forget that an organization needs both: excellent, efficient operations *and* first rate innovation. To make both work you need to acknowledge that those who thrive on innovation are generally not the best to drive efficiency and effectiveness – and vice versa. The long-term success of your organization will depend on both, and on both working together well. That is perhaps an even greater challenge, because each of those people has different values and believes – but that is another story.

If you are still sure that creating an innovative organization is truly what you aspire to then, above all, you need to make sure that you not only ask others in the organization to behave as described above, but that you, first and foremost, are the one displaying these behaviours. *Leading for innovation, by example, is* your *responsibility.*

About the author

Bettina von Stamm is hugely passionate about understanding and enabling innovation, particularly in large organizations. For this purpose she has set up her own company, the Innovation Leadership Forum (ILF), part of which is a networking group to exchange and further knowledge about innovation (current members: BASF, British Gypsum, Cancer Research UK, Cargill, GSK Consumer Health, ICI Paints, Marks & Spencer, Mars, The National Health Innovation Institute, National Starch, Nestle, Ordnance Survey, Smith & Nephew, Unilever, and Warburtons). She also enjoys the role of a 'catalyst' in large organizations (for example DSM, Hibernian, Mars, Ordnance Survey and the Financial Ombudsman Services), to speed up the creation of innovative organizations, and keeping a hand in academic research on her favourite topic. In addition she teaches innovation and design management at a number of leading universities in the UK and Germany and shares her passion for innovation at conferences, workshops and other events. For more information you may want to visit the ILF website on www.innovationleadershipforum.org.

Channelling talent to innovate

For many organizations the gap between the rhetoric of innovation and the reality is still huge, says Alison Gill, co-founder, Getfeedback.

Insight, inspiration and ideas

To create an organization that has innovation as part of its DNA requires a focus on thinking, not doing. Innovation is a brain game of which the basic components are insight, ideas and inspiration. By providing an environment that encourages talent to push their thinking beyond the boundaries of the possible, add insight to ideas and be inspired by challenging the status quo, leaders will fan the flames of innovation. To create this culture, leaders need to eradicate bad thinking practice in their organizations. Short-termism, days crammed with activity from 8 am to 6 pm, protection from failure and hierarchy will hinder, not help, innovation. Creating a culture of effective thinking requires a focus at three levels.

1. The individual

There are considerable differences in how individuals approach problem solving and creativity. An appetite for experimentation, comfort in ambiguity, the motivation to persevere, and openness to new experiences all help and can be taught. Learning how individual differences impact the creative process and developing individuals in the required skills are important.

The organizations that will succeed are not the ones that attract talent, but the ones that have learnt how to make talent profitable. (Lowell Bryan: Innovative Management, The McKinsey Quarterly, 2008, 1)

2. The team

Innovation is rarely a solitary pursuit; it is the result of collective thinking in teams, and the more diverse the team the better. Premature solutions, insufficient information, poorly structured questions and the vagaries of group think are hazards that get in the way of effective innovation and must be replaced with disciplined group thinking process.

3. The organization

Innovation must be on the leadership agenda as a clearly articulated component of the vision and architecture of the organization. Leaders must seed innovative thinking by identifying strategically the areas of the business that will most benefit from innovation. With this clarity leaders can chose to assign ongoing responsibility to all employees or to specific teams, for example by aligning innovation to the organization's talent process. Management thinking today typically supports networked structures where wealth creation through innovation is the responsibility of the masses.[1] However, getting it right in smaller groups, or 'skunk works', helps many organizations to get started.

Once a year Bill Gates takes a whole week to review suggestions for innovation and product development from his 80,000 employees. (BlessingWhite Intelligence: Leadership Insights Series: Innovate on the Run)

Embed real team thinking

Getting people to think far enough in to the future and differently enough is one of the greatest challenges of innovation. Brain power (which most organizations have by the ton) needs to be harnessed by applying proven group thinking process.

Regardless of the size of your organization, start with the leadership team and embed simple thinking disciplines there. When the top team is thinking effectively together the rest of the organization gets clear leadership that thinking discipline matters. To get started, first think of the size of the team. The optimum size for a thinking team is six; this is for two reasons: one of attention span and one of capacity. To tackle innovation, ideally your team should be formed of people with diverse perspectives. A leadership team is typically diverse; if your business is small and you don't have a formal leadership team, bring together a group of representatives (customers, suppliers, investors and employees) to support your innovation.

With your team structure in place you can begin the team thinking process. Team thinking has six independent stages each with a specific outcome. The stages go from one, creating a shared understanding, to six, defining success measures and planning. Starting with a simple problem statement such as, 'What are the barriers to innovation in our business?' gets stage one started. In stage one the team must give individual air time for each person to explain their perspective. At each stage the team must dig deeper to uncover the assumptions that they or others are making about the organization, the issue or the solution. Team progress through the stages will differ depending upon the complexity of the challenge and the team's collective ability to demonstrate the leadership behaviours that enable team thinking. In the early stages the verbose must learn to be succinct and organize their ideas in a way that helps others to understand; the dominant talkers must learn to suspend judgement and work hard to truly understand the thinking of other team members; and the persuasive must learn that consensus is the root of all evil when it comes to innovation.

Here are the six stages of Getfeedback's Intelligent Team Thinking Process:

1. Creating a shared understanding of the challenge.
2. External analysis and information search.
3. Information analysis and shared understanding.
4. Concept formation and solution creation.
5. Solution analysis and decision criteria.
6. Success measures and planning.

As the stages progress some members of the group will struggle to hold multiple perspectives, while others will be desperate to prematurely close on a solution without fully considering the pros and cons of different options. At different stages of the process the team must make use of different thinking techniques such as individual and group brainstorming, visualization, SWOT and PESTLE. Used effectively, these tools and others like them help to change thinking from convergent to divergent and to broaden perspectives appropriately. Additionally, the team will need to establish a code of conduct that holds the groups accountable for maximizing the contribution of all team members.

The six principles of optimized team thinking are:

1. Optimum team size for thinking is six people.
2. All team members must suspend hierarchy and operate as equal peers.
3. A toolkit of interventions/techniques is required to aid the appropriate mindset relevant to each stage.
4. A code of conduct that helps the team to moderate their behaviours to maximize contribution.
5. The team must always dig deep to uncover the assumptions that they or others are making about the organization, the issue or the solution.
6. Avoid the pitfalls of group think, consensus and premature conclusion.

Many innovations today are the result of collaboration between multiple organizations, academics, practitioners and employees. Take the development of SMS for example; no one organization can claim independent rights to this innovation. A group of five to eight people from Vodafone, Nokia, IDEG and Cellnet led the collaborative process.[2] Embedding team thinking as a discipline helps an organization succeed at innovation because it teaches individuals to respect diversity, dig deeper to uncover the assumptions that they or others are making about proposed issues or solutions and it creates a value for thorough thinking. Given that the majority of innovations today will involve collaboration either across an organization or across markets and geographies, effective group thinking discipline is a foundation of success.

Leverage individual differences in creativity and problem solving

For the purpose of innovation there are three specific measures of individual difference which are important to consider; the first is that of cognitive ability (intellectual horse-power), the second cognitive style (a preference for adaptation versus innovation) and the third leadership behaviour.

1. Cognitive ability

Cognitive ability is a key predictor of future success in large complex roles. It can be assessed through timed psychometric tests designed for the most part to assess how well someone processes and uses information. There is some controversy about the use of cognitive ability tests as the theory suggests a ceiling to career advancement. However, for the purposes of embedding thinking discipline, cognitive ability scores can be used to ensure individuals learn how to optimize their thinking; lower scorers may, for example, need more time to sift through data and consider options.[3]

2. Cognitive style

Cognitive style refers to the way that people solve problems. Creative management reader Michael Kirton, the author of a tool known as the Kirton Adaption-Innovation (KAI) Inventory[4] posits that individuals can be located on a continuum of cognitive style, ranging from adaptor to innovator. Adaption is characterized as a preference for improving existing practice and innovation to solve problems that challenge accepted practice. The more adaptive will search within a limited area and produce fewer

Table 2.4.1 Adaptors and innovators: style differences

Adaptors	Innovators
Do it better	Do it differently
Working within an existing framework	Challenges and reframes
Fewer, more acceptable solutions	Many solutions
Prefer well-established situations	Set new policy, structure
Essential for ongoing functions	Essential in times of change

acceptable solutions, while the innovative will scatter effort creating many solutions. Forming a team of all innovators often creates multiple ideas and perspectives but they may struggle to conclude. A team of all adaptors, on the other hand, will probably produce a single more conventional solution worked through to a greater level of detail. Compiling a team that spans the continuum will present a challenge to get the group to work together. However, with expert facilitation this can be highly productive because of the greater diversity in problem-solving methodology.

3. Leadership behaviour

Leadership behaviour can be divided in to four distinct dimensions: inspiring outstanding performance, anticipating the changing business landscape, collaborating and connecting, and creating real focus and commitment to action. To successfully innovate requires all four dimensions of behaviour. Throughout the team thinking process particular behaviours are critical to success. For example, empathy (the ability to listen and encourage openness and honesty) is crucial to build trust and respect amongst team members; forming concepts (the ability to link information to explain trends and form solutions) is critical to build on ideas amongst the team; and presentation (the ability to convey ideas with clarity and simplicity) is critical to aid knowledge transfer. Leadership behaviours that are typically highly valued by Western management, for example influence and building confidence, are less helpful to team thinking. Used too early, or at the expense of other behaviours, they cause premature solution creation and closure through group consensus, which is frankly useless if innovation is your goal.

One-dimensional leadership just won't cut it if you want a truly innovative organization. The process of team thinking provides an excellent vehicle to develop multi-dimensional leaders.

Bridge the gap between rhetoric and reality

For many organizations the gap between the rhetoric of innovation and the reality is still huge. When you look at the principles on which old management practice was designed – hierarchy, standardization and specialization – you realize why. By bringing people together in collaborative teams specifically challenged to innovate and by introducing them to the principles of thinking discipline you will start to bridge the gap. The result will be a rich and stimulating work environment in which insight is a highly valued commodity, inspiration is gleaned from tackling real-life business issues and learning is associated with a focus on solving challenges that make a monetized difference to the organization's future.

About the author

Alison Gill is co-founder of talent management consultancy, Getfeedback, which specializes in behavioural change. She describes herself as an academic entrepreneur, having formerly lectured on performance psychology at a number of academic institutions and run a number of successful businesses. She is qualified as a performance psychologist, a triple Olympian, and an adventurer. Ali is interested in intelligent action. Decisions informed by the right information are the bedrock of Getfeedback's business.

For enquiries regarding this chapter please contact the author, alison.gill@ getfeedback.net. Full contact details can be found on our website: www.getfeedback. net.

Notes

[1] Gary Hamel with Bill Breen, *The Future of Management,* Harvard Business School Press, 2007
[2] Finn Trosby, *SMS The Strange Duckling of GSM,* Teletronikk, 3, 2004
[3] The Getfeedback 3T Report: *Talent Management Defined for Today and Tomorrow. A Guide to Talent Management for Now and 2010*
[4] M J Kirton, *Adaptors and Innovators*, London: Routledge, 1994

Building the right team

Innovation does not happen on its own, says Dr Luke Whale, Managing Director at C4Ci. You have to involve the right mix of people to bring an idea to fruition.

One of the greatest challenges innovators face during the realization of their dream is recognizing the moment in the process when they need further help. Many ideas and innovations fall by the wayside due to the originator being so infatuated with their idea that help is sought far too late in the process when the opportunity has either diminished or disappeared. Successful innovation on the other hand is typified by early recognition by the originator that a team of skilled participants will become involved and that together they will likely make the single most significant contribution to the process. The level of interaction and trust between the originator and the extended group of skilled individuals with whom they consult is critical and cannot be valued too highly. Too often in C4Ci's experience of bringing innovation to fruition, we have seen lone innovators trying to develop their brainchild for too long, then become reticent to let go and involve a wider group to refine the idea and to facilitate the changes necessary for it to succeed. It is clear to us that any innovation cannot thrive in the company of the originator alone; it has to feed off an extended family of trusted third parties who will provide the horsepower for the innovation to properly develop, mature and take root.

Innovation is not invention per se but should be considered as the process embodying the rapid or procedural improvement of any current market leading product, process or tool. It is therefore the improvement of what exists already, so with this as the starting point there are some fundamentals to appreciate:

- The new or improved product has a predecessor.
- The predecessor has an established market, customer base and user profile.
- Within that market there is an established performance, which could either be poor, satisfactory, good, or excellent. Essentially the predecessor will have a known performance level and a track record.
- Other individuals and companies will have contributed to the predecessor's success and this may provide a resource capable of appraising the credibility and viability of the improved product.
- The predecessor will inevitably have interacted with other products and systems so it is vital that any innovation will be able to do the same or, better still, offer a further level of innovation in this respect also.

Using the principles of multi-disciplinary consultancy and interaction, it is generally necessary for a development team to be constituted to bring the innovation to commercial fruition, consisting of the following key functions in addition to that of the *innovator.*

Anatomy of the team

1. *A customer or current user (of the predecessor):* this individual should be able to clearly articulate the pros and cons of what it seeks to replace and be able to realistically assess the value and cost of the innovation compared to the existing offering. They are also likely to be involved in prototyping the innovation prior to general release.
2. *A manufacturer:* the product, if it is a physical entity, will need to be manufactured. This could be a relatively easy process, or conversely an enormously costly exercise requiring capital expenditure and extensive change to physical processes, with the consequent challenges and risks that this will entail.
3. *A respected (and cynical) peer group:* all innovations need to be challenged with detailed analysis and critical appraisal. This individual or group can often deliver fresh, down to earth thinking that can take the idea to the next level, and which the innovator will often have failed to see.
4. *A sales and marketer:* commerce and trade underpin any innovative intent and this individual will be able to reconfigure both the key and peripheral benefits of the innovation into a message that can be delivered to the market to persuade the end user to change.
5. *A supply channel partner(s):* partners who can assist with prototyping and field trials and who are also willing to become an active promoter of the innovation are essential to successful initial sales. These could potentially be the 'first adopters'.
6. *A robust sponsor:* innovation can be expensive and a robust business plan that is properly financed is essential. Often the sponsor will become a significant beneficiary of any ensuing success.
7. *A big picture visionary:* very often when the pressure builds and the volume of work dramatically increases, it is very easy for team members to develop tunnel vision

and lose sight of the broader interaction of the product, its value and position in the market. This individual is retained to concentrate on these important interactions, to see how they are developing and is also likely to monitor and foresee other developments that are coming down the road that need to be addressed. This individual should be able to see the time/value span of the product and as a result determine the overall investment value.

8. *A backroom team:* without which most innovations will fail to become a commercial reality. Behind the (10 per cent) inspiration from which the concept was born, and the refinement and review processes that the above team will bring, this group of people will provide the (90 per cent) perspiration required to do all of the technical and commercial due diligence necessary before the innovation is truly market-ready.

Wherever possible combine right side and left side brain thinkers within the team to create a healthy balance, otherwise the group dynamic will either be risk averse or will never be able to nail anything down or get it commercialized. Try to make sure the group has a mixture of personalities, experience and skills.

At the head of this team there will of course need to be a chairperson or manager to set the agenda, arbitrate in the case of disputes, and provide constant encouragement and motivation. Whether they are drawn from the team itself, or from outside it, the team leader must above all be commercially astute, a good people manager and respected by all.

What key principles should the team embody?

Once the development team is in place, it is important that the correct environment is established for them to carry out their work. From C4Ci's experience, the following guiding principles are key:

- *Reality check:* the team should be able to provide a constant and objective reality check of the value of the innovation versus what is currently available. The objective of the innovation is for it to enter the market and replace or enhance the existing solution and it must therefore be an easy replacement *or* a complete change if the benefits justify.
- *Graciously accept defeat:* the adage 'to flog a dead horse' may be appropriate here. It is vital that emotional attachment to any idea or innovation gets left at home, otherwise vast sums of money and resources can be needlessly wasted pursuing a personal dream. All stages of development need to be assessed and objectively analysed so that an idea cannot haemorrhage resources if it's not looking good.
- *Humility and magnanimity:* the innovator must allow and welcome the development team's input to create an environment whereby an innovation, original or amended, can become successful.
- *Pursuit of an optimum solution:* strive for optimum performance for the application under consideration and not for excellence beyond the value that is required or valued in the market.

■ *Pragmatism:* the innovation has to be deliverable. It may well have to fit with other products, processes, people or software that the predecessor interacted with – the new solution will generally have to do the same.

■ *Passion:* to drive the product into the marketplace a huge amount of personal energy and enthusiasm will often need to be expended. Getting people to change habits and processes is more challenging than one thinks – it is often the hardest element. People like to stick with the devil they know, so individuals that are passionate about the product and the changes it can effect will be essential.

■ *Total belief:* once again, essential for others to become committed and act as advocates for the change.

With the team in place and the key principles by which they will operate established, a solid and coordinated development process can be delivered. An overlap of skills within the group should be seen as an advantage as it enables an informed debate from different perspectives. This is particularly important when identifying points of interaction with other products and processes, as it is extremely dangerous to assume that one discipline will automatically understand the needs of another. Always therefore seek an informed and experienced resource within a discipline that isn't afraid to be negative or take an opposite view; demand this throughout the process to constantly check the product's veracity or viability.

Summary

■ Pick a balanced but mixed team of individuals and skill sets.
■ Be tenacious when the idea is looking promising at the concept stage.
■ Admit defeat and move on if it's only got one leg!
■ Undertake constant reality checks and don't be afraid of negativity or cynicism – it is what you will encounter when the product launches in the marketplace!

About the author

Luke Whale is a director and founding shareholder of C4Ci (Consultants for Construction Innovation), a multi-disciplinary consultancy practice specializing in bringing innovation to the construction industry. He is an engineer by training, and is now responsible for managing the company's affairs in UK and Europe. Tel: +44 (0)7950 181664; e-mail: luke.whale@c4ci.eu.

Employee inventors

Avoid the cockroach trap, says Jacqueline Needle at Beck Greener.

'If you build a better insect trap, you should beat a path to your lawyer's door.' So said Mr Justice Laddie in 2004 as he sought to determine who of four candidate inventors had invented a cockroach trap. He also had to decide between one university and two companies as to who was entitled to own the patents for the trap.

New ideas and inventions are potentially of great importance to companies, and a new product can be the bedrock of growth. The last thing the company needs is an expensive and long dispute involving the courts as to who made the invention and who owns any related patents. A company needs to encourage its inventors while avoiding the cockroach trap.

Inventors and the law

Inventions arise out of the activities of people and, in law, it is always possible to determine which individuals invented any particular innovation. The right to own that innovation, and the right to hold patents and other IP rights for it, arise from the inventors. However, in the UK, the statute determines who is entitled to own those rights. For example, an employing company will own the inventions of its employees arising in stated circumstances, and will be entitled to own patents for those inventions. Furthermore, it is not possible to vary the effect of the statute by contract or other agreements.

The first group of inventors whose inventions will be owned by their employers are those who are 'paid to invent'. Their job as research scientist or development manager gives them duties from which inventions might reasonably be expected to result, and the inventions arising from those duties belong to the employing organization.

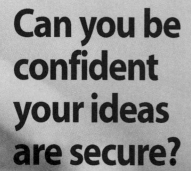

The second group of inventors whose inventions are owned by their employers are those with a special responsibility to the employing company. These inventors will be the company directors, for example, or those in senior management. Again, the employer only acquires ownership if the inventions were made while the senior employees were performing their duties.

Tactics to avoid the law

In the early part of the 20th century the ownership of inventions was determined using the common law principle of 'master and servant'. Perhaps this is responsible for a belief, amongst some employers, that they are entitled to claim all the inventions of all of their employees. Contracts of employment for caretakers, therefore, have included a provision such as 'it is acknowledged by the employee that the performance of the above itemized janitorial duties is likely to lead to invention'. Academic contracts have been known to state that 'the lecturer acknowledges that he has a special obligation to further the interests of the employer's undertaking'. Each of these contract terms is an attempt to ensure that the employees are within the language of the statute such that any inventions they make belong to their employer.

The courts are willing and able to delve into the circumstances of an employee's duties, and they will declare such contract clauses void if they are not in accordance with reality or are wider than is necessary to protect the employer's legitimate interests.

Avoiding the courts

The language of employment and other contracts is important, and a sensible employer will ensure that there are clauses covering inventions. However, to protect both employer and employee, those provisions need to honestly reflect the reality of the situation. The employer needs to accept that some employees, for example, the sales force, do not have duties from which inventions are expected, and their contract will be free of provisions about inventions arising out of their duties. The employer also needs to be aware that, from time to time, someone is taken from their usual duties and given a task, perhaps a 'blue skies' opportunity, from which inventions and innovations might arise. A written record agreed by both employer and employee as to what that task is needs to be created, and as it is likely that innovations will arise, that should be acknowledged by both parties.

The common disputes that reach the courts (and in 2007, Yeda's case went all the way to the House of Lords), are disagreements as to who owns an invention and disagreements as to who is the actual inventor or devisor. Employers must seek honesty from their employees when an invention arises. It has been fairly common for the head of a research department or the professor in charge of a university project to be named among the inventors almost as a matter of courtesy. However, no matter how eminent, and no matter how supportive, the leader is only one of the inventors if they proposed the actual inventive concept and in all other circumstances they must be omitted from the list of inventors.

Good housekeeping

A company that employs people to develop new and existing products, and to otherwise innovate, needs to recognize that inventions may result. The company should employ good housekeeping techniques to avoid future problems, and should:

- Have a contract of employment for each potential inventor acknowledging that their duties include invention, and that those inventions will belong to the employer.
- Make a written record when an employee is assigned special duties which may result in invention, the record to be signed by the employee and to acknowledge that the inventions will belong to the employer.
- Identify in any contract of employment, or in any record of special duties, employees who are sufficiently senior to have a special obligation to the company.
- Require all potential inventors to keep notebooks to record their day-to-day activities, and thereby provide a contemporaneous record to settle any disputes as to who made an invention.
- Impress upon employees the need for scrupulous honesty when assessing the contribution of members of a team to an invention in view of the need to accurately identify each true inventor.
- Provide a culture where inventions and inventors are valued so that employees will report inventions at an early stage for patenting and adoption by the company.

Encouraging and rewarding invention

In Japan, the patent law requires an employer to reward an inventor when a patent application is filed. This has led to increasing numbers of patent applications being filed. For example, in 2005 in the UK, businesses filed about 25,000 patent applications, whilst in Japan, which has a population about double that of the UK, they filed an astonishing 350,000 patent applications that year. Many of those Japanese patent applications are consolidated for filing abroad. For example, five Japanese patent applications each naming an individual inventor might become a single European patent case naming a team of five people as inventors. It is clear that offering rewards to inventors does encourage invention, but it needs to be done in a manner that does not distort the inventing and patenting activity.

The United Kingdom Patents Act does not provide for inventors in this country to be given rewards for inventions they make for their employers. The UK provisions give compensation to an employee inventor only if the patent, rather than the invention, is determined to be of outstanding benefit to the employer. This is a test which it is almost impossible for an inventor to meet.

Of course, not all rewards need to be monetary. Many employees value recognition as highly as other rewards. A company might have 'an inventing employee of the year' award. This could recognize one or both of the employee providing the largest number of commercially valuable ideas in a year, and the employee providing the idea most likely to prove to be commercially valuable.

Monetary compensation can be offered, but perhaps only after a patent has been granted for the innovation. Not only does this promote invention, it also encourages the inventor to provide assistance during the patenting process.

The caretaker invents

We have seen that the employer has no right to the inventions of those who do not invent as part of their duties, for example, the caretaker or the sales staff. While those employees might not be paid to invent, they spend a large part of their time working for the company and thinking about its activities. If any such staff come up with an invention it is likely to be relevant to the company's business. Furthermore, as the innovation has come from a source whose business perception will be different from those who normally drive the company, there is a very good chance it will be potentially valuable.

The company is advised to develop and publish a strategy for dealing with inventions that belong to employees. This should say that the company cannot deal with inventions that are not relevant to the business. The company should also state what it will do when faced with an employee-owned invention. For example, it could agree to fund a first patent application in the name of the inventor, but only if a patent attorney thinks the idea patentable. It could also agree to hold a first trial within the company for all such inventions, while reserving the right not to take any further action or incur any further costs thereafter.

About the author

Jacqueline Needle, a partner of Beck Greener, is a well known member of the UK's profession and is one of the select group of patent attorneys in the UK with a Litigator's Certificate, which gives her the right to conduct litigation in IP matters in all of the English courts. She is an electrical and electronic engineer and experienced in patent drafting and prosecution. Further details: e-mail: jneedle@beckgreener.com, tel: 207 693 5600, or www.beckgreener.com.

IP Health Check

Most SMEs lack the understanding to exploit the full potential of their intellectual property, reports Miles Rees at the UK Intellectual Property Office.

In 2006 Andrew Gowers was commissioned by the government to review the UK Intellectual Property system. One of his recommendations (No 27) for the UK-IPO was to develop a pilot IP audit scheme based on the Genesis pre-diagnosis scheme run by the French IP Office.

Scope

The UK-IPO chose to call their product 'IP Health Check' rather than 'IP Audit' because we were concerned that the term 'audit' is usually associated with financial investigations into a company and we wanted to emphasize the benefits our scheme offered UK businesses. The scheme offered Health Checks throughout the UK: 20 in England, 10 in Wales, 10 in Scotland and 10 in Northern Ireland, which were due to be completed in 2008.

The criteria were chosen for selecting the businesses: they had to be small and medium-sized enterprises (SMEs, which are businesses with fewer than 250 employees) and have either no registered IP rights or less than four registered pieces of IP. Ideally the businesses should be in a technical field, but this was not a strict requirement.

Delivery partners

The scheme has been run using regional business advice organizations as delivery partners in each of the regions. These partners had access to local businesses and were able to select the relevant ones using our criteria. The intended role of the partner organizations was to approach the companies, provide them with information about the Health Check scheme and act as intermediaries by arranging the company visits.

The Health Check

The main objective of the Health Check is to discover what IP has been created by the company, what IP is currently being used and is already protected, and finally where opportunities may lie for further exploitation of intellectual property and intellectual assets. Each Health Check is a three-stage process.

Stage 1 (one day) – research

This stage involves desk research and preparation to establish what, if any, IP is registered by the company and to gain an understanding of the business environment.

Stage 2 (one day) – the visit

The objective of the visit is to establish a full picture regarding the creation, use and management of IP. We seek to identify:

- level of IP knowledge;
- IP currently protected;
- IP that could be protected;
- IP that is redundant;
- usage and terms of IP;
- ownership and contracts;
- procedures when disclosing confidential information;
- IP ownership;
- use of third-party IP;
- licensing agreements;
- exploitation of IP;
- IP threats and opportunities;
- management procedures.

Stage 3 (one day) – the report

We prepare a report summarizing the IP assets identified and advising on whether the company should consider seeking formal protection of those IP assets not protected, through patent, trade mark or registered design applications. It also contains advice on copyright and offers practical suggestions on how the company can improve its management of IP on the basis of these findings the report will provide recommendations on general good practice so as to maximize IP benefits and minimize the associated risks.

Personnel

The team that visited the companies and delivered the Health Check was made up of one or two IP generalists taken from the IPO's Business Outreach and Education department along with an examiner from a core IP area, normally from our patents or trade mark directorates.

Awareness of intellectual property and intellectual assets

In 2006 the UK-IPO conducted a survey of 20,000 UK SMEs. This research showed that SMEs and the mass of micro-enterprises, which form the cradle of IP, small companies and future large companies, are in the main effectively unaware of the IP system. This lack of understanding is perhaps best illustrated by the fact that only 11 per cent of respondents were aware that publication of an invention before filing a patent application could prevent a valid patent being obtained.

Our initial finding from the Health Check scheme supports this research. Many of the businesses we visited had a basic understanding of IP but really lacked sufficient knowledge to maximize its true potential within their business.

Trends

The Health Check pilot demonstrated to us that there are widespread preconceptions and misconceptions about the role IP plays in businesses. These are some of our findings:

- UK businesses are deterred from applying to protect their IP by a perceived cost that far exceeds the actual cost.
- Most UK businesses are not aware of the various courses of action available to them when faced with a third-party infringement of their IP as an alternative to taking legal action through the courts.
- Most UK businesses do not provide training to employees about IP or their employees' responsibilities in protecting the company's IP.
- Businesses are not using IP portfolio systems, meaning that a lot of IP information that's important to the company is either lost or not easily accessible.
- UK businesses do not know the value, either monetary or commercial, of their IP or their intellectual assets.
- UK businesses are not managing their intellectual assets and intellectual property as diligently as they are their physical assets.

The future

The pilot IP Health Check Scheme has provided the UK-IPO with a valuable insight into how businesses are currently using IP, where we should target our resources to improve its awareness, and how we can best help businesses to get the most from their intellectual property and intellectual assets.

To meet the challenges the UK-IPO faces in improving businesses awareness and application of IP, we are developing a training programme for UK Trade & Investment's International Advisers, Business Link Advisers in England and their counterparts in the UK's devolved regions.

We're also planning to launch an online IP Diagnostic Tool that will help raise awareness and understanding of intellectual property and encourage users to consider what action they should take to better exploit their intellectual property and intellectual assets. A full report detailing the Health Check finding will be available during summer 2008 on the IPO website.

About the author

Miles Rees works in the Business Outreach & Education team in the UK Intellectual Property Office. The UK-IPO is responsible for the establishment and maintenance of the national framework of intellectual property rights. Intellectual property encompasses patents, designs, trade marks and copyright. More information about the UK-IPO is available at www.ipo.gov.uk or by telephoning 08459 500 505.

We have helped to deliver
428 422 patents into this world.

Centre for IPR in Sweden

PRV
SWEDISH PATENT AND REGISTRATION OFFICE

72-hour innovation

What does it take to complete the innovation process in 72 hours, asks Christina Nordstrom, knowledge management specialist at the Swedish Patent and Registration Office.

Can you create a completely new product in 72 hours? And can you do this even though you're not a professional inventor? Professor Kaj Mickos is convinced you can – that anyone can produce an innovation. In his TV programme for Swedish Television, *The 72 Hour Race to Innovation*, he wants to prove this by putting ordinary people to the test in a systematized process he calls the 'Innovation Plant'. The participants have 72 hours to pass the test and a team of experts at hand to help them turn the wheel of innovation and create new products. By visualizing the process on TV, he also wants to inspire and motivate the general public to actually start developing their own ideas.

> *I've often been criticized by many for being too pragmatic and not enough of an academic. But I'm an action scientist who interferes with everything I study. It is in the learning process we create great things. (Kaj Mickos)*

Kaj Mickos holds a professorship in innovation technique. During his career he has guided approximately 2,500 people with great ideas, lacking the tools and the knowledge, through the innovation process – shaping their ideas into products.

Although Mickos started off as a behavioural scientist, he has always carried a strong fascination for the phenomenon of innovation. With time this has developed into an interest for systematizing the process. Not only did he want to find the best way to execute and handle innovation processes, he also developed a production system for innovation he calls the 'Innovation Plant'.

A couple of years ago Professor Mickos wanted to take his Innovation Plant a step further, to prove that his method actually works. To do this, he needed to put his systematized method to the test in a powerful way and decided to demonstrate that it's possible to produce innovations and have products ready for the market in 72 hours.

As he had based a big part of his concept on the thesis that anyone can be an inventor and that it is the willpower and enthusiasm of ordinary people that drive development, his process needed to be 'democratic'. This meant involving lay people to come up with the ideas and use the knowledge of experts to turn the idea into a product that was ready to go to market. Another prerequisite for this method was the ability to work in a virtual production centre.

His first attempt was very successful and *The 72 Hour Race* became a powerful proof of concept for Mickos. Since an innovation process like this normally takes up to a year, *The 72 Hour Race* had been a serious challenge. It also helped him point out that the art of invention no longer is an individual sport, but a team sport.

So, how did the race find its way into Swedish television? Actually, by chance. Mickos was travelling to the north of Sweden and started talking to the passenger beside him, telling him about his latest project. It turned out his flight companion had connections within the television industry and immediately saw the potential for a TV programme.

After several meetings and discussions Mickos joined forces with the interested parties and started a new production company called 72 Hour Race Productions. Mickos made strong demands about not turning it into a reality show where people would be voted off the programme, but to create an inspiring programme that would help people believe in their strength to make things come true. In other words, a true public service programme with a clear educational focus for the general public.

Through the years Mickos has worked on different assignments where he has had the opportunity to execute innovation processes, experimenting and testing different ways of doing things. He has also carried out full scale experiments that have constituted vital learning processes. For him, it's in the learning process we create great things:

> I've always felt that I've done things I'm not really capable of doing. In return, this has led me to believe that this goes for anyone and everyone. It's my conviction that anyone can be an inventor, regardless of how much knowledge you have. As long as you have access to a network of specialists and you're able to work in a structured way – following a systematized method – your idea will, in the end, come out as a product.

The 72 Hour Race has been created into a TV production from the Innovation Plant concept. It is meant to enable people with different backgrounds and experiences to develop and commercialize their own ideas for new products and services within 72 hours. The contenders are not professional innovators but have well-specified problems to be solved and ideas that are judged on the basis of potential commercialization.

According to Mickos, the ultimate objective for an innovation is to create cash flow. Hence, enterprising is more important than the innovation itself. This is one reason for speeding up the innovation process and adjusting it to new conditions in the market. Another aspect is the environmental threats we face today, which makes it critical to find new, more environmentally friendly ways of manufacturing products. Mickos says:

> *The world of innovation has been and still is in a state of intense change. The whole information and communication technology has developed at an enormous pace and the internet revolution, where users can control and create certain content, is spreading to other areas. So, when you talk product development it's critical not to focus on what you are about to develop. Instead, my interest lies in how we are going to develop our product, creating theories of action. How we do things is key.*

The Innovation Plant process consists of multi-disciplinary science teams with IPR, design, construction, packaging, finance and marketing specialists working together to make the wheel of innovation spin. There a very few people who can execute the full process all on their own, so the focus in Mickos' model lies on the process itself, not the tools. In the hub, you find the process leaders who coordinate and help drive the process.

In the TV programme each team consists of three contenders, who together make up a dynamic and creative group of lay people who struggle against the clock to develop one or more products and services, ready for commercialization before the 72 hours have passed. The contestants were selected for the show by a board of competent business counsellors from different Swedish organizations and the criteria were based not only on good ideas but on personality, charisma, the ability to communicate, willpower and strength.

During the 72 hours expert counsellors, consisting of two process leaders, all educated by Professor Mickos, and one industrial designer, were available to give advice within their specific fields. The panel were also available to give overall advice and, at the end of each episode, give a final opinion on the idea and its potential for commercialization.

Apart from the expert counsellors on site, the team had access to a back-office function. This consisted of additional specialists such as designers, prototype builders, intellectual property rights specialists and representatives from the Swedish Patent and Registration Office. In addition, the team also had access to a group of facilitators, who they would call if they urgently needed something brought into the studio. There was no time to lose.

On site the team had access to a 3D-writer for rapid prototyping and, in Sri Lanka, forecasters would perform market research when the team slept, ready for delivery in time for breakfast. On day three they needed this information when inviting companies for a sales pitch where they presented not only the prototype, but market numbers, sales forecasts, estimated production costs and possible distribution channels.

When turning an idea into a product this fast you wonder if quality suffers. But according to Mickos quality only consists of the ability to get a patent and that you actually produce something new, something that doesn't already exist. However, at the end of the day quality of a product is ultimately defined in the market, and whether it's possible to sell or not. This is why the contenders in the TV show still had the possibility to go on after the show and commercialize their products and services. It could well turn out that their product is successful on the market, even though the panel didn't select it in the TV programme.

The greatest challenge in every innovation process is the patent. Most ideas die before the process has even started, if they're not eligible for a licence. This is why the first step consists of an IPR specialist confirming eligibility for patent protection. During *The 72 Hour Race* for example, the Swedish Patent and Registration Office has performed quick novelty searches to make the assessment possible in such a short time. When the assessment process is done the innovation process can start, even though the idea may evolve into a product different from that originally planned. Even though the product may eventually not qualify for a licence, it's still protected during the process and the inventors can get at least three years head start if it's successful in the market.

This is also why the road to a final product or service during *The 72 Hour Race* is more important than the final result. It's the process that is meant to inspire both contenders and the TV audience, giving them the possibility to improve their skills in developing an idea. Also, the innovation process is being visualized to inspire viewers to develop innovation projects of their own, as well as to follow new teams in the next episodes.

The 72 Hour Race has been broadcasted in 10 episodes on Swedish Television channel 8, where one hour summarizes 72 hours of intense innovative development. The different races have resulted in 30 patent applications and almost all products are already on the market. Mickos says:

> It was great to see the teams in action and the great things they produced as teams. More importantly, it was a real joy to see how it seriously changed the participants' lives. It set off processes that made them find the strength inside they never knew they had. Hopefully this goes for the TV viewers as well. If so, we have definitely reached our ambitions with The 72 Hour Race programmes.

The 72 Hour Race has now been designated a 'format', which means it can be sold to other TV channels and other countries.

For further details see: www.prv.se.

3

Open innovation

Passionate about innovation

Inspired at Durham University, Dr. Arnab Basu founded Durham Scientific Crystals at NetPark, Sedgefield, County Durham. Now the company is breaking new ground in defence and medical imaging as well as transforming the future of airline security with better airport screening technology.

www.northeastengland.co.uk

Left: Dr. Arnab Basu, Managing Director, Durham Scientific Crystals
Right: Durham Cathedral

Passionate people. Passionate places.

north east
england

Open innovation

It is now inevitable that much of the knowledge a business needs will sit beyond its organizational boundaries, says Lorelei Hunt, Director of Innovation at the South West Regional Development Agency.

Open vs closed innovation

Open innovation describes a process by which companies actively pursue externally generated knowledge and bring it into the business, and allow internally generated knowledge to flow outwards, in order to increase the rate of innovation in the business. This is in distinct contrast to older, closed models of innovation in which new technological knowledge was developed internally, in corporate research and development (R&D) laboratories and retained within the business.

Once a source of real competitive advantage, available only to firms that could afford the necessary investment, the closed innovation model is increasingly seen as slow and insular. The ability to keep up with the speed and complexity of innovation and to maintain the necessary specialist knowledge base in an increasingly mobile labour market is becoming ever more difficult and costly. It can be relatively inefficient if potentially worthwhile technology is not exploited, because it is not a fit with the company's product portfolio. In open models, companies look for external opportunities to exploit unused technologies through licensing or other arrangements.

The growth in information technologies (including the internet) and the opening of global markets have facilitated the diffusion of information and further encouraged open innovation – not only by facilitating desirable information flows but by increasing the difficulties in preventing information from spreading. As a result, companies have to learn to take advantage of a development they cannot stop.

In practice, there are many open innovation models covering a broad spectrum of activity. These range from the idea of 'open source' intellectual property at one end, where intellectual assets are made freely available to anyone who can make use of them to develop new products and services; to models where new IP is openly traded into and out of the company using formal mechanisms such as licensing, technology transfer agreements or strategic alliances.

External sources of innovation can cover a wide range of organizations and individuals, including companies that might be seen as competitors in other fields. The role of suppliers and consumers is increasingly significant. Dissatisfied customers might be equally important in the process of user-driven innovation.

Open innovation in a knowledge economy

Post-industrial, knowledge-based economies are increasingly reliant on the exploitation of intangible assets – on knowledge of all kinds – for business growth and wealth generation. In such an environment it is inevitable that much of the knowledge a business needs will sit beyond its organizational boundaries. New ways of working are essential if companies are to be able to access and make use of that knowledge. Traditional, closed models of innovation will be increasingly less able to generate competitive advantage when much of the knowledge required is outside the organization.

There has also been a real shift in the nature of the knowledge-based assets that create value for businesses, so that brand becomes more important than patents, for example. As the rate of innovation accelerates, getting to the market first can be more important than protecting knowledge. This creates further challenges to conventional models of closed, R&D-based innovation. In an increasingly knowledge-driven world we need to look at issues in new and different ways to create value. This requires companies to look for good ideas and new knowledge wherever that is located.

Culture change

Open innovation needs a different company culture and thinking than traditional or closed innovation. The move towards open innovation models has been supported by the change in the nature and structure of organizations, with vertical disintegration of the business value chain, concentration on core competencies and increased outsourcing. Businesses are increasingly collaborating to offer combined, value-added solutions to their customers, often in alliance with companies they are competing with in other markets. In other areas we see new, 'open book' relationships between manufacturers and their suppliers and new types of symbiotic relationships within supply chains.

This has led to a blurring of organizational boundaries and the development of new competencies within businesses that place an increased emphasis on the ability to work collaboratively, to network and to look outward as well as inward for solutions to businesses issues. Increasing globalization means that businesses are on the lookout for clever ideas wherever these originate. Global capital and labour mobility create new dynamics that require new, more outward-focused approaches, facilitated by culturally diverse workforces and driven by the need to address a variety of new markets.

How open is open innovation?

Others are more sceptical about the concept of open innovation, pointing out that even companies like IBM and Procter & Gamble, which are seen as leaders of the open innovation movement and report significant business growth as a result, still keep substantial areas of their activity 'closed'. In reality, business models based on open innovation are likely to use a variety of mechanisms. Companies can donate their patents to an independent, third-party organization, put them in a common pool or grant unlimited licence use to anybody.

Open source innovation is most commonly applied to software, where it is openly available to anyone who wants to use it and the user community freely contributes upgrades and improvements. There are debates, however, as to how open such models really are, and how accessible the products are beyond a narrow, technically proficient, user community. New, blended models are emerging, such as IBM's Eclipse platform, which IBM is advocating as a case of open innovation, where competing companies are invited to cooperate inside an open innovation network.

Open innovation and SMEs

While there are small and medium-sized enterprises (SMEs) with significant R&D capacity, their scale of activity is inevitably less than for some of the businesses we have mentioned so far, and open innovation has always been a necessary part of the business model for these businesses. More open attitudes to innovation on the part of larger firms provide new opportunities for businesses, either to find markets for intellectual property (IP) they have generated or to commercialize knowledge generated elsewhere.

The vertical disintegration of large corporates and increasing outsourcing also create new opportunities for SMEs to provide specialist services. When the core product is knowledge based, there are fewer advantages from economies of scale and many more opportunities for profitable activity at the SME level. Collaboration between SMEs to meet the varying needs of larger customers becomes a key feature as mobile knowledge professionals can take their core skill to wherever the work is and form new alliances. Knowledge is a very portable commodity.

There can be significant barriers preventing SMEs from practising open innovation. European research has shown company culture to be the most significant single restraint upon SMEs seeking to innovate, but resources such as time and access to investment are also significant. South West RDA is working to ensure that its SMEs have access to the right kind of management and leadership training to enable them to understand the challenges ahead and how to adapt and change to meet them.

This works alongside a range of initiatives designed to provide practical support to businesses seeking to innovate. This includes schemes in which we share the risk of R&D investment with SMEs, such as our Great Western Research project which co-funds three-year research studentships, and the national Grant for Research and Development scheme. In the past three years, this scheme has awarded £4.5 million of funding in grants to over 50 South West businesses. We are currently evaluating this scheme to understand its total impact, but we know that some of our clients have already attracted millions of pounds of follow-on funding and created substantial numbers of new jobs as a result. We will use information from the evaluation to help us increase the number of companies applying for the scheme to further boost innovation and business growth in the South West.

The Agency supports the European Enterprise Network, which includes the former Innovation Relay Centres. These actively broker relationships between SMEs across Europe that have complementary technology, as well as a range of other networks such as Beacons SW, which enable businesses to see the benefits of collaboration and build their networking skills.

We are currently working with UK-IPO on piloting intellectual asset audits to better understand how we can work together to assist our SMEs to recognize, manage and protect their intellectual assets. This is a critical first step in being able to trade these assets effectively in open innovation business models.

The notion that open innovation can create competitive advantage at the level of the business, by encouraging an environment in which ideas for innovations can emerge or go to market from outside the company as well as inside, can be extended to consider open innovation systems at a regional level. In such a system, a regional innovation network consisting of a range of different actors can offer an environment that facilitates and encourages collaboration between companies. This is likely to be particularly valuable to SMEs, which might have difficulty in sourcing a business partner with complementary technology, or in building a relationship with a large business that might be a potential customer. It also helps to bring academics generating new research and thinking into contact with those who might be able to put that knowledge to use and generate real economic benefit from its commercialization.

At the business and at the regional/national level, open innovation allows for new ideas and knowledge to contribute to innovation and for the exploitation of neglected intellectual capital. This is increasingly important as we search for multi-disciplinary solutions to complex problems and to new solutions for consumers' demands for complete packages that might provide products and services in a high value-added combination.

This is part of the thinking behind the designation of the six Science Cities in England and why South West RDA has been so keen to support the Science City Bristol initiative. By bringing academics, businesses and the public sector together we can ensure that the science assets of the City region are used to generate wealth and economic growth.

There is a need to achieve culture change at regional level to ensure that the South West looks outwards to source the best ideas wherever they are found, and seek new markets for their goods and services across the world. This forms a key theme in the new EU-funded structural programmes for the South West, which place a considerable emphasis on (and will make substantial investments in) encouraging the internationalization of South West businesses. This will ensure that South West businesses recognize and respond to competitive forces and use the spur these provide to innovate and grow.

Bibliography

http://en.wikipedia.org/wiki/Open_Innovation'Categories: Innovation

Regional open innovation system as a platform for SMEs: a survey, Marko Torkkeli, Tiina Kotonen, Pasi Ahonen, *International Journal of Foresight and Innovation Policy,* Vol 3, Issue 4/2007

Chesbrough, H (2003) *Open Innovation,* Harvard Business School Press, Boston, MA

www.research.ibm.com/eclipse/

About the author

Lorelei Hunt is currently Director of Innovation at South West Regional Development Agency. Her current portfolio includes a wide range of activities aimed at encouraging innovation in regional businesses to build a knowledge-based regional economy. The South West RDA leads the development of a sustainable economy, investing to unlock the region's business potential. Find out more at www.southwestrda.org.uk.

LONDON
SCHOOL *of*
HYGIENE
&TROPICAL
MEDICINE

Our aim is to contribute to the improvement of health worldwide through the pursuit of excellence in research, teaching and advanced training in national and international public health and tropical medicine.

The spectrum of diseases studied is wide and there is innova research working on topics which include:

- African trypanosomiasis (sleeping sickness)
- Blue Tongue Virus
- HIV/AIDS and other sexually transmitted diseases
- Counterfeit antimalarials
- Chagas disease
- Leishmaniasis
- Malaria
- Tuberculosis
- Schistosomiasis (bilharzia)
- Vaccine development and evaluation
- Vector biology and disease control

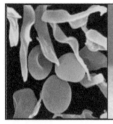  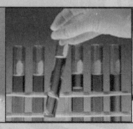 

About the London School of Hygiene and Tropical Medicine

LSHTM is Britain's national school of public health and a leading postgraduate institution in Europe for public health, international health and tropical medicine.

Part of the University of London, the School is an internationally recognized centre of excellence with a remarkable depth and breadth of expertise.

Innovation for improving health in the developing world

Quinton L Fivelman

London School of Hygiene and Tropical Medicine, Keppel Street, London, WC1E 7HT, UK

London School of Hygiene & Tropical Medicine is Britain's national school of public health and a leading postgraduate institution in Europe. Part of the University of London, the School is an internationally recognised centre of excellence in tropical medicine, public health and international health. Our mission to contribute to the improvement of health worldwide is achieved by investing in high quality, innovative research in these areas, in particular the neglected tropical diseases (see Table 1).

There is an urgent need to develop and deliver new tools (drugs, vaccines, and diagnostics) for the prevention and treatment of neglected parasitic diseases responsible for an enormous burden of poor health in the developing world. For example, since 1975, only 13 of the 1,223 drugs developed have been for neglected diseases. One of the main factors resulting in this shortfall is that drugs and vaccines for diseases such as malaria, tuberculosis (TB), leishmaniasis, schistosomiasis (bilharzia) and human trypanosomiasis (both Latin American Chagas and African sleeping sickness) tend to have low market returns. This makes it difficult for commercial firms to pay for the expensive investment into research and development. The majority of new drugs and vaccines are developed by the pharmaceutical biotechnology sector, but there is little market incentive for these companies to pursue drug discovery research for these common infectious diseases.

The discovery of leading compounds with the potential to become useful drugs is a critical first step to ensure a sustainable global pipeline for new treatments. The lack of new drugs entering development for tropical diseases has been blamed on the so-called 'translational gap' – the gap between basic science research, which is usually publicly funded by research grants or charities, and clinical development which is usually funded by pharmaceutical companies. This has recently been changing. The creation of various public-private partnerships (PPP) such as the Medicines for Malaria Venture (MMV); the Global Alliance for TB Drug Development; Foundation for Innovative New Diagnostics (FIND); and the Drugs for Neglected Diseases Initiative (DNDi), has galvanised the development of new therapies. These PPPs between charities, large pharmaceutical companies and small biotech firms are run more like a business, but are not for profit. Academic institutions, such as LSHTM, interact within these partnerships allowing for cross-fertilisation of ideas, skills, knowledge and compounds resulting in more focused research with a clear 'lab to market' route in mind. These partnerships have also placed increased emphasis on the high-risk early discovery phase for these diseases which large pharma have often neglected. LSHTM has been actively engaging with many of these ventures and, in the case of MMV, has led to valuable lead compounds.

The School is a world-leading centre for research in tropical diseases. Using our multidisciplinary expertise (which includes clinicians, epidemiologists, statisticians, social scientists, molecular biologists and immunologists) we have been actively increasing our patent portfolio. Patents are vital to protect intellectual property generated through the expensive investment of university research; and can be valuable for attracting commercial partners or to secure follow-on funding. The School has recently filed patents related to public health and human or animal pathogen research. Patents cover areas including malaria, blue tongue virus, gastrointestinal pathogens (*Campylobacter, Clostridium difficile*) and counterfeit antimalarial detection.

Unattractive, low-margin but high-volume markets can be fertile ground for spurring innovation – the fight against TB is a case in point. Control of TB remains one of the most serious challenges to global health and the emergence of mutated strains of *Mycobacterium tuberculosis* that are resistant to the major anti-TB drugs poses a deadly threat to control efforts. The School's TB research includes development and evaluation of innovative tests for diagnosis of TB and the detection of drug resistance. In collaboration with PPPs such as FIND, the School is actively researching novel antigens and methods for the early detection of TB. The correct diagnosis of diseases such as TB and malaria is a crucial first step towards improving health and efficient use of resources.

Vaccines are often cited as the medicine of choice for poorer markets. LSHTM uses a range of technologies to identify and develop potential vaccine candidates. Genomics-based mutagenesis techniques involving the pathogens that cause malaria, *Leishmania*, TB, and enteric bacteria are improving our knowledge of these pathogens. The production of virus-like particles through application of a baculovirus-based expression system (mimics a virus shape but lacks genetic material so it does not multiply in host) has led to the development of vaccine candidates against SARS, Blue Tongue Virus (BTV), Rift Valley Fever, rotavirus and influenza. Further research of BTV has resulted in a highly protective protein-based safe vaccine which is undergoing trials. BTV is an insect-vectored emerging pathogen of wild ruminants and livestock and is increasingly having a severe economic impact on European agriculture and poses a threat to the UK.

Unforeseen public health challenges can be vital in sparking innovation: Malaria is a tropical disease that kills more than one million people each year mainly in the endemic countries. Measures taken to control malaria include insecticide treated bednets and the most successful drugs to treat malaria are produced from the Chinese shrub *Artemisia annua*. Sadly they have been extensively faked as they are expensive – i.e. tablets without active ingredient in them have been made by people intent on monetary gain without regard for human life. Reports from SE Asia indicate that around 50% of the drug artesunate (an artemisinin derivative; ART) sold is indeed faked. Currently available tests to check for the amount of insecticide on bed nets or the quality of drugs are expensive due to the technology used, thus limiting their use where they are most needed. We have development two simple, easy to use, robust, inexpensive and rapid, colour assays that could be used in the field to check the quality of ARTs namely; artesunate, artemether and dihydroartemisinin. These assays are highly specific as they only detect and measure the ARTs component of in the formulation. Generally the monitoring of insecticides on bed nets is restricted to reports from health staff and questioning the net users. At present there is no simple test to determine the amount of insecticide on the nets. We have developed a test that will give an indication of the amount of insecticide on the nets and an added advantage of our test is that it will also indicate compliance of internal residual spraying of walls with insecticide to help evaluate the quality control of the interventions in the fight against malaria.

The large market of people at risk of infectious diseases in the developing world should be seen as both a challenge and opportunity. To meet this demand, innovation at the basic science level needs to be actively encouraged. Investment in academic R&D through research councils and philanthropic funding can provide valuable sources of innovation eventually leading to new therapies. Increasing investment into tropical disease research at LSHTM research councils and charities such as the Wellcome Trust, MRC, BBSRC and Bill & Melinda Gates Foundation is allowing for improved allocation of resources towards improving our understanding of pathogen biology. There is a good deal of high-quality research into tropical diseases; but translating these discoveries into valuable new treatments is a complicated, expensive and long process. 'Proof of concept' awards and seed funds have also become extremely valuable in allowing universities to bridge this gap. These small grants allow scientists to support the translation of often risky novel and inventive ideas from fundamental research to commercial demonstration. The scientists can then approach PPPs, the biotech sector, or charities to obtain follow-on or translational funding to develop market viability for these products.

In addition to the need for novel drugs, many people still die in developing countries due to diseases that can be prevented with drugs or vaccines easily available in developed countries. This is due to many factors but the high cost of essential medicines, poor drug quality and an inadequate healthcare infrastructure are often cited as main reasons. The development of new drugs to tackle tropical diseases needs to go hand in hand with a strategy to allow affordable, easy access to the general population for which it will benefit.

There is a vast discrepancy between the standards of health in developed and developing countries. This is increasingly being recognised as one of the most important challenges facing the developing world. Today, over a billion people are affected by neglected tropical diseases that disproportionably affect poor and marginalised populations. Despite considerable advances in medicine, over six million people die each year from the 'big three' diseases: malaria, HIV/AIDS, and TB with countless numbers of children dying due to preventable diseases such as diarrhoea. With one in five of the world's population living in extreme poverty, urgent help is needed to improve public health by tackling disease. Good health and wellbeing is essential for economic development eventually leading to a reduction in poverty.

\

References and Further Reading

Neglected Diseases Outlook. *Nature*. 2007; **449**:157-182
Doing better at doing good. *Nat Biotechnol*. 2008;**26**:357

Table 1: A list of the most common human tropical diseases

African trypanosomiasis (sleeping sickness)*
Ascariasis (roundworm)
Chagas disease (American trypanosomiasis)*
Dengue Fever*
Guinea worm (drancunculiasis)
Hookworm*
Leishmaniasis*
Leprosy*
Lymphatic filariasis (causes elephantiasis)*
Malaria*
Onchocerciasis (river blindness)
Schistosomiasis (bilharzia)*
Trachoma*
Trichuriasis (whipworm)
Tuberculosis*

* = researched at LSHTM

Connect and develop

Richard Wilding discusses Procter & Gamble's Open Innovation Programme.

For nearly 170 years, the Procter & Gamble Company (P&G) excelled as a traditional innovation company, carrying out the bulk of its research and development (R&D) in-house to develop products for the world's consumers. Beneath the surface, however, this model encountered difficulties in meeting the demands of 21st-century business – much of the home grown innovation was under-utilized (for example, only 10 per cent of P&G's patents covered products marketed by P&G) and P&G's business model was also struggling to deliver the levels of organic growth demanded of modern companies.

P&G's present CEO, Alan Laffley, stepped in at a challenging time in the company's history. In seeking to realign P&G's businesses to face the demands of the new millennium, he realized that a radically new approach to supplying P&G's innovation pipeline was needed. Taking his lead from other innovative companies such as IBM, he announced the dawn of a new era of open innovation for the consumer products giant or, in P&G language, a move from research and develop towards 'Connect & Develop' (C&D).

C&D means many things but, above all, it means recognizing that others outside P&G can innovate as well as, perhaps better than, P&G itself and that they can sometimes do it faster and cheaper. If they can, then why not 'connect' with them? For example, why spend years developing a cosmetic skin imaging device from scratch, if a medical device company already has such a 'cooked' technology that could be quickly adapted and used instead – a potential win for both parties. C&D can also mean licensing P&G's under-utilized intellectual property rights to unlock value for both P&G and third parties.

From humble beginnings before 2000, C&D has mushroomed to feed P&G's escalating appetite for external technology. A highly motivated global team of 'technology entrepreneurs' scours the planet looking for the next potential innovation, and dedicated websites allow selected partners to suggest technical solutions for joint development with P&G.

It is hard to over-emphasize the shift in culture that C&D has engendered in P&G. From a relatively safe player that eyed innovations 'not invented here' with suspicion and that wanted to own the results of all external collaborations outright, was born a company that has learnt to take more risks, to play for bigger rewards, a company prepared to share with external partners to leverage the benefits for all participants. It cannot be pretended that the path was not rocky, that no mistakes were made, but P&G has evolved as a result such that, today, over 40 per cent of all P&G initiatives incorporate technology brought to the company via C&D. Today, P&G is happy to say that many of its innovations are 'proudly found elsewhere' (www.pgconnectdevelop. com).

In 2004, P&G launched a new line of Pringles® potato chips printed with designs and trivia. Two years previously, a proposal to do this had been mooted within P&G, but it was clear at that time that the expertise to bring such an execution to market did not exist within P&G. By putting out feelers, a connection was made to a university professor in Bologna who had developed an ink-jet process for printing edible images onto food that P&G was able to license and adapt to its needs.

About the author

Richard Wilding, Senior Patent Attorney, Procter & Gamble, www.pg.com.

Old industries, new solutions

Steel, coal and textiles are industries that are having to reinvent them-selves. Jim Farmery, Head of Innovation at Yorkshire Forward, reviews how expertise is being accessed through research centres.

The days of the industrial revolution saw manufacturing techniques change at a rapid pace, one that has not let up over the last 100 years. In fact, the e-business revolution is changing the way we do business so quickly that we are achieving advances in technology in a five-year period that would have taken 20 years in the latter half of the last century.

As companies strive to keep abreast of these advances, constantly upgrading the way they operate while competing with rivals in emerging economies in China and India, they have to learn to work smarter. Keeping ahead of the game by bringing new products and services to market is the only way to survive in a global marketplace.

Changes in the global economy have meant that over recent decades the Yorkshire and Humber region has been challenged to look again at its strengths as its traditional industries like coal, steel and textiles move their focus overseas. The region has some incredible examples of entire industry sectors changing markets – the point being that it's just a question of economies of scale, and if whole industries can innovate, why not individual businesses.

"The focused approach of the Yorkshire Forward Engineering Design CIC provided us with the results we wanted – faster, more accurate assessments of component design. The system is now used extensively across our business."

Lou Gill, Fatigue Group Team Leader
BAE Systems

Collaborate to innovate,
innovate to compete

Yorkshire and Humber's academic excellence and industry expertise has established the region as one of the leading European centres for innovation, in some of the world's fastest growing industry sectors.

The Yorkshire Forward Centres of Industrial Collaboration (CICs) and KnowledgeRICH service help both large and small businesses. By harnessing the technical expertise of the world-leading R&D facilities based in Yorkshire and Humber, they translate knowledge and facilities into business benefits. Expertise ranges from short-term measurement through to applied R&D, and covers the very latest technologies.

WORKING WITH NATION-WIDE BUSINESSES OF ALL SIZES.

These include:

BAE Systems, Clariant Ltd, Carrs of Sheffield, DuPont, Firmac, Galpharm, JRI, Peratech, Ping Golf, Robert McBride, Robinson Paperboard Packaging, Rockware Glass, Smith & Nephew and Tesco.

For further information on Yorkshire Forward's innovation programmes, please visit:
www.yorkshire-forward.com

YORKSHIRE FORWARD

Yorkshire *Alive with Opportunity!*

The Region's Development Agency

Meeting the needs of a changing market – playing to your strengths

Fifty years ago, Britain, Germany and Sweden were world-class steel producers, and they still are. However, even with a worldwide reputation for excellence in steel manufacture Yorkshire's steel industry has had to evolve to meet the demands of a changing marketplace. Over time steel production in emerging economies began to corner the market in bulk manufacturing. This forced the region's steel production and engineering sectors to reinvent themselves as a metals industry that includes nickel and titanium alloys as well as steel alloys. They had to rethink their production and marketing strategies, concentrating on their reputation for excellence and refocusing on specialized production and finding niche markets.

New key markets in the medical devices, automobile and aviation industries have a huge demand for new technologies and metals, providing South Yorkshire with a unique opportunity to maximize its strengths in an emerging field. To support this activity, building on South Yorkshire's steel heritage and supporting the industry's need to innovate, a joint venture between UK Coal and Yorkshire Forward enabled the development of an Advanced Manufacturing Park (AMP) on a former colliery site between the steel towns of Rotherham and Sheffield.

In close proximity to the University of Sheffield, the AMP has become a respected research and development centre for companies working in the metals and engineering sectors. Offering innovative companies unique access to expertise within the university, it is attracting world-class business, including the Advanced Manufacturing Research Centre (AMRC), a collaboration between the University of Sheffield and Boeing that provides first-class research facilities for companies. The AMRC has already helped local company Claro Precision Engineering Ltd to optimize production times by introducing new speed and feed solutions, saving time and money.

Demand for quicker, lighter aircraft, smaller precision-made components and more cost-effective production techniques means that in some cases even the newer metal alloys are being superseded by non-metallic engineering materials like composites and polymers. More than 50 per cent of the A380 aircraft is non-metallic.

This constant evolution of the industry has led to Yorkshire Forward's investment in the 'Factory of the Future' that is currently under construction on the AMP. The aim is to provide facilities to prototype and test new products and production methods. This will help companies within the advanced engineering and materials sector to keep innovating without going to the expense of dedicating vital production equipment to research and development work.

The AMP is also the location for an Environmental Technologies Centre. This is being set up to help new businesses in the growing renewable energies market to become established and tap into the research and development expertise around them. This Yorkshire Forward-funded project, due to be completed late in 2008, comes out of the region's strategy to be at the forefront of the development of new technologies – helping businesses to tap into a global £400 billion emerging market while contributing to a reduction in greenhouse gas emissions. Yorkshire and Humber is home to three of Europe's largest coal-fired power stations that generate 12 per cent of the UK's energy, so it's important to find a balance between keeping the lights on and saving the planet.

In addition to providing bespoke premises, which incidentally are being built on sustainable principles, for companies working in the environmental technologies sector, the aim is to enable the companies to bring their research to market. Longer term, selling the technology to other countries like India and China will widen global capacity for reducing greenhouse gas emissions and provide new markets for further innovations.

Finding a new direction

These may seem like extreme examples to a small business, but the principle is the same: know what your strengths are, build on them and adapt them for the future. It may sound easy when your strengths and assets have a clear market demand, but even more complex examples of reinvention can be found in Yorkshire and Humber.

The City of York has a history of building trains and making chocolate, but both of these industries have declined in recent times, so the city needed to reinvent itself. As a city of historical interest, surrounded by beautiful countryside, the obvious answer was to build on the existing tourism industry, which it has done, but the city still needed an industry base, which it has achieved through the development of the university – known worldwide as Science City York.

The ethos behind Science City York is to create a place where technology and business can learn and grow together in some of the region's fastest growing sectors – bioscience, creative industries and IT. Since its inception in 1998, Science City York has helped to create 80 new technology companies and more than 2,800 new science and technology jobs.

Science City York has had financial support from Yorkshire Forward for science business development, an extension of the innovation centre, establishment of a bio incubator, and an IT incubator. The success of this turnaround in the city's primary industry proves that your reputation as an expert in one sector is not your only option: with careful planning you can develop in a completely new direction just as successfully.

New businesses like Cizzle and Forsite Diagnostics – both of them were established following scientific breakthroughs by university researchers. Chris Danks, former scientific researcher at the Central Science Laboratory in York, developed an in-field testing kit to detect crop diseases. Five years on he is now Chief Executive of Forsite Diagnostics, and the company has become an integral part of the Science City York bioscience technology cluster. Through Science City York's business networks, they are now actively partnered with five other Bioscience York cluster members.

The success of this company is not unique. Many businesses are born out of research, and the people who own the intellectual property often have a scientific rather than a business background.

Making the most of expert assets

What is clear is that scientists and businesspeople can learn from each other. To nurture this interaction in Yorkshire and Humber, Yorkshire Forward has invested in 11 Centres of Industrial Collaboration (CICs), which are commercially managed but based within the region's universities. The centres are linked to the expertise within the universities – for example, the Engineering Design CIC is based at the University of Hull and the Materials Analysis and Research CIC based within the Materials and Engineering Research Institute at Sheffield Hallam University.

The aim is to strengthen the relationships between business and academia, and bring more new products to market. Over the last five years the CICs have helped to develop more than 1,700 projects with businesses and generated in excess of £40 million of research income. This is a great start – one which demonstrates what can be achieved if the right levels of support are put in place.

Grants for research and development that have been made available for companies over the last three years are also proving to be successful. A £200,000 development grant has resulted in a trailer that is capable of carrying up to 30 per cent more pallets than a conventional trailer for one Yorkshire company, SOMI. This product will enable hauliers to move more goods in fewer vehicles, helping to reduce CO_2 emissions.

Innovations like the SOMI trailer are great news for the logistics sector, which needs to find ways to improve its carbon footprint. Logistics is an expanding sector. Yorkshire and Humber's location at the centre of the country, and the added advantage of the Humber ports complex, means that the transport infrastructure is a key economic asset. Distribution hubs are springing up alongside the motorway network, and traffic to the ports is increasing. To support the growing logistics industry, which is recognized as one of the city's industrial strengths, a new Logistics Institute has opened at the University of Hull.

These successful large scale sector innovations have demonstrated what can be achieved, and paved the way for a Regional Innovation Strategy, a blueprint for driving forward innovation in the region over the next 10 years. The main themes within the strategy are: growing the region's innovation culture; developing a region-wide innovation environment; targeted European engagement; and pan-northern activity.

Only 10 per cent of the region's companies currently have research and development links to universities, which seems low, but I am encouraged by the fact that this figure is 2 per cent higher than six months ago. However, the region's future economic growth is dependent on more businesses understanding the importance of innovation, and taking steps to change the way that they do business.

If chemical companies that had spent generations producing dyes for West Yorkshire's wool producers can develop into specialist manufacturers working with the pharmaceuticals industry, I am confident that Yorkshire and Humber's 21st century businesses can innovate and succeed.

About the author

Jim Farmery is the Head of Innovation for Yorkshire Forward, the Regional Development Agency (RDA) for Yorkshire and Humber. RDAs are responsible for the sustainable economic development of the English regions. They achieve this by helping people to find jobs, encouraging new businesses to start up and grow, developing towns and cities and helping businesses to find new markets. Further details: www. yorkshire-forward.com.

Sourcing ideas

By searching patents you can identify innovative products and map the technological landscape within your market. Dean Parry at Patent Seekers discusses the techniques for gaining this strategic information and putting yourself ahead of your competitors.

With over 50 million patents on worldwide patent databases, there is a wealth of information (much of it not available anywhere else) for companies to explore and utilize. These databases provide information on patents that may be in the application stage, granted or dead; they are all published for the public to view:

1. If a patent is in the application stage this means it may or may not be granted (has been put in force) and there are many reasons why it may fail, eg lack of funds, failure to meet statutory requirements or the invention lacks novelty and/or inventiveness.
2. If a patent is granted, this means it has been put in force at some stage. However it does not mean that it is currently in force. The patent may have subsequently died.
3. A patent may have died for many reasons, eg its 20-year life has ended, it's been revoked due to evidence put forward against its validity or there was a failure to pay renewal fees. However, there are certain situations where a patent can be reinstated and certain inventions can gain extended protection via supplementary protection certificates (SPCs), eg pharmaceutical inventions.

The above information can give companies access to the latest technological innovations, market trends and the companies that have control over areas of a particular technologies. If a particular patent relates to a product of interest, a company can discover the owner and see whether the patent is granted and in force.

THE UK'S FASTEST GROWING SPECIALIST SEARCH COMPANY

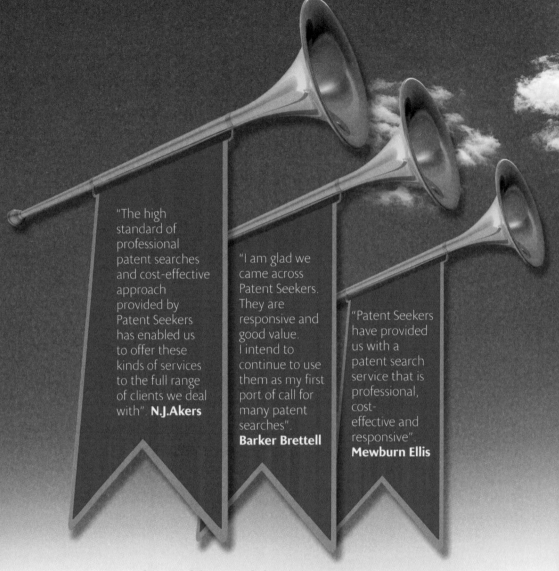

"The high standard of professional patent searches and cost-effective approach provided by Patent Seekers has enabled us to offer these kinds of services to the full range of clients we deal with". **N.J.Akers**

"I am glad we came across Patent Seekers. They are responsive and good value. I intend to continue to use them as my first port of call for many patent searches". **Barker Brettell**

"Patent Seekers have provided us with a patent search service that is professional, cost-effective and responsive". **Mewburn Ellis**

We don't like to blow our own trumpet, so we thought we'd let our clients do it for us.

Patent Seekers is the UK's fastest growing specialist search company. We work on behalf of Patent Attorneys and other organisations and businesses based in Europe and North America. Our staff are all qualified, professionally trained patent analysts (including former UK Patent Office Examiners) providing patent search services for their specific areas of expertise. We work in teams to ensure attention to detail, each follow meticulous processes as well as utilising multiple databases. One of our teams specialises in Pharmaceutical, Biotech and Chemical searches whilst another provides the same level of expertise for Electrical, Electronic, Software and Mechanical. If you have a requirement for any of our services or want to find out more information about Patent Seekers, please get in touch.

Patent Seekers Ltd., Suite 53 Imperial House, Imperial Park, Celtic Lakes, Newport NP10 8UH.

Tel: +44 (0)1633 816601
Fax: +44 (0)5602 048146
Email: mail@patentseekers.com
www.patentseekers.com

| INVALIDITY | INFRINGEMENT | STATE OF THE ART | NOVELTY | DESIGN |

PATENTSEEKER
The UK's Fastest Growing Patent Search Com

Searching patents

There are a large number of patent databases available to carry out different levels of patent searching and analysis. The best places to start a search would be Espacenet or the SIP databases. These allow free searching to be carried out by using keywords, classifications and company names.

Any patents found through these databases may not give the full picture because each patent may have many patent family members, eg a UK patent may have other patents connected to it via countries outside the UK such as Germany, France and the United States. These family members would need to be found for each patent.

Once all the patents have been found for, say, a particular company, the results can be displayed based on the number of patents for subject matter, countries, publication dates, etc. These can be displayed as a patent map or landscape, which show trends and how patents may be linked.

Making decisions based on patent information

Patent information, maps or landscapes can provide vital strategic information to companies:

- Trends for a particular technology, ie the number of patent applications for a particular subject matter over time.
- Potentially identify the next generation of products your competitors are developing.
- The companies most active within a particular field (and when they were most active).
- Partnerships between companies working on a technological area.
- Areas of technology that have very few patents could indicate a good option for research.
- Areas of technology that have a large number of patents may indicate a high probability of litigation or a very high cost for due diligence (identifying any patents in force for a particular subject matter).

The above information can be used to develop a working strategy to either avoid potential problems and/or to identify new products and new areas for research.

Final word

Companies that regularly analyse patent information in their area of technology automatically have a big advantage over their competitors. They are able to see areas lacking in development and may even be able to identify where the next innovation should be. So the best advice for companies developing a product and/or developing a market strategy would be to know your market, the patents that control it, the companies that own them and the patent applications that may control it in the future.

Patent strategies for open innovation

Mark Cohen, Head of Intellectual Property Services, Sagentia
IPservices@sagentia.com

Open innovation activities in technology-dependant companies are accelerating. This presents new challenges when determining an appropriate way to protect intellectual assets, either for out-licensing, or when in-licensing and further developing a third party's technology. It is increasingly important, therefore, that companies take a structured and systematic approach to Intellectual Property (IP) management.

There are a number of challenges related to gaining appropriate IP protection for the open innovation space, including:

- Identifying the optimal set of patent filings necessary to give comprehensive protection to a technology across the broadest range of uses whilst avoiding a single point of failure.

- Breaking up the filings to allow a 'pick and mix' approach to out-licensing elements of a particular technology.

- Ensuring appropriate ownership of further developments of the licensed technology, so that a purchaser that carries out additional development gains protection or reward for that development, whilst allowing these developments to be exploited outside the purchaser's industry.

Six IP Zones

Sagentia's experience in developing IP strategies for companies operating in the open innovation space has led us to develop the 'Six IP Zones' framework. This approach addresses the above challenges and can be used to identify the optimal set of filings to protect a technology and allow its exploitation in both conventional and open innovation models.

- Zone 1 protects the platform technologies which underpin the overall product or development. Platform technologies are those which have applicability and utility across many product types.

- Zone 2 protects combinations of Zone 1 and other technologies to form subsystems and products.

- Zone 3 identifies additional 'surround' elements which may be used to further protect technologies and products in Zones 1-2, for example methods of use, methods of manufacture or packaging.

- Zone 4 looks to the future and protects further development of Zone 1 and 2 technologies and products. It seeks to optimise what has already been protected, to anticipate competitor reaction and to prevent the generation of competitive blocking IP.

- Zone 5 adds value to Zone 1 technologies and Zone 2 subsystems by looking outside their initial areas of application for use in other products and industries.

- Zone 6 looks at competitive alternatives to the Zone 1-5 IP and seeks, wherever possible, to generate blocking IP to restrict their exploitation.

Housekeeping

Before applying the zones, some basic housekeeping is advisable.

Firstly, all technology developments should be preceded by a patent landscape study to ensure the development is either:

- unique and protectable (no patented or public domain knowledge is evident); or

- marketable (public domain knowledge exists but no valid patents remain).

For the latter, a business decision must be taken to determine whether other methods of protection, such as brand or channel ownership, may be used to give informal protection or differentiation. If existing, valid patents are found during this initial patent landscape study, further analysis will be needed to determine whether these patents can be licensed or whether the development will need to work around them. If the licensing route is chosen, the R&D programme must be reconsidered accordingly.

Development staff should be given a good grounding in the identification and capture of novel intellectual property. They do not need to fully understand legal or strategic aspects, but must know what to do when encountering something apparently novel and useful. It is down to the legal function, R&D managers and technology transfer specialists to determine the most appropriate way to protect and exploit these developments.

The involvement of technology transfer specialists at an early stage of IP generation is vital to prevent platform technologies being inappropriately filed in product or application specific patents.

With this housekeeping completed, application of the IP zones can begin.

Applying Zones 1 and 2: Protecting platform technologies, subsystems and products

The initial step in identifying Zone 1 and 2 IP is to disaggregate the overall product or technology into subsystems and enabling elements. This should be done by both function (what is achieved) and technology (how it is achieved). Next, each identified element should be assessed to determine if it has applicability outside of the targeted product or application. Technology transfer specialists or external consultancies can often provide valuable insight here. Typical Zone 1 technologies include novel new materials or sensor types.

Applicability outside of the targeted product or application identifies the IP as being in Zone 1, rather than Zone 2; it is these Zone 1 filings that will be the initial out-licensing candidates.

With Zone 1 IP identified, a set of ideal patent filings should be generated. Where possible, consideration should be given to several filings covering different aspects of the same technology to avoid a single point of failure during and after the patent prosecution process. These filings can then be related to the IP landscape study conducted earlier to determine the likelihood of patents being granted. Where there is existing IP, the set of ideal filings will need to be modified to take this into account.

Zone 2 filings should be built up in layers, using combinations of Zone 1 and other technologies to initially build subsystems and then products. If specific combinations of Zone 1 technologies reveal utility outside the targeted product or application, these combinations should be considered as belonging to Zone 1. With the subsystems and products identified, the next step is to repeat the identification of a set of ideal patent filings, relate these to the existing IP landscape and amend accordingly.

The filings for Zones 1 and 2 should be lodged with the appropriate patent office simultaneously. This should prevent potential issues associated with the creation of prior art and obviousness between the sets of filings, subject to the specific demands of the local patenting system. The U.S. Patent Office, with its continuation system, is usually optimal when using Six IP Zones.

Zone 3: Ring fencing Zones 1 and 2

Moving to Zone 3 requires additional analytical tools. Lifecycle mapping of the product is a useful tool to identify Zone 3 IP. In short, all the activities associated with the product are mapped out, from manufacture through to usage and disposal. This lifecycle map is then analysed to see which steps may offer additional IP opportunities, for example whether there are novel methods of use or mechanisms to recycle the product. This is likely to be a multilevel approach, with the initial lifecycle map identifying broad areas of IP opportunity and specific deep-dives identifying where actual novelty lies. Zone 3 IP may relate to the product itself (such as methods of use) or may add additional protection to Zone 1 technologies (such as methods of manufacture) to further add value when exploiting Zone 1 IP outside of the core business.

As with Zones 1 and 2, a set of ideal Zone 3 filings should be identified and then assessed in light of the external patent landscape and modified accordingly. Preferably Zone 3 documents should be filed during the 18 months between filing the Zone 1 and 2 documents and their publication.

Zones 4 and 5: Future generations and new uses

Zones 4 and 5 move from the analytical to the creative. In Zone 4 (future generations), techniques including voice of the customer analysis, technology roadmapping, ideation and functional analysis are used to identify how Zone 1-3 technologies and products are likely to evolve. The outputs can give guidance as to the R&D programmes needed to capture future product and technology generations, and stay ahead of the competition. With good planning, broad patent filings can be made early in the development process for Zone 4, which are then narrowed down as the operational parameters for the technology become clearer.

In Zone 5, functional analysis, ideation and other techniques are used to determine new uses for Zone 1 technologies. Rather than file numerous broad patent applications for multiple uses, it is better to hold back and investigate the market first to identify the most relevant sectors and applications. With these identified, provisional patent applications can be made and discussions with targets can begin under a non-disclosure agreement. The provisional applications can be converted into full applications when the scope of any collaboration and shape of the technology usage are understood. If the Zone 1 technology is to be exclusively licensed for a specific application, transferring ownership of the corresponding Zone 5 patent is a useful way of giving the buyer exclusivity whilst still maintaining control over the base technology.

Out-licensing and ongoing development

For companies that are aggressive about out-licensing, it is common for Zone 5 to be investigated in parallel to Zone 3, generally by the technology transfer function.

Once the technology is out-licensed, it may be further developed by the out-license partner. A major issue is that of ownership and exploitation of these ongoing developments. There are no fixed resolutions here, but an optimal and relatively benign route is the developer back-licensing the improvements to the originator and other license partners, assuming there is no overlap in areas of operation. This may be for royalties or as part of an overall cross licensing agreement, as is common in the semiconductor industry.

Zone 6: Ring fencing competitors

Zone 6 seeks to prevent competitors entering the space targeted by the new developments in Zones 1 and 2. IP landscaping and commercial intelligence are used to identify competitive alternatives to Zone 1 and 2 technologies and products. Analytical and creative techniques are then used to identify how the threats from these might be mitigated. Examples of mitigation include:

- Purchasing or exclusively licensing threatening IP owned by a non-competing third party, thereby preventing a competitor from acquiring it and generating an alternative product.

- Improving a lower quality competitive technology to become a rival; gaining patent protection for these improvements, and thereby locking the technology owner out from that development path.

Sagentia's 'Six IP Zones' approach has proven to be a robust framework for maximising the value of IP when operating in an open innovation environment. With careful application, it can help construct a patent portfolio that confers comprehensive protection, and is optimally structured for technology trading.

Useful links

Free patent and research databases

Espacenet: http://ep.espacenet.com/
Software for Intellectual Property (SIP): www.patentfamily.de
US Patent Office search facility: http://www.uspto.gov/patft/index.html
GoogleScholar: http://scholar.google.com/

Commercial patent databases

PatBase covers full-text on GB, EP, WO, DE, FR and US documents and covers more than 75 countries: www.patbase.com
Delphion covers full-text on WO, EP, DE and US documents and covers INPADOC: www.delphion.com
Dialog provides extensive worldwide information on patents and research papers: www.dialog.com

Classification information

http://ep.espacenet.com/
http://www.wipo.int/classifications/fulltext/new_ipc/ipc7/eindex.htm

About the author

Dean Parry (BSc, MSc, MIMA, MIEEE) is Technical Director of Patent Seekers. He is an expert patent analyst and gives advice on technical research to small businesses and companies worldwide. He has helped build technical defences for some of the highest profile patent disputes in both Europe and the United States. He is a former cybernetics researcher and UK Patent Office examiner, and a member of The Society of Competitive Intelligence Professionals (SCIP).

Patent Seekers Ltd is now one of the leading suppliers of prior art search and analysis in the UK, supplying patent attorneys and multinational companies world-wide. It specializes in validity and infringement searching and regularly works on high-profile cases to help companies defend against infringement action in European and US markets.

Further details: Patent Seekers Ltd, Suite 53 Imperial House, Imperial Park, Celtic Lakes, Newport NP10 8UH Web: www.patentseekers.com, e-mail: mail@ patentseekers.com, tel: 01633 816601.

The role of universities in enabling innovation

In the 21st century universities will be the drivers of economic prosperity in the same way that textile mills were at the outset of the industrial age says Dr Robert Singh, commercial development officer at the University of Hull.

It is widely acknowledged that in order for the UK to be prosperous in the globalized economy, it must be a leader in innovation. Innovation adds value to business, allowing adaptation to new challenges and promoting sustainability in the face of changing market demands and growing environmental pressures. Innovation is often thought of as the successful application of new ideas or knowledge and in this context universities must be seen as key resources for the generation of new knowledge that can prime innovative commercial activity. UK universities produce world-class research and it is no surprise that the government's recently released 'Innovation Nation' White Paper[1] indicates that this extensive knowledge base should be harnessed for economic benefit. Indeed, it has been said that in the 21st century universities will be the drivers of economic prosperity in the same way that textile mills were at the outset of the industrial age. This comment may be particularly pertinent with the increasing trend for companies to adopt open innovation models under which they are looking to external organizations to feed their R&D pipelines.

Universities have, of course, always been synonymous with ground-breaking research and discoveries. However, historically, a lack of structured interaction between universities and industry has often led to ideas diffusing out of institutions

The University of Hull
Knowledge Exchange
'Our knowledge is your business'

www.hull.ac.uk/business

For information on
commercial development
please contact Dr Robert Singh
01482 466012
r.singh@hull.ac.uk

in an unmanaged manner. Although this is one route for dissemination, it has been recognized that a more formal proactive approach to the transfer of knowledge from academic environments into industry is more likely to lead to successful collaboration, mutual benefit and long-term sustainable relationships. The larger academic institutions in the United States were the early leaders in development of knowledge transfer activity. This followed the Bayh-Dole Act[2] of 1980, which gave US universities control of the intellectual property (IP) resulting from Federal Government-funded research. In the last decade there has been considerable change in the way UK academic institutions approach knowledge transfer. Government funding, significantly the Higher Education Innovation Fund,[3] has pump-primed technology transfer in the UK and enabled universities to develop dedicated teams and resources. While models and formats may vary, most UK universities now have knowledge transfer offices (KTOs) that act as the interface between the university and industry.

Universities have been criticized in the past by industry for not understanding business needs, being too slow to respond and for over-zealous valuation of their IP. While some of these perceptions linger, the development and professionalization of knowledge transfer mean that universities are now much better equipped, in terms of appropriate expertise and processes, to meet this challenge.

An industry of provision of knowledge transfer support to academia has evolved in recent years with some institutions outsourcing all of their knowledge transfer activity to third-party providers through various pipeline agreements. The focus of such transfer companies is necessarily on financial gain, since many are accountable to shareholders, rather than purely exploitation of IP and engagement with business. Many of these organizations have been very successful at adding value to university-generated commercial opportunities and they now form an important part of the knowledge transfer network.

KTOs are an effective bridge between universities and commercial partners, developing relationships and dealing with negotiations and agreements. They also have an inward-facing role as they are responsible for the identification and evaluation of new inventions and other commercially valuable aspects of the research output. These may range from simple devices to complex molecules. Significant examples of such innovations from the University of Hull include the use of broadband ultrasound for the detection of osteoporosis developed by Professor Chris Langton; and the pioneering work of Kyoto Prize winner Professor George Gray, CBE, allowing the synthesis of new types of stable liquid crystal. This technology forms the basis of all modern liquid crystal displays and is a field in which the University of Hull continues to have considerable strength and reputation.

Following disclosure of a new invention, KTOs will evaluate it, arrange for appropriate IP protection and develop it as a commercial opportunity. Industrial partners may be involved in collaborative development or license the right to use the IP in order to add value to their business. Alternatively a spin-out company may be a more appropriate route for developing the product or service and taking it to market. Through this function, KTOs enable exploitation of university knowledge and ideas so that they are used in practical commercial applications. In addition, this activity also increases the level of interaction between academia and industry, promoting the development of strong collaborative relationships.

Knowledge Transfer Partnerships is a national scheme funded by the Technology Strategy Board that involves the embedding of a recent graduate within a company to carry out a very specific business improvement project under the careful supervision of both a company and a university mentor. The innovative work adds value to the company's business but also provides a mechanism for recruiting highly skilled staff, as up to 80 per cent of KTP Associates are retained by their host companies. Through one such scheme, the University of Hull enabled caravan chassis manufacturer Bankside Patterson to develop the first cost-effective, fully corrosion-resistant galvanized frame in the market. Since this new product has reached the market, Bankside Patterson's annual turnover has increased from £6 million to an anticipated £20 million next year.

For companies wishing to access a university's knowledge base, KTOs act as the point of contact to match their need with the expertise present within the university. In addition, brokerage services, such as the Yorkshire Forward's KnowledgeRICH scheme, can provide a means of fielding a specific enquiry to several institutions simultaneously.

Universities are also increasingly turning their attention to student and graduate enterprise. Hull has received regional and European funding support for a new Enterprise Centre, which will open in July 2008. This will encourage the creation of student and graduate start-up companies to follow on from increased provision of enterprise education. It will also provide direct access to the range of expertise and facilities required at that vital 'pre-incubation' stage of new businesses.

While teaching and research remain at the heart of every university, recent developments including the Sainsbury Review of Science and Innovation[4] make clear that realizing the social and economic benefits of this core activity is vital to ensuring the future prosperity of the nation. Effective knowledge transfer will allow universities to play a critical role in future innovation ecosystems.

About the author

The Knowledge Exchange is the University of Hull's knowledge transfer office. As well as being responsible for the management and commercialization of the university's IP portfolio it also facilitates access to specialist knowledge within the institution, enabling companies to apply it to their products and processes. The university performs work for companies on a consultancy basis or, if more appropriate, in the form of a collaborative research arrangement. In addition, Hull hosts many successful Knowledge Transfer Partnerships (KTPs).

Dr Robert Singh is the Commercial Development Officer for the University of Hull and is responsible for the management and commercialization of the university's IP portfolio. He has a background in life science research, completing a BSc at the University of Leeds, PhD at the University of Bristol followed by a postdoctoral research position at the University of East Anglia. Prior to joining the University of Hull, Robert worked within a patent attorney private practice. Further details: Commercial Development Officer, Knowledge Exchange, The University of Hull, Cottingham Road, Hull HU6 7RX, tel: +44 (0) 1482 466012 fax: +44 (0) 1482 465299, e-mail: r.singh@hull.ac.uk.

Notes

[1] Department for Innovation, Universities and Skills 'Innovation Nation' White Paper, March 2008.
[2] Bayh-Dole is codified in 35 U.S.C. § 200-212, and is implemented by 37 CFR.
[3] Funding programme administered by the Higher Education Funding Council for England for higher education institutions to support their knowledge transfer activities and interactions with business and the community.
[4] *The Race to the Top: A Review of Government's Science and Innovation Policies*, Lord Sainsbury of Turville, October 2007.

Model agreements

To ease the difficulties in reaching agreement about the form that the IP will take in a research project, a series of model agreements has been developed for use in collaborations between companies and universities. Lawrence Cullen at the UK Intellectual Property Office reports.

To improve innovation performance, it is essential to increase collaboration between business and university. However, the complexity and cost of negotiations relating to intellectual property (IP) can be a serious barrier to setting up such collaboration. This was one of the key findings from the UK government-sponsored Lambert Review of business–university collaboration in December 2003. This review was chaired by Richard Lambert, former editor of the *Financial Times* newspaper, former member of the Monetary Policy Committee of the Bank of England and currently chairman of the Confederation of British Industry (CBI), the voice of business in the UK.

To help overcome this barrier, the Lambert Review recommended the development of a set of model agreements to help business and universities understand the issues involved in handling IP under a number of different collaboration situations. This set of model collaboration agreements, known as the Lambert Model Agreements Toolkit, was launched in February 2005. Following an update in October 2005, a review was carried out in February 2006, which found that a wide range of UK organizations were making use of the Toolkit. These include universities, small and medium-sized Enterprises (SMEs), large corporations, regional development agencies (RDAs) responsible for innovation, and technology transfer training organizations.

Purpose

The Lambert Toolkit is designed to help businesses and universities save time and effort in the negotiation process and increase the likelihood of a consensus between all parties. Use of the Toolkit is voluntary.

The Toolkit is important because the rapid pace of change in science and technology is generating new opportunities for business in the UK and in Europe. Great strides are being made in areas such as bio- and nano-technologies, information and computer technology, new materials and new fuels. To take advantage of this progress, our economies have to be able to transfer knowledge effectively, both in terms of people and know-how, between those who have generated it and those who are best placed to exploit and develop it commercially.

Solutions and applications developed through such collaborations will usually have a high intellectual input, be knowledge-intensive and provide high added-value to a business. This value is usually protected through the use of IP rights such as patents, trademarks, copyright and registered designs. Hence the model agreements are extremely important guidance tools for UK businesses and universities to ensure they get the IP right. Making it easier for embryonic businesses to handle what is seen as a complex issue will improve their chance of survival.

The Toolkit

The Toolkit comprises five model agreements and three supporting tools. Each Lambert Model Agreement (LMA) describes a different scenario for collaborative working between business and university. The five scenarios covered by the model agreements are summarized in Table 3.6.1.

Table 3.6.1 The five Lambert Model Agreements (LMAs)

LMA	Terms	IP owner
1	Business has non-exclusive rights to use in specified field of technology and/or geographical territory; no sub-licences	University
2	Business may negotiate further licence to some or all university IP	University
3	Business may negotiate for an assignment of some university IP	University
4	University has right to use for non-commercial purposes	Business
5	Contract research: no publication by university without business's permission	Business

The three supporting tools help potential collaborators identify all the issues they need to take into account when deciding which one of the five model agreements is most suitable for their particular circumstances. The *Agreement Outline* provides a checklist of all the issues that a potential collaborator needs to think about in preparation for negotiating a collaboration agreement. Some of these issues need to be considered internally within the business or university before entering negotiations and some of them need to be covered during the negotiations themselves.

The *Decision Guide* is an interactive question and answer tool that helps users to identify the most appropriate LMA to use as a starting point for their negotiations. It focuses on three key areas and how they interact with each other. These are:

1. the ownership and rights to use the results of the project;
2. the financial and other contributions made by the commercial sponsor; and
3. the university's use of the results for academic purposes.

Having a clear idea of the position in these areas helps users to identify which model agreement most closely meets their needs.

By combining the responses to the questions in the *Decision Guide,* it is possible to identify which of the LMAs may be the most appropriate starting point. If a project is of critical commercial importance to the commercial sponsor, and cannot take place without using the sponsor's technology or intellectual property, the *Decision Guide* directs the user to consider LMA4 or LMA5. Where publication of the results would have a serious impact on the competitive position of the sponsor and the sponsor wishes to ensure that publication does not take place, the user is directed to LMA5. If a project is of a more speculative nature or not of such critical commercial importance and is more about developing a relationship with the university academic, then the user is directed to consider LMA1, LMA2 or LMA3. The *Decision Guide* can be used as many times as a user wants to explore different combinations. It is not a precise or exhaustive guide but it is very helpful at focusing the user's thinking on what they really want from a collaboration.

The *Guidance Notes* provide a commentary and explanation of the terms used in the agreements and an explanation of some of the legal issues. This makes sure that both parties understand the issue and avoids confusion.

Using the Toolkit

The best way to use the Toolkit is to take a stepwise approach where:

1. They use the *Agreement Outline* to identify *all* the issues they need to consider in order to have an effective collaboration agreement.
2. They use the question and answer approach in the *Decision Guide* to decide which of the five model agreements provides the best fit with the circumstances of their collaboration.
3. They use the *Guidance Notes* to check that they understand the meaning and relevance of the terms and clauses used in the model agreements.

Using this approach, it is possible to identify quickly the important and relevant issues in any proposed collaboration, and to gain a better idea of the type of collaborative agreement best suited to the purpose in hand. Thus when negotiations with the potential collaborator begin, the common issues can be agreed without delay and both parties can then focus their time and effort on resolving the critical issues. The model agreement serves as a starting point and is designed to reduce the cost and time spent negotiating. The text of these agreements is not 'set in stone'; they can be adapted to take into account the particular circumstances of each collaboration.

The stepwise approach is designed to make sure that potential collaborators have identified and thought about all the relevant issues before beginning negotiations. This is important because it allows those issues that are not contentious to be agreed quickly. If both parties have very different expectations from the potential collaboration, illustrated, for example, by their selection of very different model agreements as starting points for negotiation with each other, this rapidly becomes clear. Both parties will then be able to decide quite quickly whether to continue or not.

None of the LMAs deals with the joint ownership of IP. The Lambert WG considered that it is more difficult for the business and the university to manage this together efficiently. The Toolkit adopts a simpler approach that relies on one of the parties owning all the IP as a single entity, with the other party receiving appropriate payment and access as agreed. Also, third parties seeking to license a technology may often find it easier to deal with a sole owner of all the IP.

The Toolkit in practice

The Toolkit has been used across the full range of companies and universities – SMEs and large corporates such as GlaxoSmithKline (GSK) as well as well-established universities such as Oxford and Cranfield and new universities such as Hertfordshire. For example, GSK have used over 100 LMAs in over 13 countries. All five types of model agreements have been used, while agreements 1 and 4 are the most common.[1] They have enabled otherwise lengthy negotiations to be concluded in relatively short timescales. For example, GSK secured one contract from start-to-finish in just forty eight hours.

In a survey of academic use 72 per cent of respondees reported that the LMAs had produced significant savings in resources. The University of Oxford have used the agreements with both SMEs and large pharma companies. The University of Hertfordshire has used the Toolkit to review its policy on collaborations with industry. As a newer university with less experience in this area, it found the Toolkit to be a useful benchmark. The LMAs have provided answers on how to deal with issues on ownership of IP, confidentiality and publication of material by students. This has resulted in the successful negotiation of eight agreements with SMEs.

Business support and development bodies such as the Regional Development Agencies have also begun to use the Toolkit. The Lambert Agreements have been used by the South East England Development Agency (SEEDA) as the standard agreements for their Proof of Concept Funding Scheme (PoCKeT) where local businesses are put in contact with an HEI partner anywhere in the UK to assess commercial viability (seven projects in the period May 2005 to February 2006; £25,000–£30,000 per project). In each of these cases an LMA type 4 or 5 has been used where the industry collaborator will have ownership of the IP. SEEDA expects to have 20 to 30 such projects each year in this programme and that the standard agreement for each collaboration will be a Lambert agreement.

Recent updates

The update to the Toolkit in October 2005 provided examples of other agreements that users had found helpful when putting a collaboration in place. These are listed in Table 3.6.2 and cover specific issues that may arise when setting up or in the course of a collaboration.

These other useful resources (OURs) as they are termed, will help users to tackle a range of related issues that often arise during collaboration projects. Such issues include, for example, ensuring confidentiality, negotiating a licence, and use of samples provided by one collaborator to the other. These OURs are provided as examples only and, though consistent with the five model collaboration agreements, they were not subject to the same level of scrutiny and development by the Lambert WG.

Collaboration in Europe

Inspired by the example of the Lambert Model Agreements Toolkit and drawing on similar work from other European states such as Denmark and Germany, in 2006 the UK, as part of its presidency of the EU, led a working group that developed the CREST Cross Border Collaboration Toolkit, which highlights the issues that a collaborator in one European country must address when considering a collaboration with a business or university counterpart in another European country.

This toolkit uses a Decision Guide approach similar to that used in the Lambert Toolkit. It also includes a Checklist of Cross Border Issues that the user can use to check if a proposed collaboration agreement adequately addresses the cross-border issues. Actual suggested clauses are not possible because of the differences in legal systems and contract law between countries. This Toolkit also includes fact-sheets for 20 countries in Europe identifying the key issues that a person needs to know about when considering a collaboration with a partner from that country. This Cross Border Collaboration Toolkit was published in September 2006 and a fully interactive internet version is now available at http://ec.europa.eu/invest-in-research/policy/crest_cross_en.htm.

Conclusion

The Lambert Toolkit has provided a useful and practical tool to make negotiating a collaboration agreement easier. It helps save time, effort and resources. It makes it easier for potential collaborators to identify any major issues or differences of approach early on in the process of negotiating the collaboration agreement, so as to be able to concentrate on resolving those issues or differences. The sooner this is achieved, the sooner the work can begin.

Table 3.6.2 Other useful resources for business–university collaborations

	Resource	Example of when used
1	Sample Patent and Know-how Licence	Where the sponsor and the university have reached agreement that the sponsor should be granted an exclusive licence to use identified IP in the results of a research collaboration [see Lambert Model Agreement 2].
2	Sample Patent Assignment	Where the sponsor and the university have reached agreement that the university will assign IP in certain results of a research collaboration to the sponsor. [see Lambert Model Agreement 3]. It is based on the assumption that the assignee will pay a one-off sum for the assignment of the patent, but the parties may agree revenue sharing or other payment terms.
3	Sample Materials Transfer Agreement	Where a sponsor has agreed to allow the university to use certain materials in connection with a research project.
4	Sample Consultancy Agreement	Where there is an agreement between a commercial sponsor and an individual academic researcher, under which the individual researcher undertakes to provide consultancy services to the sponsor. It records a private arrangement between the researcher and the sponsor.
		The researcher assigns the intellectual property rights in the work they do as a consultant to the sponsor in return for payments made by the sponsor. In order to be able to assign those rights, the researcher must own them. That normally means that they must not have been developed in the course of their employment by the university; if they have been developed in the course of their employment, those rights will usually belong to the university.
5	Sample Non-Disclosure Agreement	Where a business and a university wish to exchange confidential information as part of their discussions about a potential research project before they have entered into a collaboration agreement.
6	Sample Equipment Loan Agreement	Where the business sponsor has agreed to allow the university to use equipment in connection with a research project.
7	Sample Confidentiality Notice	A user would include a simple example of the kind of notification on the front page of a document to indicate that it and the information provided are confidential.

Future work

The LMAs and toolkit focus on bilateral collaboration agreements between a single business and a single academic partner. Work is currently underway to provide model agreements that would be suitable for use by a larger number of partners working in a consortium. Such multipartner consortia increasingly arise in research and development projects funded by the UK Technology Strategy Board and by the European Community under its Framework Programme 7 and Joint Technology Initiatives.

The Innovation Directorate of the UK-IPO (Jim Houlihan) are continuing to support the Lambert IP working group in developing the tool-kit. The Group plans to launch a new website which will incorporate the multi-partner agreements within the website of the Department for Innovation, Universities and Skills later this year.

Note

[1] LMA 1 – The University owns IP in the Results and grants the Sponsor a non-exclusive licence to use the Results in a specified field. LMA 4 – The Sponsor owns IP in the Results and University has the right to use the Results for academic teaching and academic research.

The Toolkit can be accessed through the website of the UK Intellectual Property Office (UK-IPO, the new name for the UK Patent Office) at http://www.patent.gov. uk/education/education-hfe/education-agreements.htm or through the government website at: www.innovation.gov.uk/lambertagreements.

To order a free copy of the Toolkit on CD ROM and obtain further information on any of the above, contact the Awareness, Information and Media team, UK-IPO.

About the author

Dr Lawrence Cullen has a wide experience of IP practice and policy issues. He is a Deputy Director in the Patents Directorate of the UK Intellectual Property Office (UK-IPO) where he is in charge of the group that deals with patent applications in the pharmaceutical, organic chemistry and biotechnology fields. He took up this post in July 2007. Prior to this he was a Principal Hearing Officer in the Trade Mark Registry at UK-IPO (2006–2007) where he dealt with disputes between parties over trade marks. From 2001–2006 he was a Senior Policy Adviser in the Intellectual Property & Innovation Directorate (IPID) of UK-IPO. Dr Cullen was a member of the Lambert Working Group on Intellectual Property that developed the Lambert Model Agreements Toolkit in February 2005. He was co-chairman of the EU-CREST group that produced the CREST Cross Border Collaboration Toolkit in October 2006 to simplify setting up collaborations between partners in different EU countries. Dr Cullen was educated in chemistry in Ireland and the UK and has worked as a research scientist in universities in France, UK, Germany and the United States.

Coordinating global IP

Differences between IP jurisdictions can cause complications in managing international growth, says Dominic Hickman at Rouse & Co.

Coordinating and managing IP in one jurisdiction can be difficult enough, but start operating in a number of countries and suddenly it can be much more of a challenge. Problems with language, time zones, acceptable standards, local customs and diverse management styles can all combine to make life 'interesting'. There are clearly great advantages to operating on a global scale, such as gaining access to a larger market, cost savings, tax advantages, etc. Provided the IP is kept under control by being handled efficiently, effectively and consistently, managing a global portfolio doesn't need to be a headache.

Businesses that need to manage IP internationally fall into three main groups (although there are overlaps):

1. established multinationals: these are businesses that operate in many jurisdictions, eg large energy companies, retailers, financial organizations;
2. businesses based in one region or country that plan to expand into a global market; these may be new companies or businesses that have developed their home territory and want to emulate their local success elsewhere; and
3. businesses based in one territory or region that wish to have some functions performed overseas, whether this is manufacturing in China, software development in India, R&D in Japan or call centres in Eastern Europe.

There is no simple formula for successful IP management in different countries, but there are a number of common issues to consider and pitfalls to avoid. As with managing and making the best of any asset, careful planning can make the difference between success and failure.

Types of business operation

Established multinational businesses

For most multinational businesses, the most important IP assets are often brands. Having a unified brand across many jurisdictions is often viewed as vital to success. Inevitably, this will involve careful management of trade marks. To be successful, management of an international trade mark portfolio requires both central coordination and input from local advisers in the countries of interest. The local advisers could be country or regional managers from within the business, or local agents and lawyers.

Central coordination will provide consistency of brand format and quality of the goods/services being provided under the brand, and will ensure the filing strategy matches the business strategy. Central coordination will also allow the business to make the most of priority filing dates and ensure that patent coverage matches production and sales plans. The local advisers will oversee or perform the filing activities and day-to-day administration of applications, as they will be familiar with the nuances of the local IP registries.

Local advisers can also play a vital role in making sure the global brand is translated correctly, both linguistically and culturally. There is nothing more likely to undermine a marketing campaign than a brand which, when translated into the local language, means something that differs wildly from the image the brand owner wishes to convey or is actually offensive (as is not entirely unknown). In some circumstances, it will be better to have some unified brand elements that are identical in all territories (eg, a single logo and colour scheme) but have local variations (eg, the product name in a local language). This may be a compromise, but should serve to ensure the brand message will be the same everywhere. The key is to consider in which territories the brand is to be targeted, and then check with local advisers in those territories that the brand will be publicly acceptable (and available for use) before embarking on a trade mark filing and marketing campaign.

Expanding international businesses

Businesses expand into new territories in two main ways: by opening/acquiring new foreign operations, or by franchising/licensing to overseas operators. The expansion may involve using the same brands and brand values (a unified model), or it might require developing a completely different local presence that looks and acts independent from the parent, to serve a different market (a devolved model).

In operating a unified model, there may be a need for more elaborate (and more robustly enforced) quality control measures to prevent brand values (and therefore business value) being eroded. One issue that is sometimes neglected is registration of licences or franchise agreements with the local IP office. In some countries, this is necessary before royalties can be paid out of the country.

The devolved model is broadly similar to setting up a new operation in the business's home territory. The only difference might be that the IP is controlled at a distance.

With either approach, the brand management issues discussed above will be important. In both cases, consideration must be given to the ownership of IP. Some businesses require all to be IP owned by a single entity. In other cases, local ownership of locally developed IP is preferred. Often this is a tax-driven decision, but whichever approach is taken, it is important that the contractual arrangements (within the group as well as with third parties) match the intention. Particular care needs to be taken with third parties; for example, advertising agencies or design houses. There should be a clear assignment to the relevant business of all the IP in work done by contractors.

These issues do, of course, also arise in arrangements in the business's home territory. However, there is a greater danger of neglecting them when they are at a greater distance: 'out of sight, out of mind'.

Outsourcing

IP is often given little consideration when business functions are performed by third parties overseas. A business will sometimes focus more on the cost savings that can be achieved and consequently neglect the stewardship of the business IP.

At its most simple (and most common), outsourcing merely involves having goods manufactured in another country. Inevitably, as part of this process there will be a licence (either as part of the contract or implied) of designs and other technology and know-how to the manufacturer. The manufacturer may contribute to the development of those designs or to the design of tooling required for product manufacture. Ideally, the business will ensure that in the contracts, the IP in the manufacturer's developments and tooling is owned by the business. This will help the business in dealing with counterfeit issues, for example where the manufacturer continues to make the products after the contract has ended and sells them on to other customers.

Other steps that can assist in preventing or dealing with counterfeits include ensuring that, so far as is possible, technology being shared with the manufacturer is protected by patent rights, covering the country of manufacture as well as countries where sales are planned. If the manufacturer will apply the business's trade marks to the product or its packaging, the trade marks should be registered in the manufacturer's territory (in addition to sales territories) and should be actively policed and enforced.

Where it is a service that is being outsourced, for example IT support or customer service call centres, there are other IP issues to consider. Copyright in operating manuals, software, and in written and electronic materials should all vest in the business, not the service provider. This should all be set out in the contract.

Common themes

Whatever the type of business, there are some common issues that need to be considered when coordinating an IP portfolio on a global scale. Some of these may seem trifling, but without careful planning, they can cause real problems. Some of these issues apply equally to other aspects of the business, but for some reason they are often neglected when it comes to IP.

Seeking local advice can prevent many difficulties. The advice may be to establish what IP is or is not registrable, or to ensure that brand manuals and standard operating procedures are consistent with local laws and practices. It may be to perform some due diligence on a potential service provider or to assist in stopping counterfeiting. Unless the business already has the expertise to deal with these issues, local assistance will be invaluable.

An international business must be aware of local customs, laws and practices. These can be relatively straightforward, such as knowing the dates of the national holidays. Setting deadlines that expire around Chinese New Year can result in enormous frustration for Western businesses operating in Asia. Some local customs may be less obvious, but just as important.

Robust reporting structures are vital. If the business needs to take swift action to deal with an infringement, or an allegation of infringement, the relevant decision maker must be informed promptly. Good reporting is also very important in maintaining quality control and consistency and for ensuring that business opportunities are not lost simply because no one in authority knew about them quickly enough.

Language can often be an important consideration. If there are problems in communicating clear instructions, or if things are translated poorly, all sorts of difficulties can arise. It is not unknown for trade mark registrations to end up covering the wrong goods and services, simply because of a mix-up in translation.

Perhaps the most important aspect of managing IP globally is making sure the IP policy is truly global, not just a local policy that is being imposed worldwide, without building in the flexibility to cope with the subtle, and not so subtle, differences that exist in different jurisdictions. In developing the strategy, it is important to be aware of and sensitive to these differences; what works in one territory may not work in others.

Coordinating and managing IP at a global level can be challenging. Careful planning and investing time in getting it right can save a lot of difficulties. A successful global IP strategy will provide for the consistent, effective and efficient use, protection, exploitation and enforcement of IP wherever the business operates.

About the author

Dominic Hickman is a commercial lawyer working with Rouse Legal, the UK legal arm of leading global IP consultancy, Rouse & Co International. He has extensive experience negotiating and drafting all forms of IP agreements and working with multinational clients on international aspects of IP. Further details: Rouse Legal, 1st Floor, 228–240 Banbury Road, Oxford OX2 7BY, UK, website: www.iprights.com.

Collaborative ventures

Open innovation should improve speed to market, but collaborative ventures can end up in a tangle, says Dominic Elsworth at Hargreaves Elsworth.

Many partners in collaborative ventures end up in a tangle about who exactly owns the IP. If open innovation really means faster times to market at lower cost, then collaborative ventures have to work smoothly. Before considering how to operate collaborative ventures it is first worth looking at some more fundamental questions, as one must know the answer to these before considering how to operate such a venture.

Why collaborate?

While collaboration is often talked about as a goal in itself, in fact organizations only ever collaborate for one reason: each party needs something that the other has. Research teams at different universities may have reputations in different fields, but a potential area of research may cross more than one field. To obtain a research grant it may be necessary to show that the research will be carried out by a team of people with experience in all the fields. Hence, the universities come together. In the more commercial world a product may need development for a particular application. This may require knowledge of the product and the application, and such knowledge may not be held by one organization, hence the organizations in question collaborate. At a more basic level, the nature of the innovation to be embarked upon may be such that the costs are so great they cannot be borne by one party alone, a situation that often arises in the defence sector.

Considerations for potential collaborators

Any collaborator should understand the motivations of its fellow collaborators. Such understanding may be gained from open discussions prior to collaboration begins. It may also take the form of research and investigations into the potential collaborator.

Such research and investigations will pay dividends when seeking to negotiate a collaboration agreement. For example, if the investigations show that the collaborator has connections in particular markets, be they defined by geography or technology, it should then not come as a surprise if the collaborator seeks rights to exploit the outputs of the collaboration in those markets. They may also uncover a potential collaborator's real motives for collaboration.

Who brings what to the collaboration?

Organizations would not be collaborating unless each was bringing something to the venture. To avoid the possibility of disagreements down the line it is important for the collaborating parties to identify what they each bring to the venture. Of course, this will include details of the capabilities of each organization. It is also important that each party identifies what intellectual property it owns so that there can be no argument at a later date that a piece of technology resulted from the collaboration rather than the efforts of one of the collaborators alone.

How will the collaborative venture be managed?

Collaborative ventures need to be given continual impetus, with clear targets for each collaborator.

One very important aspect of management is how knowledge arising from the collaboration is managed. This is very much a management issue and involves the provision of resources that allow information to be stored in a manner where it can be accessed easily by all collaborators, the scheduling of regular meetings between collaborators, and the establishment of reporting structures to provide for the screening of new knowledge for patentable inventions.

Who gets what?

Another vital aspect of any collaborative venture is for the parties to agree the rights of each party both during and after the venture. Is each party to have equal access to all outputs of the collaboration, or will the access depend on which collaborator came up with the particular idea? While unequal access may appear fundamentally opposed to the ethos of collaboration, there is no one correct answer. For example, there may be very good reason for collaborators to have rights in different territories or technical fields.

How is intellectual property resulting from the collaboration to be owned and what will be done with it?

In terms of patents, to determine ownership one must go back to the person who is the inventor and then look at how rights in the invention and to the grant of a patent may have passed from the inventor, which may occur by virtue of employment or by assignment. Under Section 3 of the Patents Act 1977 the right to an invention made by an employee in the course of employment belongs to the employer. Hence, if the collaboration is between two businesses, under normal circumstances the businesses would each enjoy rights to the inventions of their own employees. A collaborator must satisfy itself that the key personnel of its fellow collaborators are in fact employees, and if not that other arrangements for the transfer of inventions and the right to patents have been put in place. This is a particularly difficult area for universities. Businesses collaborating with universities should seek undertakings that intellectual property rights arising from work performed by the university do belong to it.

It would often appear equitable for collaborators to own jointly patents resulting from collaboration. In some cases this works, but joint ownership of patents comes with its own pitfalls, one of which is that each joint owner may work the patent for its own benefit without reference to the other joint owner. Further, in many countries licences cannot be granted without the authority of all joint owners, whereas in other countries any joint owner may grant licences without reference to other joint owners. While this arrangement may work well for some collaborators, for others it may undermine the whole venture. It is often better for collaborators to set up a company in which they each own shares. The patents are then owned by a single legal entity and the questions regarding joint ownership do not arise.

Collaborators must consider what will be done with the technology resulting from the venture and what the rights of each party in terms of commercialization will be. They also need to satisfy themselves that their fellow collaborators will not use the technology in a manner that might not be consistent with their values.

People

People are often the reason for collaborating. What happens if a key member of staff of your fellow collaborator leaves? Is there still a reason for collaborating? What happens if a key member of staff of one collaborator wishes to leave to join another collaborator (which may be the reason why the other collaborator wished to be involved in the venture)? Such questions should be considered before entering into any agreement.

Who pays?

Collaborators should not only agree how costs associated with intellectual property rights are to be funded, but also those who will be responsible for managing those rights. They also need to establish what should happen in terms of ownership in the event that one collaborator wishes to withdraw from the venture.

What about other work?

Other than where two organizations merge, collaboration is usually project-specific, even if the collaboration results in a spin-out company. This means that each collaborator will have ongoing business to attend to outside the collaboration. Where this business involves the development of new technologies it is vital that the boundaries between what rightly belongs to the collaboration and what rightly belongs to the collaborators are clear to all collaborators.

The golden nugget

For a collaboration to be successful for all collaborators, it must not be possible or even desirable for a collaborator who comes up with the golden nugget to attempt to keep it outside the collaboration.

All these issues should be dealt with in a Collaboration Agreement. Furthermore, such an Agreement should be in place at the outset. There is often a strong desire to get on with the work of a collaboration, and let the negotiation of the Agreement run alongside. This is a dangerous policy that collaborators should resist.

About the author

Hargreaves Elsworth is a Patent Attorney practice established in Newcastle upon Tyne in January 2002 by its founder, Dominic Elsworth, a Registered Patent Agent, Trade Mark Agent, European Patent Attorney and European Trade Mark Attorney.

The ethos of the practice is to bring to its clients a service of the highest quality, tailored to specific business requirements, at a reasonable cost. The practice provides both UK and international clients with advice and support services in all areas of intellectual property law, and in particular patents, trade marks, designs and copyright, know-how, and technology transfer. Further details: www.heip.co.uk.

4

Radical breakthroughs

Value-driven growth

Break the rules and redraw the market. Dr Tim Jones of Innovaro discusses the potential of value innovation.

Innovation is now firmly on the corporate agenda and is seen by companies, analysts, governments and consumers alike as a primary source of competitive differentiation. Innovation leaders, those companies that are able to better understand emerging opportunities, access and exploit new technologies, develop successful new products and services or even change their business models, are the corporate heroes of today. As Wall Street analysts and company management place ever more demanding expectation and growth targets on organizations, innovation is widely seen as the most successful route for delivering organic growth.

In the world of innovation there has been an assumed linkage between innovation success and sustained growth. Over the years, various academics in the United States and Europe have found correlations between innovation activity and corporate growth, while numerous government departments have mapped share price growth of high investors in research and development against FTSE, NASDAQ and Dow Jones indexes. Add into the mix the OECD, World Bank, KPMG and PWC analysis and the guiding view for those involved in innovation has been that, as a means to generate successful, share price-influencing growth, it is largely more successful and more sustainable than a purely merger and acquisition strategy.

SERVICE DESIGN, INNOVATION AND DOTT 07

As well as looking at traditional science based Research and Development, One NorthEast has also done a lot of work around service and innovation design.

Designs of the Times 07, or Dott 07 as it was known, was a celebration of design which challenged perceptions of the impact design and innovation can have on people's lives.

It saw a number of projects carried out covering various topics: farming in Middlesbrough town centre; re-designing more environmentally friendly schools across the region; reducing the carbon footprint of a house in Ashington; exploring how design can improve the lives of those suffering from Alzheimer's disease; and speculating on how robots could be taking over our lives.

The event, run by the Design Council and One NorthEast and the first of its type, was a major success and has certainly left a legacy on the region.

Move Me looked at how people from a small rural community, Scremerston in Northumberland, get to where they need to go without new cars and roads, and where public transport is infrequent and expensive.

Tied in with Dott 07, the challenge was set for a team of designers to make transport more accessible to the villagers as well as making it more environmentally friendly.

Working with the villagers to identify the problems – which included buses being few and far between, confusing public transport times and the expense of taxies – the team looked at solutions which could also be applied to other areas around North East England.

What they came up with included a 'Give or Get a Lift' card, which trusted community services providers like teachers, midwives or football coaches to give lifts to people who were on their route; and simplified transport timetables printed on easy to read leaflets which anyone could pick up.

By thinking about the design and innovation process simply the solutions to the problems became much easier to achieve.

There couldn't be a better time to get efficient about energy. The price of fuel has soared, and more people are struggling to afford to keep their homes warm enough for them to stay comfortable and healthy. The government is also regularly reminding the public that domestic carbon emissions need to be reduced.

Average carbon emissions from a domestic household in the UK each year, with no energy reduction appliances or insulation, would fill 30 double-decker buses. The government has set a target to reduce the amount of energy used by domestic households by 60%.

With Dott 07 in full swing, a team of designers took on board the challenge of turning a standard terrace house in Ashington, Northumberland, into an energy efficiency show-piece – known as the Low Carb Lane project.

People in the street knew little or nothing about energy efficiency – both in terms of the benefits it can bring to the environment but also the cost savings for them. They believed it would be too technical for them, too expensive, they were reluctant to invest when they didn't own the home, and they found their energy bills simply too complicated to understand.

But by refurbishing 'House X' to be more energy efficient, the team was able to see a:

- 10 per cent energy consumption reduction by installing more energy efficient appliances
- 20 per cent reduction with loft or cavity-wall insulation
- 15 per cent by generating themselves, perhaps through solar panels or wind power
- 15 per cent with behavioural changes, including switching the TV off standby at night, boiling less later in the kettle, and understanding how to control their energy bills.

The results showed residents in the street real benefits to being more energy efficient, which have been taken on board and introduced.

These projects highlight how One NorthEast and our partners are turning the challenge of being more innovative into a real strength within the region.

LYNSEY ROBINSON
SERVICE SECTOR MANAGER

Over the past eight years, as the Innovation Leaders analysis (www. innovationleaders.org) has been undertaken, a unique set of companies have been assessed and tracked in terms of revenue and margin growth as well as share price rise or fall. The results have been quite revealing: half of the companies identified as Innovation Leaders in their respective sectors back in January 2005 subsequently demonstrated an increase in share price of at least 50 per cent over the succeeding two years. In addition, the top five performers over this period all had growth in share price of over 60 per cent. Between 1 January 2005 and 1 January 2007:

■ Apple's share price increased by 163 per cent.
■ Google's share price increased by 139 per cent.
■ Rolls-Royce's share price increased by 89 per cent.
■ Toyota's share price increased by 64 per cent.
■ Canon's share price increased by 61 per cent.

Over the same period, the Dow went up by 15 per cent, NASDAQ by 20 per cent and the FTSE 100 by 9 per cent. As a portfolio, the Innovation Leaders shares have in fact exceeded the performance of all the major indexes for the past seven years.

The rise of the Innovation Leaders shares has since continued apace. Between 1 January 2007 and 1 January 2008, the 2006/7 Innovation Leaders overall portfolio went up by 12 per cent while the Dow only managed 7 per cent, NASDAQ achieved even lower growth of 4 per cent, with the FTSE 100 bringing up the rear with a growth of only 3 per cent. The top five performers over this period were:

■ Apple, whose share price increased by another 135 per cent.
■ Nokia, whose share price increased by 91 per cent.
■ Google, whose share price increased by 52 per cent.
■ Adidas, whose share price increased by 36 per cent.
■ Reckitt Benckiser, whose share price increased by 25 per cent.

Innovation success, as demonstrated by the Innovation Leadership analysis, is clearly not only directly related to share price growth but, by comparison to all major indexes, also enables companies to outperform their peers. Across economic booms and recessions alike, innovation has consistently delivered sustained growth.

Value innovation

Many of the organizations that have successfully focused on innovation to drive organic growth have been using value-driven innovation as a key source of sustainable advantage. Some, such as Virgin, have achieved this from a core cultural heritage; other such as RyanAir and NetJets through following or leading changes in market forces. However, other companies have embraced the evolving 'value innovation' approach as a core part of their strategic toolkit and, in doing so, have also realized significant gains. How and why this has been achieved may provide useful lessons for all.

Customer value

The Virgin Group has, largely from its inception, 'championed the customer' in the products and services it provides and how these are delivered. Whether this be convenient, pay-as-you-go mobile telephony through Virgin Mobile, high-value business class travel through Virgin Atlantic, or easy to understand, reliable financial products through Virgin Money, a common element that the Virgin brand has offered the world has been exceptional value for the customer – albeit simultaneously profitable for the provider. As Virgin has continually entered new markets, sometimes more successfully than others, providing value has often been linked directly to Richard Branson's leadership or a corresponding cultural norm within the organization. Whichever, numerous would-be or incumbent competitors have not been able to replicate it and so have lost market share and customers. Virgin's USP has become a passion for value and, as this is ingrained throughout the organization, many would see that it has been a key driver of success – and one than cannot be easily copied.

Cost models

Several companies have delivered value in providing new variations of opportunities that have emerged as markets have evolved. In the mass-market airline business, RyanAir in Europe, and Frontier and JetBlue in the United States, all saw Southwest Airlines making a mark in low-cost mass economy air travel. Although Southwest has about the same number of aircraft as United Airlines, it operates over 3,000 flights a day, double that of United. Moreover, Southwest has reported annual profits for 31 straight years. RyanAir, Frontier, JetBlue and others have adopted and adapted Southwest's approach and strategies. They have successfully acted as catalysts for change, have created largely low-cost business models and have successfully exploited them wherever they can. In the case of RyanAir, this has driven profitable growth to a point where its market capitalization eclipsed that of British Airways. Although a wide range of other would-be operators have tried to emulate this success, many of those seeking to compete in the same markets have failed to gain the same advantages either through being late into the game or having insufficient scale to operate in a sustainable manner.

Likewise, at the other end of the airline market, NetJets has reinvented the value equation of point-to-point business travel through providing all the convenience and flexibility of a corporate jet with none of the responsibilities of hiring pilots and scheduling maintenance – and all for a price that is only a slight premium on standard business class. With a fleet of over 500 aircraft now in operation serving 140 countries, NetJets' success has led to incumbent airlines trying to halt the drop in corporate customers by introducing business class-only flights and start-ups such as Silverjet trying their own variation. However, as both the first value-changer in this high-end of the market and also the first to achieve the necessary scale to fulfil a wide range of corporate travel demands, NetJets clearly has the current advantage.

Re-inventing the boundaries of value

While the above organizations have inherently innovated around value primarily from strategic and cultural perspectives, other companies are using a more process-driven approach. Following on from the initial 1997 *HBR* article and the subsequent best-seller *Blue Ocean Strategy,* both authored by W Chan Kim and Renee Mauborgne of INSEAD, several companies have been successfully innovating around value through following what has become an increasingly recognized process of 'value innovation'. As in the example of hotel company Accor highlighted in the original *HBR* article, by first gaining a clear view of what differentiating features of a product or service are really important to their customers, and then identifying how and where the associated value curve can be changed to exceed expectations in key 'purchase decision influencing' areas, some companies are able to fundamentally change the value proposition they are providing. They are better able to match customers key 'real' rather than 'perceived' needs to the products or services they are providing and so push the value boundaries, or even reinvent them, with significant financial benefit to all. One of the best current examples of this approach, and beneficiaries of the associated impacts that it can deliver, is Samsung Electronics.

From copycat to market leader

Samsung Electronics is part of one of the largest multi-billion dollar corporations in the world which, in 2007, exceeded the US$100 billion mark in annual sales for the first time in its history. This makes it one of the world's top three companies in the electronics industry where only two other companies, Siemens and Hewlett-Packard, have posted larger revenues. If you are talking innovation, Samsung walks the walk and is now the established leader in consumer electronics, providing a range of leading-edge premium products and, in its own words, is 'leading the digital convergence revolution'. In so doing Samsung has made a remarkable transformation from copycat manufacturer to become Asia's most valuable technology company.

Samsung spends more than US$6 billion on research annually and recognizes that many of its products, such as semiconductors and flat-screens, are now basic commodities. So part of its focus is on producing iconic devices for the next generation as Sony's Walkman was in the 1980s and the iPod is now. Samsung today also owes much of its success to its Value Innovation Program.

Since its strategic decision to become a 'rule breaker' and create a corporate culture of 'innovation is everything' in 1993, Samsung has successfully driven itself up-market making a world-leading shift from innovation follower to innovation leader. In achieving its ambition to become the world's best company, Vice Chairman Jun says, 'it's all about innovation – in every aspect of our business, we must innovate continuously on six parallel tracks'. These are:

1. *Product Innovation* to deliver a continual stream of stylish, innovative products that deliver unexpected delight.
2. *Technology Innovation* to quickly develop and retain key technologies and core R&D investments that separate the company from its competitors.
3. *Marketing Innovation* to create fresh approaches at every level of customer contact, continue to build the brand and drive sales.
4. *Cost Innovation* to control costs in ways that complement and encourage innovation and increase market impact worldwide.
5. *Organizational Culture Innovation* to create work environments where everyone shares the freedom to learn from mistakes and succeed.
6. *Global Management Innovation* to develop highly localized product strategies that link strong local insight and key market presence with an ability to accelerate the decision-making process and rapidly seize major opportunities worldwide.

To help identify the core opportunities to out-compete its peers, Samsung opened a dedicated Value Innovation Program Center in Suwong. This is an integrated five-floor facility where value innovation is taught as a process and applied across many product lines. While the second, third and fourth floors are available for project teams to work on value innovation projects, ranging from strategy development to new business models to new products, the first floor is devoted to value innovation training and the fifth floor is a mini-hotel where teams often stay until the project is finished! Identifying and exploiting value innovation opportunities across all six innovation tracks, this facility has fast become a key source of new concepts that have helped grow market share and margins.

Key products from Samsung's Value Innovation Program have included the SGH T-100 wireless phone, which sold over 10 million units; a 5-inch plasma display and the world's first 40-inch LCD TV, which represented breakthroughs in size and wide-angle viewing; and the SPH-E3200 digital camera phone which had no antenna. All of these products changed the value curve for the most important customers in their respective markets and are making significant contribution to Samsung's increasing revenues, margins and market share.

Conclusion

Samsung highlights that, when the market opportunity, corporate capability and core customer insights are aligned, companies can use a disciplined approach to identify and deliver value innovating concepts. Looking at Samsung and other Value Innovation leaders some common characteristics are evident:

- CEOs champion innovation and their personality influences what the companies do and how they do it.
- Company growth strategy and business models are clear to all employees.
- Decisions are made quickly with little dithering.
- Cycle times from concept to finished business model, product or service are being reduced from months, even years, to weeks.
- The organizational culture and working environment both support risk taking with innovation permeating the company.
- Ideas are sought after and welcomed from anywhere – within and outside the firm.
- Value Innovation can occur anywhere, at any level, at any time.

Value Innovation has evolved into a more sophisticated and reliable approach, able to help companies innovate better and differently. The capability in using the approach is now being seen by some as a key tool in their strategic planning process both for the short and long terms. As part of their innovation portfolio, more organizations are seeking to better understand the value innovation methodology, link it to key differentiating consumer insights and so identify market-breaking concepts. For many companies, there is an increasing recognition that if you don't value innovate in your space, someone else will. As the global innovation landscape accelerates, such strategic and organizational developments will be the drivers of change in the future innovation space. They will be the future sources of higher margins and sustained growth, and so may well be the core of many future innovation leaders' credentials.

References

Kim, W C and Mauborgne, R (1997) Value innovation: The strategic logic of high growth, *Harvard Business Review*, Jan-Feb, pp 103–12

Kim, W C and Mauborgne, R (2005) *Blue Ocean Strategy,* Harvard Business School Press, Boston, MA

About the author

Dr Tim Jones is Principal and founder of Innovaro. For nearly 20 years he has been active in the conception, development and introduction of a wide range of both evolutionary and revolutionary products and services. He has worked with many of the world's leading innovation companies, creating and developing new ideas, leading development teams, defining new strategies, designing new organizational structures and creating innovation-centric cultures to build new and improved innovation capability. He is a regular speaker at corporate events focusing on such topics as innovation leadership, innovation strategy and future trends in society and technology.

Based in London with offices in Amsterdam, Cambridge and Munich, Innovaro is Europe's leading innovation strategy and insight firm working with major global organizations to help improve business performance through innovation. It is an expert in helping organizations identify new innovation spaces, define and implement new innovation strategies, generate better ideas and renew their organizational capability. Innovaro has a growing reputation in helping companies see over the usual horizon to identify major new growth opportunities for the future and regularly runs programmes for clients across the technology/consumer/societal interfaces. Further details: www. innovaro.com.

Early-stage winners

Start-ups are a powerful source for technology breakthroughs and new market opportunity, says Ian Ritchie at Coppertop.

Innovation is a characteristic required by all modern business to survive and prosper. Without innovation, businesses tend to wither and die, as new approaches, new technologies and new communication methods overtake them and make them more and more irrelevant.

The UK has been obsessed for many years with our 'R&D Gap' – the fact that UK industry spends around half of the amount per capita on research and development that some of our industrial rivals in Germany, Japan or Scandinavia do. But in fact, R&D spend is not synonymous with innovation.

It is unlikely that very much of the revolution in new approaches to the selling of insurance, for example, led by businesses such as Direct Line, was down to anything that could be classified as R&D. In fact a great deal of innovation is down to start-up companies, and this is the area in which the UK is a leader. The UK has by far the most developed venture capital community in Europe, the biggest outside of the United States, and has developed a very healthy environment for the start-up of new businesses.

The most recent statistics indicate that the UK was the home of 37 per cent of the venture capital deals completed in Europe in the first quarter of 2008, compared with 18 per cent in Germany and 11 per cent in France. The leading sectors attracting investment are the internet, followed by biotechnology and healthcare, and then communications, all areas in which innovation is strong.

And start-ups can innovate in both technology breakthroughs and new market opportunity. In many cases a new start-up company can create a new innovative way of doing business that an established company cannot undertake – often because it might well be damaging to its current business model.

I can take two examples from my own experience to show how innovation can be managed to create wealth in start-up companies: Voxar and Digital Bridges. The companies have either led in technological change (Voxar) or in market innovation (Digital Bridges) and I was the founding chairman of both businesses. I also aim to demonstrate that innovation is not easy and that both companies had to change their products and business model in order to survive and prosper.

Voxar

Voxar was founded in 1994 by a graduate of the University of Edinburgh, Andrew Bissell, who had developed some innovative software technology for the display of three-dimensional (3D) images on standard personal computers without the need for special graphics enhancement. We could use this technology in a number of applications, but after an exhaustive analysis of the possibilities we chose to specialize in the display of medical images from MRI and CT scanners.

At that time we could see that although MRI and CT scanners take a volumetric view of the target part of the human body, the images distributed to the consultant, usually on large sheets of film to be viewed on a light box, were two-dimensional images, chosen by the radiographer to represent the most significant parts of the total scan. We decided that it might be very valuable for the consultant to be able to view the original volumetric image, and to manipulate and manage the original 3D image in order to undertake a full investigation of the individual scan. That was the simple part of the task – the more difficult was to make it actually happen.

We had made a crucial decision to appoint a chief medical adviser, a research-based medical consultant in Boston, and he helped us identify the key features required. Advice from real users were vital in the design of our product – we learnt, for example, that making it really easy for consultants to fill in the insurance billing forms quickly and correctly was a key requirement, every bit as important as the manipulation of the images.

But major problems emerged as we tried to market the product. We discovered that many hospitals had long-term contracts for film-based image systems that meant there was no incentive to switch to the more modern networked displays that we required to run our software. We had to contend with medical conservatism, where it was by no means accepted that existing methods of viewing images were not perfectly effective. So, our ability to sell our solutions directly to the medical market was constrained – innovation was not enough. The world was not beating a path to our door, despite our having a much better 'mousetrap' to offer.

Fortunately the medical world was changing, film-based systems were being replaced by networked computers configured as 'Picture Archiving and Control Systems' (PACS) and a number of major medical equipment companies, such as General Electric, Kodak, Philips and Fuji were actively selling these PACS products. And, in most cases, these companies did not have a 3D solution to offer and were willing to license solutions from Voxar. By 2002 we had licensed our software to all the major global PACS manufacturers with the exception of GE, which had its own technology. The company was successfully sold to Barco of Belgium in 2004.

Digital Bridges

In the case of Digital Bridges it was essentially market opportunity rather than technology breakthrough that inspired the formation of the company. The founder, Kevin Bradshaw, had identified in 1999 that mobile phones were becoming more sophisticated, and in particular that WAP was becoming a standard feature in modern mobile phones. He thought that the WAP platform was suitable for the development of simple computer games, and that young people were used to using their phones for entertainment and, crucially, paying for it, and would be keen to play engaging new games on them. The company was formed in early 2000 and set about to become a world leader in games for mobile phones.

We discovered that life was not so simple. WAP was over-hyped by the mobile operators and the performance was so poor that it was not widely adopted by their customers. We also discovered that although the mobile operators could have, in principle, introduced charging systems for our type of product download, they wouldn't. Sales didn't take off as planned and we were left pondering what to do next.

One aspect of mobile phone use that was being widely used was SMS messaging and, unlike WAP, it did have a built-in billing model that was already being successfully applied by third-party companies to sell entertainment products such as ringtones. We developed SMS games and games that relied on SMS messaging to collect the subscriptions, and had a limited success with that. But it was not until mobile phones started to appear with support for programs written in the Java language that the market opened up.

The advantage of this was that a program written in Java should, in theory at least, be able to run, unmodified, on any device. Of course, it didn't happen that way and huge customization was still required to suit different screen sizes and audio capability.

However, the company successfully gained market share, becoming one of the top five global publishers and was rebranded to 'iPlay'. It was sold in 2007 to Oberon Inc, a publisher of casual gaming on the internet that was keen to extend its reach onto the mobile phone platform.

Lessons learnt

The lessons of these two experiences are:

■ Identify a key innovative technological or marketing advantage that is not yet exploited by large multinational corporations.
■ Listen to the users. They will tell you what works and what doesn't. Be responsive to their needs.

- Keep close to market developments. In both these cases, market success really began when external factors (PACS systems or Java phones) became an industry standard way of doing things. Both companies were ready and willing to substantially change their business model quickly to exploit the opportunities presented by these important market changes.
- Keep an eye on the exit opportunities. It is most likely that a successful start-up company will become attractive to an industry leader that already has a market presence.

Innovation should not be measured by crude 'R&D metrics'. The strength of the UK economy lies partly in the strong venture capital community that is willing to invest in early stage innovative companies. With careful attention of the development of their market, and a willingness to adapt quickly to exploit market developments, such innovative companies can create exciting new enterprises that take their place within the modern economy.

About the author

Ian Ritchie is Chairman of Iomart plc, Computer Application Services Ltd, Scapa Technologies Ltd, the Interactive Design Institute and Caspian Learning Ltd and a director of Iomart plc. He has also been active in venture capital as a director of Northern Venture Trust plc from 1997 to 2001 and as a member of the advisory board of Pentech Ventures from 2001. He has served as Chairman of Judges for the Young Software Engineer awards since inception, the Winners on the Web awards, and as Chairman of the Scottish Financial Director of the Year awards. He has also been a judge on the joint UK Research Council's Business Plan awards, The Economist *Innovation awards, and the Royal Academy of Engineering MacRoberts Awards (the UK's premier award for engineering innovation). Ritchie was awarded a CBE in the 2003 New Years Honours list for services to enterprise and education. Further details: www.coppertop.co.uk.*

Our prescription against patent infringement and counterfeiting

Before commercializing your idea, make sure you have the right patents, designs and trademarks for your innovations.

Doing this creates a reliable safety net around your ideas and your precious intellectual capital.

Brann can help you build it, and provide you with high quality commercial and legal agreements.

INTELLECTUAL PROPERTY LAW FIRM

BRANN AB BRANN@BRANN.SE WWW.BRANN.SE
STOCKHOLM +46- (0)8-429 10 00
GÄVLE +46- (0)26-18 63 20
LUND +46-(0)46-271 77 00
UPPSALA +46- (0)18-56 89 00

BRANN

What investors expect to see

It is easy for venture capitalists to say 'No' to inventive ideas. Barry Franks at Brann reviews what you have to get right.

The one thing that all innovations have in common is that they all need resources to bring them to the marketplace – to commercialize them. It doesn't matter if you are an individual inventor or a Fortune 100 company – at some point you will have to invest money in your innovation and the key question is: where will that money come from?

Many companies and even some individuals have sufficient resources to commercialize their innovations themselves and the decision about whether or not to commit time and money to such a project can be taken internally – just like for other investments. However, in most cases, especially for individual inventors and small and medium-sized enterprises, some form of external investment will be required. Normally this can be obtained in three ways.

The first is by borrowing money, for example from a bank, family, friends or individual investors who will expect their investment to be paid back at a future date (usually with interest) but will not take part in the running of the business.

The second way is by entering into a partnership agreement with a company which, in exchange for a licence to exploit the innovation, will contribute some of the money and/or resources necessary to turn the innovation into a marketable product.

The third way, which will be dealt with in more detail below, is to form a joint venture in which an investor (a 'venture capitalist') is given a share of the company and *a say in the running of the company* in return for investing capital.

There are many inventors pitching for investments from a limited number of venture capitalists, and to be successful it is important for an inventor to understand what a venture capitalist wants and to make a pitch that satisfies these requirements. It is very easy for a venture capitalist to say 'No' to a new project and it is the inventor's task to make it even easier for the venture capitalist to say 'Yes!'

So what is a venture capitalist looking for when deciding whether to invest in a project? I suggest that the minimum requirements that such an investor usually wants are:

■ an exit mechanism to get a return on the venture capital investment;
■ preferred rights in relation to the shares that it holds in order to minimize the consequences of failure; and
■ a reasonable degree of control over the company's activities to ensure the business is being run following sound commercial practice.

Exit mechanisms

The inventor must identify a plausible exit strategy for the venture capitalist. The investor will want to know precisely how they can realize the capital gain on their investment when they leave the business. Investors expect to wait from three to seven years for their investment to be realized. The options for a successful exit by the venture capitalist are:

■ floating the company – either on the local stock exchange or increasingly on an international stock exchange;
■ the original investors or other persons buying out the venture capitalist; or
■ the business being sold – often to a competitor.

Preferred rights

Usually the initial investors want a preferential right that gives them priority over other shareholders in being paid if the company is wound up. Furthermore, experience shows that young companies often need several rounds of investment to bring a product to market. Each round of investment adds to the number of shares of the company in circulation and causes a dilution of the value of the original shares. The venture capitalist will wish to have (at least some) shares that will not be diluted during further investment rounds.

The inventor has to negotiate the amount of equity to be allocated to the investor in return for the actual investment (that is, allocate a percentage of the business's issued share capital to the investor in return for them providing the actual venture capital), in line with the anticipated financial return for the investor. As arriving at the actual share allocation is by way of negotiation between the parties, generally, the more the inventor can assure the venture capitalist that their proposed rate of return will be achieved, the less onerous the conditions on the inventor. As always, the higher the risk the more equity the venture capitalist will expect to receive for the investment. However, if the inventor has an existing or anticipated strong cash flow, then the venture capitalist is likely to receive a lesser percentage of shares.

Reasonable control of the company

Often the investor will nominate a director to the company's board of directors or even demand a majority of all the seats to be able to control the board's decisions. In this way, this investor becomes a partner in the day-to-day management of the business. If the business grows, so too will the value of the venture capitalist's investment. If the business fails, the investment is lost – because unless the investment is made as a loan, there is no automatic right to repayment of the original investment.

As well as board positions, the investor may require that the business be managed in a predictable way and, if certain specified events occur (such as major contracts or further share issues), there will be specific contractual mechanisms (possibly in the form of a Shareholders Agreement) in place to enable the venture capitalist to protect their investment (and the expected high returns on that original investment).

Before entering into a joint venture agreement, an inventor is advised to consider if they are willing to agree to these demands – if these requirements agree with their goals and desires. If they do, then an agreement with a venture capitalist might work.

The first step to such an agreement depends very much on the inventor's business plan. The investor needs to be reassured that the investment will not be exposed to unnecessary risks. The investor therefore needs to be comfortable with, and trust, the people seeking the venture capital. After that they need to see a risk evaluation and return analysis that they are comfortable with, preferably presented by a business owner and/or CEO with a good track record – that is, an owner/CEO with relevant experience in the industry for this business and who has a management team with a high level of relevant skills and competence levels. The evaluation should show a strong potential for revenue growth (perhaps over 20 per cent per year for the next three to seven years) with realistic time-frames and, last and not least, an IP portfolio able to protect those aspects of the business that determine the venture's success.

The business plan, which shows what the investment is to be used for, must include:

- focused, realistic strategies for the next five years including times for milestones such as proof of concept, working model, first prototype, etc;
- a good marketing plan that illustrates strong market opportunities and methods of realizing them, possibly an initial focus on the domestic market (but with potential for expansion internationally); and
- revenue projections, pricing and gross-margin strategies that offer a potential pre-tax return of between 30 and 50 per cent.

How to use IP to scare off investors!

The value of an IP portfolio cannot be over-estimated. Without adequate IP protection it is impossible to prevent competitors copying a successful commercialization of an innovative product or service and, as they don't have to make the same investments in R&D, selling it at a lower price.

Even the most unsophisticated investor realizes this and the inventor must be prepared for deep and probing questions about their IP portfolio. The three areas that are most likely to scare off a potential investor are unclear IP ownership, unclear scope of protection, and inappropriate/missing scope of protection.

IP ownership must be clear – and this unfortunately often conflicts with national or international funding schemes in which the greater the number of international and university–industry institutes that are involved, the higher the chances of getting funding. Investors fear that the chances of negotiating a successful agreement drop rapidly as the number of people who are involved increases. In an example where the IP was jointly owned by three universities, one start-up company and one established company, negotiations become too complicated and time-consuming and, despite being very interested in the technology the potential investors become frustrated and gave up. They really only wanted to deal with one person or exceptionally two. Therefore inventors should select their initial partners carefully (and not just so as to be able to show a long list of loosely associated people who are hot profiles in academia) and, if possible, before approaching investors all IP rights should be transferred to a technology holding company which should be able to negotiate on behalf of all the parties and which licences the IP to the commercializing company. An advantage of having IP in a separate holding company is that in the event of the risk-taking commercializing company failing, the separately owned IP is safe from the demands of the failed company's creditors.

The investors will want satisfactory answers to the following questions:

■ Who is the named inventor/designer? Have *all* the inventors been identified? Are there people named as inventors in patents who actually didn't contribute to the invention? Correct identification of inventors is a legal requirement in the United States.
■ Are there possible unhappy collaborators? A disgruntled partner can make it difficult or expensive to reach any kind of agreement.
■ Have *all* the inventors assigned their inventions to the (holding) company? It can be time-consuming and expensive to get assignments signed if the inventors are no longer working with the invention, have moved abroad or have died.
■ Are *all* necessary rights held in the same company? The issue of a patent doesn't necessarily mean that it is possible to use the invention – there may be earlier rights that need to be licensed-in.
■ What do the agreements between co-inventors say about IP ownership and their possibilities for sub-licensing? In some countries each co-inventor can act independently of the other co-inventors. Unless this right is restricted by a contract between them there is the possibility of co-inventors individually licensing their invention to competing companies.

Investors will often get a third-party analysis on patentability or even a full due-diligence. If the inventors haven't already done their own analysis then they will most likely be at a disadvantage during negotiations as they will look unprofessional.

A patentability analysis should be able to provide positive answers to the following questions:

■ Does the IP cover the commercial product/process – not just the idea? The invention must not only be technically interesting but it must add some value to the product.
■ Has IP with these claims been granted anywhere? Granted claims in at least one country are seen as a favourable factor.
■ Does the IP cover the right fields – both technical and geographical? Are patents and applications filed in the major markets and do the claims cover the specific product as well as wider fields. Note that claims that are too broad can be a source of worry as more prior art can be cited against them.
■ Does the IP include patents *and* registered trade marks/domain names *and* registered designs? An IP portfolio should contain many different types of IP to give comprehensive protection.
■ Is the IP valid? This means not only checking for patentability/registration issues but also if all necessary fees and annuities have been paid.
■ Is it possible to design-around the IP? This can also include an analysis of possible competing technologies and their pros and cons.
■ What in-house IP will be needed in the future to cover improvements? This can include a plan showing an ongoing IP strategy to cover further products or identified gaps in IP coverage.
■ Is there a need to license-in any IP? If so, is the IP owner willing to license it?

Unfortunately IP owners don't always take logical or commercially-based decisions. A Swedish company that produces sun-shades for computer monitors has been trying vainly for many years to get a licence from the private owner of a US patent covering such shades. The IP owner apparently prefers to (un-successfully) tackle the whole US market using their own limited resources instead of receiving royalties from the Swedish company, which is well established in Europe and which has to refuse orders originating in the United States for its product.

Doing this analysis can prevent expensive mistakes – like those made by a small biotech company that had obtained a revolutionary patent based on new scientific findings and was about to launch a product based on them. Unfortunately, when a competitor beat them to the market with a similar product they were not able to stop them as the patent claims only covered the scientifically interesting findings – they didn't cover that commercially interesting product.

The correct and timely acquisition of IP can be powerful protection – witness the case of a Swedish company that invested 1 million Swedish Crowns (€100,000) in moulding tools at a Chinese subcontractor. When the Swedish company decided to transfer production to another manufacturer because of delivery problems, the original subcontractor could not make unauthorized copies as the product was protected by patents and registered designs in the major markets – including China.

However, the presence of IP cannot help if there are other monopolistic factors affecting the market. A company that was granted a patent for environmentally friendly wooden paper-clips was thwarted by its intended supplier in its efforts to mass-market them. This wood-veneer company realized that it was the only company in the world able to produce veneers that were both sufficiently strong and flexible enough to make the paper-clips and raised the price of its raw materials. So much that a finished paper-clip would have cost €2!

About the author

Barry Franks, VP Patents at Brann AB, started his career in IP in 1983 as Examiner at the European Patent Office. After nearly 10 years he moved into private practice in Sweden and then spent seven years as an IP Counsel for GE Healthcare (in Sweden and the UK) before returning to private practice. Direct phone +46-(0)18-56 89 34; Cellular phone +46-(0)70-685 2053; e-mail barry.franks@brann.se.

Brann AB is a full-service provider in the field of IP rights, backed by comprehensive knowledge and experience of IP law. Founded in 1949 in Sweden and employing over 90 IP specialists, Brann also benefits from a comprehensive global network of foreign contacts built up over the last six decades. Web: www.brann.se.

Claims for novelty and originality

Incorrectly drafted patents can be a disaster, says Keith Beresford at Beresford & Co.

A patent, or more accurately a patent specification, is a legal document. Like others, such as contracts, its structure and language determine its effect and therefore its value. Given a commercially valuable invention, a patent carefully drafted to meet the requirements of both the patent law and the commercial environment in which the invention will be exploited can be of immense value. Incorrectly drafted it can be an expensive disaster. Some examples of expensive disasters will be described later.

What does a patent do?

In the EU, the answer is to be found in the national patent laws of the individual states. These have been harmonized to the provisions of a treaty called 'The Community Patent Convention', which dates from 1975. In the UK, Section 60 (1) of the Patents Act 1977 is the relevant one. It says the following *commercial* activities in the UK infringe if carried out without the agreement of the patent owner:

(a) If the patented invention is a product, making, using, selling, offering to sell or importing the product, or keeping the product.

(b) If the patented invention is a process, using the process or offering it for use plus (and of great importance) if the patented process is for *making* a product, importing the *direct* product of the process, selling it, offering it for sale, or keeping it, even if the product of the patented process itself is not in any way novel.

The above activities are called 'direct' infringement.

There are some supplementary provisions in Section 60 (2), which specifies activities that constitute 'indirect' infringement. Indirect infringement arises if someone, without the agreement of the patent owner, supplies or offers to supply (in the UK) to someone in the UK an item for use in putting the invention into practice in the UK when the supplier knows (or it is obvious) that the item is intended for this purpose. The item does not have to be novel in and of itself. However, indirect infringement can be difficult to prove because you have to prove the mental state of the supplier.

So a patent gives the owner the right to prevent, through legal action in the courts if necessary, competitors from performing the above activities, or to collect royalties on those activities through a licensing arrangement.

What determines what the patented product or process is?

This is done in the patent specification. In the case of many inventions the patent draftsperson can choose whether to define the invention as a product or a process or both. For example, if the invention is some improvement in a machine for manufacturing a product, the invention can be defined in the patent specification:

(i)   as the machine itself (and that becomes a product invention); or
(ii)   as the process which the machine carries out in manufacturing the product (in which case the patented invention becomes a process); or
(iii) both.

If he or she chooses (i) but not (ii), they would be unable to prevent (or collect royalties on) the importation of the product of the patented machine. If they choose (ii) but not (i), they would be unable to prevent manufacture of the machine in the UK for export, but of course he or she could prevent its commercial use in the UK because the commercial use of the machine would involve performance of the patented process.

So we are beginning to see how the value of the patent is directly dependent on the interaction between the way the patent specification is drafted and the law of infringement. And we are beginning to see that without knowledge of the law of infringement it is impossible to ensure that the patent specification is drafted to achieve the full value of the invention.

A brief discussion of the patent specification

A patent specification can be divided into three main parts:

1. An introduction, which outlines the field of the invention, the current state-of-the-art, the problem the invention aims to solve and an indication of the way in which the invention solves it.
2. A detailed description, usually with drawings, to explain how to implement the invention. This would normally consist of a description of products or apparatus and/or processes that 'embody' the invention.
3. One or more definitions (called 'claims'), which define, by their language, the product (or apparatus) or process that is to be protected by the patent.

The function of the introduction is obvious. The detailed description has two functions. First, it has to give enough technical information to a person of ordinary skill in the relevant field to develop, without further inventive activity, a product or process in accordance with the invention. Second, it has to 'support' or 'justify' the claims. More of this later.

The language of the 'claims' is crucial. If a claim is too broad, so that it reads on to previously known products or processes, the claim will be invalid. If it is too narrow, so that its language fails to cover important versions or variants of the invention, infringement can be easily circumvented. A very careful analysis is therefore necessary to determine the appropriate level of generality of the claim in order to maximize the scope of the patent while, so far as possible, avoiding invalidity through claiming over-broadly.

Because no one can know every piece of technology that pre-dates the application date of the patent, it is usual to include a set of claims of varying scope so that if the broadest ones turn out to be 'unpatentable' the narrower ones (defining the best aspects of the invention) may still be valid and of significant commercial value.

Infringing and royalty-generating activities: the essential ingredients

Patent infringement and royalty-generating activities are activities that are:

■ performed by a person or corporate body;
■ performed within the country of the patent;
■ performed in relation to a product or process within the scope of a claim; and
■ prohibited by the law of infringement of the country of the patent.

It follows that the wise and experienced patent draftsperson has at the forefront of their mind not just the *technology* that constitutes the invention, but also the *commercial environment* in which it would be exploited and the *law of infringement*, so that they can produce a patent specification that gives the maximum monopoly, the maximum opportunity for royalty collection and therefore maximum value.

Crucially, they must produce claims that define products or processes in relation to which infringing activities can be performed and whose language is broad enough to protect all of the modifications and variations on the invention that are commercially important. For example, if the invention is an improved electrical plug and socket, they should provide separate claims to the plug and the socket (assuming both are novel) because these items are traditionally sold separately; a single claim to the plug and socket combination would be of limited value.

Supporting claims by the description

Also, the draftsperson must produce a detailed description that supports or justifies their claims. For example, if the improvement in the plugs and sockets applies both to the two and the three pin varieties, the detailed description will need to explain how to implement the invention in both thereby to justify claims that cover both.

Expressed facetiously, a detailed description of how to make cream cheese will not support a claim to a process of making an apple pie. And by analogy, a detailed description of an improved three pin plug will not necessarily support a claim broad enough to cover the same improvement in a two pin plug.

With this background, we can now look at some disastrous examples of patents that went wrong.

When things went wrong

The windsurfer problem

A windsurfer is made up of two main components: the surfboard, which is provided with a universal joint or part of one, and the rig (mast, control bar and sail), which connects to the surfboard by the universal joint. In the UK, the patent only contained claims to the combination of surfboard and rig (and this was at a time when indirect infringement did not exist in the UK). In Germany the patent only contained claims to the rig.

The Windsurfer Company licensed people both to make the complete device and to make replacement surfboards because the surfboards apparently frequently break. It collected large amounts of royalties on the replacement surfboards until at some point somebody complained to the EU authorities that this was an anti-competitive trade practice because the boards by themselves were not patented. The complaint was upheld. The Windsurfer Company was fined by the EU and had to drop its royalty claim on replacement surfboards. An expensive disaster because of the mismatch between the way the patent was drafted on the one hand and the law of infringement and the commercial environment on the other.

The RDS radio problem

In the RDS radio system, a coded signal transmitted when the station is about to broadcast a traffic report causes car radios to switch to that station even if tuned to a different one. The transmitters are novel because they have to produce the signal. The receivers are novel because they have to respond to it. Obviously, massively more receivers would be sold than transmitters.

The German patent only claimed 'A transmission system comprising...'. When the German owner sued someone for importing and selling RDS receivers, the German court rejected the case because the patent did not contain a claim directed to the receiver. An expensive disaster, simply because no claims to the receiver were included in the patent specification.

The CD problem

Making CDs involves producing a 'master' (like a mould) and then stamping out multitudes of CDs from the master.

Pioneer, the Japanese company, had a patent for an improvement in the way the master was produced. It contained only a claim to a method of producing the master. It could have but did not include a further claim to a method of making CDs from a master made by the improved method.

Someone began importing CDs that had been made, in a country where there was no patent, from masters made by the improved method. Pioneer sued for infringement and argued that the CD was the *direct* product (see above discussion of infringement) of the patented process of making the master. The judge (and the Court of Appeal) disagreed. They held that the CDs were the *indirect* product of the patented process and struck the case out. Another expensive disaster.

The modelling software problem

Haliburton, the US oil equipment company, had two patents for designing oil drilling bits by computer. They were both revoked by the court because the detailed description of the implementation of the inventions did not meet the requirements of the patent law. The description appeared in fact to be made up of notes made by the inventors themselves. The judge said, 'As a description of how an undoubtedly complex model works, this is useless.'

Not only did Haliburton fail in its infringement action and thereby lose markets and damages (and its patents) but it had to pay the defendant's legal costs, which undoubtedly were extremely large. Investment, at the beginning, in a properly drafted patent specification would have avoided this expensive disaster.

Avoiding expensive disasters

The above are a few examples of patents whose value was significantly less than it could and should have been. Or in some cases zero.

To avoid this kind of problem the first step is to carry out a rigorous analysis of the invention as a piece of technology, and determine how the technology can be commercialized, in particular what novel products could be made and sold (and what processes could be performed) based upon that technology. Basically, 'How will money be made out of this invention?' and then, 'What claims are needed in the patent in order to protect these money-making activities?'

This analysis is not easy. It involves forward and lateral thinking, technical knowledge, commercial knowledge and legal knowledge. It is best done by interaction and face-to-face discussion between the inventors, the businesspeople who will be responsible for exploitation of the technology and a patent attorney, all of whom will make their contributions to this exercise. Following this, the patent attorney will be able to prepare a patent specification containing claims to each important novel process and/or novel product in which the technology would be implemented, and the required detailed description and introduction.

As noted at the beginning, a patent specification is a legal document even though its contents are technical. It cannot be drafted effectively by anyone not trained in patent law and with the requisite technical knowledge and understanding of the invention. In general, inventors cannot hope to adequately draft even the detailed description because this has to meet the legal requirement of providing support for the claims, and it is almost impossible to draft adequate claims without the requisite legal knowledge and training. Special care is necessary in preparation of the description because errors and omissions cannot normally be rectified later.

Hence, investment at the outset in the analysis and a professionally drafted fully detailed specification is what is needed. It will not only avoid expensive disasters but will actually be cheaper in the long run because properly drafted specifications are easier to prosecute through the patent offices of the world and to litigate in the courts if that should become necessary.

About the author

Keith Beresford is a British Chartered Patent Attorney, European Patent Attorney and Intellectual Property Litigator. He has a degree in physics and a Master of Law degree in advanced litigation. He is the senior partner of Beresford & Co, which he founded in 1986. The firm acts for a wide variety of clients including multinational corporations, small to medium-sized companies and private inventors. His work includes drafting and prosecution of patent applications, patent office oppositions and prosecution and defence of patent infringement actions in the courts. He handles a wide range of technical subject matter, including complex electronic and software systems, and is the author of the book, Patenting Software under the European Patent Convention, *published in 2000 by Sweet & Maxwell, London. Tel: 020-7831-2290, e-mail: mail@beresfordpatents.co.uk.*

5

Continuous improvement

Profitable niches

Grow your business by sticking to the knitting, says Gerard Burke, Programme Director at the Business Growth and Development Programme at Cranfield School of Management.

How often do you hear that small businesses must 'innovate or die'? But what is meant by innovation? Often government agencies and trade bodies peddling this advice appear to suggest that entering new markets and developing new products/ services are imperatives for small businesses. But our experience of working with nearly 1,000 ambitious owner-managers over the last 20 years is that this route to growth is a high-risk strategy. We find that 'sticking to the knitting' – selling more of your existing products/services to your existing customers and customers just like them – is more likely to lead to sustained profitable growth. Then, once you have a deep understanding of your customers' needs, innovation happens gradually and naturally.

We've undertaken two separate studies in recent years looking at market focus and financial performance that make a convincing case for this argument. Across our sample population of growing businesses, nine out of 10 of the high-performing firms, showing consistently profitable growth, focused on selling existing products and services to the market they already knew. They 'stuck to the knitting'.

A compelling strategy for the growth-hungry firm is to find a profitable niche market and bring distinctive value to the customers within it. Some of the most successful businesses on our Business Growth and Development Programme (BGP) have done exactly that:

- Pacific Direct supplies luxury branded toiletries to five-star hotels.
- Cobra Beer with its beer and wine portfolio for Indian restaurants.
- Hotel Chocolat provides delivered handmade chocolate gifts.

The niche strategy comes with three great benefits for the owner-managed business. First, niches are frequently overlooked or not well served by big players. Second, a smaller business simply cannot fight on too many fronts. If it tries, there's a danger of failing to serve properly the needs of either the diversified market or the core customers. For instance, before participating in BGP, the founders of Hotel Chocolat had twice tried to grow through diversification – and failed both times! Following BGP, they renewed their focus on the core – and the resultant growth has been exponential. Third, the business can focus on meeting the needs of a well-defined target group. This in turn builds a deep knowledge and understanding of their customers, which allows the business to be better than the competition at meeting those customers' needs.

Think of it like squeezing a lemon. When a recipe calls for the juice of half a lemon, most people will slice a lemon in two, squeeze one half and then throw away the remaining peel and flesh. If they bother to keep the other half of the lemon, they will likely as not wrap it in clingfilm and put it in the fridge – where it remains for several weeks before turning green and mushy! In other words, most people will fail to get the maximum juice out of the lemon. Many businesses take exactly the same approach with their customers. There is no plan for developing the sales relationship with larger customers, no plan to encourage smaller customers to become larger ones, and no plan for finding new customers.

Here's one example of squeezing the lemon. Hotel Chocolat takes the view that each gift order of chocolates comes with two customers: the actual customer, the person who places the order; and the potential customer, the person who receives it. Hotel Chocolat makes sure that the recipient knows all about where the chocolates came from and encourages that person to become a customer in turn.

I am not suggesting that businesses like Cobra, Pacific Direct and Hotel Chocolat don't innovate. In fact, the highest performing smaller firms are highly innovative. Indeed, these three businesses regularly win awards for their creativity and innovation. However, their innovation is regular and usually *incremental*. Their deep knowledge of their niche allows them to respond quickly to, or even anticipate, their customers' needs. As a result, they can be seen to be constantly enhancing their products and services in ways that they already know will meet with their customers' approval.

This type of incremental innovation, based on deep sensitivity to customers' needs, is usually a perfectly natural and deeply engrained behaviour within the business. In the successful growth business, there is no need for a special 'innovation process', or for one person to be responsible for new ideas. Identifying new and better ways to service their customers is simply part of what everybody does, and the business is sufficiently nimble and flexible to allow these improvements to be implemented quickly.

Of course, these high-performing businesses also occasionally diversify. But, the sort of radical innovation and diversification that often seems to underlie the 'innovate or die' message, is only undertaken once the foundations have been well laid within the core niche, and as part of a carefully thought through strategy.

FUNDING AND THE REGIONAL PICTURE

Like every other region of the UK, North East England has had to face up to the growing challenge of globalisation and the implications this has for regional economies and businesses.

Tied in with the need to create an extra 22,000 businesses, One NorthEast has taken the bold approach of turning this challenge into an opportunity, by building on our existing world-class industrial strengths with the aim of exploring new, innovative markets.

We want the region to be a place where budding entrepreneurs can realise their dreams and aspirations; where regional companies can grow and prosper; and where national and international companies come to expand operations.

The central element to this is access to funding. Without the money to develop their ideas and services, those businesses would be very unlikely to get to first base. One of the biggest challenges facing entrepreneurs in the North East is to attract private investment.

The fact is we are a long way from most of the UK's financial centres and so any business proposition coming out of the region has to be a very good bet for business angels and venture capitalists to take a risk.

That's why One NorthEast set up NStar in 2003. An early stage technology finance company, it provides high growth businesses with access to both flexible funds and expertise.

Under the NStar umbrella there are two equity investment funds totalling £33m. The £10m Proof of Concept Fund (PoC), jointly funded by the European Regional Development Fund and One NorthEast, gives loans of up to £90,000 to prove the feasibility of a product or service, while the £23m Co-Investment Fund (CoIF), funded solely by ERDF, offers larger amounts - up to £1m – for development projects.

The Proof of Concept Fund has so far helped around 120 companies; two thirds of the cash has been invested; and it is hoped the remaining funds will be awarded to innovative companies by the end of 2008.

It's important to stress that this is not a free ride. Both are equity investment funds that are loaned at near commercial rates on the basis they have to be paid back with interest or are convertible into an equity stake within the borrowing company.

In fact, by the time the funds come to fruition in 2008 it's estimated they'll have leveraged in around £60m of private investment into the companies they have supported and therefore into the region as a whole.

It's a great return – about £2 for every £1 invested – and it's vital for the future of the region's business growth because this is a legacy fund. The money repaid by those companies as they grow and prosper will be used again to fund more early stage ventures in the future.

With the objective of developing a varied, robust economy and the region's vibrant science agenda, it is not surprising the initial funds had a focus on new technology opportunities, many of them with university spin-outs and high-tech SMEs.

However, two new pilot funds recently launched by NStar recognise more burgeoning sectors in the North East where there is huge promise.

The 'Three Pillars' Fund targets business ideas within the technology sectors identified by One NorthEast as having massive potential to create jobs and wealth in the region. These are energy, healthcare and health sciences and process innovation. Designed to assist companies at the development and pre-seed stage, up to £125,000 is available.

The second, the Design and Creative Fund, is focused on providing financial support for the North East's high-growth design and creative industry sector. Businesses in the following six areas are eligible to apply:

- Advertising design and brand communications
- Performing arts (with a focus on content creation)
- Publishing (with a focus on content creation)
- New media, games and software
- Film, TV and video
- Music (with a focus on content creation).

But applications from other industry sectors are encouraged where there is a clear and significant element of design or creative content. Loans of up to £60,000 are available, with additional funding on top in exceptional circumstances.

MARK PEARSON
BUSINESS STRATEGY MANAGER

For example, Pacific Direct built a strong position in hotels before moving to servicing airlines. Business and first class airline passengers also tend to stay in five-star hotels and appreciate the same sort of luxury brands. Pacific Direct's credentials built in one niche bolstered its entry into the adjacent one and the company's infrastructure was robust enough to support the expansion.

Although innovation, or investing in new products or markets, is a higher risk strategy than competing more effectively, there are ways to manage the risks involved. The least risky innovation is likely to be the new product or service requested by existing customers. Often, the business works closely with the customer. While the business has a guaranteed sale, there is a danger that the product or service is so customized for a limited group of customers that it cannot be sold to a wider target.

The term 'innovation' often suggests something radically new. In fact, new products can equally mean simple line extensions to the core business. Look at the Coca-Cola Company. More than a century after its foundation, it still derives most of its revenues from its core Coke portfolio. And the Austrian company Red Bull has built a significant global business around one product and a handful of variants.

What appears to an outsider to be radically new or different may be a clever combination of existing features and technologies. Many businesses have built strong positions not through innovating a particular technology, but in re-presenting existing technology in an attractive way to the customer.

Nevertheless, in our experience, for the smaller, growing business, improving competitiveness usually ensures better returns than launching new products/services into new markets. Putting this into practice is normally a two-stage process: sell more to existing customers and then look to capture customers from your competitors.

So the message is: go deep *before* going broad. Unfortunately, too many ambitious businesses never make it past the first burst of growth because they start wandering too far, too fast from what they really know how to do. Entering new markets and developing innovative new products/services may well play an important role at certain specific stages of growth, but only at the right time and only as part of an overall strategy.

About the author

Gerard Burke is the Programme Director and lead designer of the Business Growth and Development Programme (BGP). BGP is the UK's biggest and most successful development programme for ambitious owner-managers. The programme is now in its 21st consecutive year of operation and during that time has helped nearly 1,000 owner-managers to achieve their business and personal ambitions. Businesses that participate in BGP grow sales and profit more quickly than their peers, and grow more quickly after the programme than they did before. For example, here's what Karan Bilimoria of Cobra Beer said about it: 'BGP has been a real turning point in my business and my career. This unique programme has given me the personal and hands-on development I required. It exceeded my expectations and was excellent value for money. I really wish I'd done it earlier.' You can find out more about BGP at www.som.cranfield.ac.uk/som/bgp.

Provided by

Invest
Northern
Ireland
Building Locally
Competing Globally

Part funded by

EUROPEAN REGIONA
DEVELOPMENT FUND

Anything you want to know about business, you'll find it here.

Starting Up

Finance and Grants

Taxes, Returns & Payroll

Employing People

Health, Safety, Premises

Environment & Efficiency

Exploit Your Ideas

IT & e-Commerce

Sales and Marketing

International Trade

Grow Your Business

Buy or Sell a Business

Your Type of Business

**NIBUSINESS
INFO**.CO.UK

Practical Advice for Business

The knowledge advantage

Dr Joanne Coyle at Invest Northern Ireland discusses how enterprises can exploit their existing resources and knowledge.

Businesses have access to an extensive pool of knowledge – whether this is their understanding of customers' needs and the business environment or the skills and experience of staff. The way a business gathers, shares and exploits this knowledge can be central to its ability to develop successfully.

What is knowledge in a business?

Using knowledge in business isn't necessarily about thinking up clever new products and services, or devising ingenious new ways of selling them. It's much more straightforward. Useful and important knowledge already exists in business. It can be found in:

■ the *experience* of your employees;
■ the *designs and processes* for your goods and services;
■ your files of *documents* (whether held digitally, on paper or both);
■ your *plans* for future activities, such as ideas for new products or services.

The challenge is harnessing this knowledge in a coherent and productive way:

■ *Market research* can be tailored to target particular customers with specific types of product or service.

■ Files of *documents* from and about customers and suppliers hold a wealth of information that can be invaluable both in developing new products or services and improving existing ones.

■ *Employees* are likely to have skills and experience that can be used as an asset. Having staff with knowledge can be invaluable in setting businesses apart from competitors. Employees' knowledge and skills should be passed on to their colleagues and successors wherever possible, for example through brainstorming sessions, training courses and documentation.

An understanding of what customers want, combined with employees' know-how, can be regarded as the **knowledge base**. *Knowledge advantage* is using this knowledge in the right way, enabling a business to operate more efficiently, decrease business risks and exploit opportunities to the full.

Basic sources of knowledge

■ *Customer knowledge* – businesses should know their customers' needs and opinions. A mutually beneficial knowledge-sharing relationship should be developed with customers. This can be by talking to customers about their future requirements, and discussing the best way to develop products or services to ensure that their needs are met.

■ *Employee and supplier relationships* – businesses should seek the opinions of employees and suppliers – they'll have their own impressions of performance. Formal surveys can be used to gather this knowledge or opinions can be asked on a more informal basis.

■ *Market knowledge* – watch sector developments. How are competitors performing? How much are they charging? Are there any new entrants to the market? Have any significant new products been launched?

■ *Knowledge of the business environment* – business can be affected by numerous outside factors. Developments in politics, the economy, technology, society and the environment could all affect the business. Consider setting up a team of employees to monitor and report on changes in the business world.

■ *Professional associations and trade bodies* – their publications, academic publications, government publications, reports from research bodies, trade and technical magazines. Trade association can be found on the Trade Association Forum (TAF) website.

■ *Trade exhibitions and conferences* – these can provide an easy way of finding out what competitors are doing and to see the latest innovations in a particular sector.

■ *Product research and development* – scientific and technical research and development can be a vital source of knowledge that can help create innovative new products, retaining competitive edge.

∎ *Organizational memory* – do not to lose the skills or experience the business has built up. Find formal ways of sharing employees' knowledge about the best ways of doing things. For example, create procedural guidance based on employees' best practice.

∎ *Non-executive directors* – these can be a good way to bring on board specialized industry experience and benefit from ready-made contacts.

Exploiting your knowledge

Consider the measurable benefits of capturing and using knowledge more effectively. The following are all possible outcomes:

∎ An improvement in the *goods or services* offered and the processes used to sell them. For example, identifying market trends before they happen might enable a business to offer products and services to customers before competitors.

∎ Increased *customer satisfaction* through a greater understanding of their requirements through feedback from customer communications.

∎ An increase in the quality of *suppliers,* resulting from better awareness of what customers want and what staff require.

∎ Improved *staff productivity,* because employees are able to benefit from colleagues' knowledge and expertise to find out the best way to get things done. They'll also feel more appreciated in a business where their ideas are listened to.

∎ Increased business *efficiency,* by making better use of in-house expertise.

∎ Better *recruitment and staffing* policies. For instance, increased knowledge of what customers are looking for will make a company better able to find the right staff to serve them.

∎ The ability to *sell or license* knowledge to others using knowledge and expertise in an advisory or consultancy capacity. To be able to do so, intellectual property should be adequately protected.

Make knowledge central to your business

In order to manage the collection and exploitation of knowledge, it is important to build a *culture* in which knowledge is valued. One way to do this might be to offer incentives to staff who supply useful market news or suggest ways customers can be better served.

As part of knowledge management, any *intellectual property* (trade marks, patents and copyright) that the business holds should be protected. This gives businesses the right to stop competitors from copying it as well as allowing businesses to profit by licensing existing business knowledge.

Protecting and exploiting the knowledge base will be more effective if the business develops efficient systems for storing and retrieving information. Files – whether stored digitally or on paper – contain knowledge that can be used to make products, services, systems and processes better and more customer-focused.

Knowledge should be kept *confidential*. Employment policies play a central role in this. For example, staff might sign non-disclosure agreements (also known as 'confidentiality agreements') when they join the business as this ensures that they understand the importance of confidentiality from day one. Employment contracts can be written to reasonably limit employees' freedom to quit and work immediately for a rival (restraint of trade clauses) or set up a competing business in the vicinity (restrictive covenants).

Sharing knowledge across your business

It's essential to avoid important knowledge or skills being held by only a few people, because if they leave or retire that expertise could be lost. Having efficient ways of sharing knowledge across the business will allow it to be more widely used and its value and effectiveness is likely to be maximized.

Knowledge can be shared through holding innovation workshops or brainstorming sessions at which staff are given the freedom and encouragement to think of ways in which the business could improve. It can also be a good idea to create a *knowledge bank* containing useful information and instructions on how to carry out key tasks. Putting this on an intranet is ideal as it will encourage staff to post news or suggestions. Training is also instrumental in spreading key knowledge, skills and best practice across your business.

Create a knowledge strategy for your business

To get the most from business knowledge, it is important to take a strategic approach to *discovering, collating and sharing it*. This is done via a knowledge strategy – a set of written guidelines to be applied across the business.

For a strategy to be effective, a business must make sure senior managers are committed to it and are fully aware of the benefits it can bring. When drawing up the strategy a business should:

■ Consider how effective the business currently is at using its knowledge.
■ Analyse internal processes for gathering and sharing information – are there successful ways of generating ideas and do staff have a good grasp of what's happening?
■ Make sure that knowledge management, acquisition and distribution is a continuing process, so that it becomes central to the business's strategy.

It is also important to identify the value of knowledge to the business. Ways to exploit knowledge for financial gain include gaining a larger market share, developing new products, or selling or licensing protected intellectual property to others. This should fit with the overall business plan.

Using information technology to gain and manage knowledge

Information technology offers powerful tools to help gain and make the best use of knowledge. Some of the systems can be complex to set up and time-consuming to maintain. A system should fit with the business and improve it without becoming a burden. Technology alone isn't the answer to sharing knowledge – it has to be managed carefully so that information is channelled properly:

- *Databases* organize information so it can be easily accessed, managed and updated; for instance, a database of customers containing contact information, orders and preferences.
- A *data warehouse* is a central storage area used for a variety of business systems, or a range of information in different digital formats. Many businesses now use digital asset management to store, manage and retrieve information, and this can be particularly helpful if you sell online.
- *Data mining* is a process in which all the data collected are sorted to determine patterns; for instance, which products are most popular and whether one type of customer is likely to buy a particular item.
- *Reporting and querying tools* create reports interpreting data in a particular way. How many sales have been handled by one particular employee, for instance?
- *Business intelligence portals* are websites that bring together all sorts of potentially useful information, such as legal issues or details of new research.
- *The internet and search engines* – these can be a powerful source of knowledge, although be certain to check the credibility of your information source.
- An *intranet* is a secure internal network for the sole use of a business.
- An *extranet* is similar to an intranet but can be extended to customers and suppliers.
- *Customer relationship management software* helps build up a profile of a customer database and enables better targeting through e-mail, telephone or postal marketing campaigns.
- *Call-centre systems* can serve large numbers of customers for selling by telephone.
- *Website log-file analysis* helps analyse how customers use websites.
- *Systems to analyse and file* customer letters, suggestions, e-mails, and call-centre responses, which will enable businesses to spot trends, improve customer service and develop new products, services and systems.

Further details can be obtained on www.nibusinessinfo.com.

to protect your innovation in Italy
contact the Italian Patent and Trademark Office
telephone 0039 06 47055616
fax 0039 06 47055635
uibm@sviluppoeconomico.gov.it

Italian enterprises and their innovative performance

Italian enterprises have once again learnt to thrive on the basis of their tacit and coded knowledge, the Italian Patent and Trademark Office reports.

Italy presents a puzzling case of technological specialization, which, over the years, has been the subject of numerous economic analyses. How can an economic model that has many of the characteristics of 'backwardness', such as a high prevalence of SMEs and a concentration of activity in traditional sectors, continue to do so well? Recently, it has even been described as 'bumblebee Italy' (Becattini, 2007).

The data and definitions that follow will make this discussion more concrete. Ninety-five per cent of Italian enterprises have between one and nine employees. Competition is strongest in traditional sectors, known as 'Made in Italy'. These include food and wines, fashion, furniture, marble, stone and ceramic tiles, metal products, machinery and domestic appliances, motorcycles, bicycles and yachts.

Italy is the leading European net exporter in these sectors, with a value of €90,4 billion in 2006 while the other 26 EU countries net exports in the same year amounted to €200 million (Fortis, 2007).[1] A significant share of the successful production of 'Made in Italy' is manufactured in industrial districts (IDs)[2] (Menghinello, 1996).

In determining the competitiveness of 'Made in Italy' and its enterprises, specific elements play a role: tacit knowledge; the creation of new intellectual property; and a capacity for creating and managing the demand for 'Made in Italy' products.

The knowledge creation for an enterprise stems from a combination of coded and tacit knowledge. The former is public and standardized and therefore transferable.[3] The latter, owing to its very nature, is tied into the context where it is created, so making it rather difficult to transfer (Cantwell, Archibugi,1997). In IDs, there are fewer such barriers: new forms of knowledge and innovation can be more freely synthesized, setting off a significant cumulative process on the basis of a shared wealth of experiences and skills.

Within IDs, however, the fundamental assumption for creating new knowledge and skills relies on social capital that stems from economic and social relationships between enterprises and local institutions (political, economic, financial and cultural). In the functioning of industrial districts, two processes are crucial: knowledge transfer and knowledge combination that render the IDs a community market (Grandinetti and Camuffo, 2006). Industrial districts operate as a meta-context where there is an intense knowledge production on the part of enterprises and a strong knowledge transfer capacity, as well, owing to the existence of cognitive overlapping. This is particularly deep for enterprises making the same product or specializing in the same phase of production: their imitative observation of each other is enhanced.

Such cognitive overlapping is fundamental to knowledge transfer and is a strong tool for new knowledge creation. The acquisition of innovation through this imitative approach leads to the creation of further new knowledge. This explains the wide range of products manufactured in IDs that have between them a complementary competition aimed at satisfying the demand for quality and luxury goods and related services all over the world.

Another two elements characterizing the IDs are people mobility and intra-district relations. Employees can easily change place of work within the district since enterprises share language, basic knowledge/generic specialization and skills. The relationships between enterprises making the same product or specializing in the same production phase, as well as those operating upstream or downstream as subcontractors or technology suppliers, are strong means to enhance innovation. This makes IDs a place where there is a high level of information flow and transparency.

All these traits make for two types of know-how: a district-specific and enterprise-specific know-how that together represent the main part of intellectual property creation within the 'Made in Italy' sectors. At the core of their competitiveness, there are learning processes inherent to the working groups of an enterprise.

According to the evolutionary theory of economic change, innovation at enterprise level is defined in a wider sense that gathers the characteristics of the whole productive system, including its organizational aspects. An enterprise is considered as a social cohesion unit or a production system and thus as a cumulative productive capacity tank (Cantwell, 1997). An enterprise therefore has the inherent capacity to learn, innovate and transform its own productive system over the years.

The learning process binds creation, absorption and adaptation of public/codified and tacit knowledge together with accumulation of the tacit capacity incorporated in organizational habits of the enterprise. However, the fact that the core of innovation and competitiveness at enterprise or ID level relies on know-how, which is rather difficult to protect, although each country generally provides rules for its legal protection,[4] implies that there is a high risk of appropriation by third parties. In addition, when know-how becomes the object of a contract, it is rather difficult to maintain the enterprise's competitive advantage.

The global economy affects the industrial districts business model. Its boundaries are opened through the participation in global knowledge networks and the internationalization of the value chain. Furthermore, as part of globalization, districts tend to take on a new configuration. They become a strategic centre for decisions and skills[5] rather than a physical location of production, operating in a larger international network of productive and commercial relations. Consequently the role of IPRs in creating, managing and maintaining competitive advantages becomes even more crucial.

For 'Made in Italy' goods, innovation, new knowledge and skills go beyond products, processes and business model. This aspect is tied not only to the distribution capacity and management (CENSIS, 2007) but also to the capacity to pick up on and, in some respects, to create consumer needs through product differentiation, sectoral diversification of production, and making products a cultural experience (Beccattini, 2007). This is the reason why in order to protect 'Made in Italy' innovation and quality there is a wider use of trade marks and designs than patents.

Together with the know-how, the other most valuable result in term of IP is the transformation of 'Made in Italy' from a concept into a brand. From a consumer perspective, when the origin of a good is related to a specific country, know-how is broadly recognized as a driving force of extraordinary quality innovation. The origin is immediately understood as a quality-giving added value to products and with a cumulative effect over time, which strengthens the evocative power of geographical indication.

As for indicating the country of origin at customs, different rules and procedures are in force all over the world. Within the EU, the adoption of the indication of origin, labelled directly on products, for community and non-community goods is not compulsory, leaving businesses to decide on whether or not to use 'Made in...' labels on their goods. Different rules apply in the United States where the labelling is compulsory but only for imported goods.

Over the years, the added-value of indicating 'Made in Italy' on goods has been assessed. Labelling products 'Made in Italy', in accordance to EU customs rules, has passed from being little or no distinctiveness, according to IP principle governing trade marks, to assume an evocative power for consumers, an evocative power typical of a mark and almost of a brand. This vision might be supported by a few principles contained in some decisions of European Court of Justice concerning the evaluation of evocative element in judgements where a likelihood of confusion on the part of the public exists. The evocation of the qualitative immaterial component through labelling products with 'Made in Italy' has produced value and it is an important source of economic growth for the country, thanks to specific commercial experiences that become cultural experiences through the IP system.

The major use of IP tools on the part of SMEs, especially in areas where IDs predominate, is revealed by the data on acquisition/disposal of 'non-produced/non-financial' assets) collected by the Balance of Payments of Technology (BPT).[6] Values registered in the BPT represent an indicator of *input* (payments) and *output* (earnings) of technology.

From 2001 to 2006, SME participation in technology transactions has strongly increased. The share of earnings for SMEs with fewer than 19 employees has gone from 21.3 per cent (2001) to 38.4 per cent (2006), while the share of payments made by SMEs with fewer than 19 employees has risen from 22.1 per cent (2001) to 42.3 per cent (2006). This shows the increased capacity of knowledge absorption, including the one created out of the district context and the capacity of the Italian SMEs to participate in international networks of knowledge.[7]

Furthermore, this type of technology transaction is particularly intense in the traditional industrial sectors that are gathered in the 'Made in Italy' concept (around 26 per cent of total earnings value and 27 per cent of total payments value).[8] The important variable consists precisely in the cumulative value of payments and earnings from technology transactions, rather than the net amount between payments and earnings. It is the cumulative value that creates the technology market, opening up possibilities for deeper innovation within enterprises. In 2006 the 'Made in Italy' sectors made a positive contribution to the credit balance of BPT.

These figures seem to bear out the strategy chosen by the Italian enterprises to maintain their market share under increasing price pressure from Asia. Their actions to improve their competitiveness have had a clear influence on the technical efficiency of their productive processes, on their capacity for product differentiation, on their diversification within sectors and on the quality of their products. It represents a recovery from the recent past: a survey concerning the period 2000–2004 of the reactions of Italian enterprises specializing in traditional 'Made in Italy' products revealed that limited number of enterprises (5 per cent) had adopted complex business strategies, which simultaneously affected all aspects of innovation (Menghinello and Papa, 2007).

The data[9] concerning applications for IPRs indicate progress in the innovative choices of Italian enterprises.[10] In the period 2005/2007 applications for IPRs made to the Italian Patent and Trademark Office have increased: 8.1 per cent patents for inventions,[11] 8.4 per cent trademarks,[12] 16 per cent utility models[13] and 29 per cent designs.[14] Also the application of community trademarks and designs originated from Italy has registered a positive dynamic: 31 per cent the former[15] and 4 per cent the latter.[16] In 2006 patent applications made to the European Patent Office originating from Italy were substantially unvaried[17] while the applications with the EPO (Euro and Euro-PCT) designating Italy have increased.[18]

Data on innovation collected by the fourth edition of the Community Innovation Survey (CIS 4) cannot provide significant information on the innovative behaviour of Italian enterprises since it only gathers data on enterprises with 10 or more employees, which therefore disregards the majority of Italian enterprises.

Bibliography

Daniele Archibugi (1997) *Innovazione e globalizzazione. Definizione, misurazione e implicazione per le politiche* in Daniele Archibugi, Gianfranco Imperatori, *Economia globale e innovazione -La sfida dell'industria italiana,* Roma, Donzelli Editore, pp 113–57

Daniele Archibugi, Marco Ceccagnoli, Daniela Palma (1997) *Innovazione e internazionalizzazione nelle imprese manifatturiere italiane,* in Daniele Archibugi, Gianfranco Imperatori, *Economia globale e innovazione -La sfida dell'industria italiana,* Roma, Donzelli Editore, pp 160–237

Giacomo Becattini (2007) *Il Calabrone Italia,* Bologna, il Mulino

Leonardo Becchetti, Andrea de Panizza, Filippo Oropallo (2003) *Distretti industriali: identità e performance,* ICE, Conferences and Seminars documentation, free available on http://www.ice.gov.it/editoria/rapporto/default.htm

Chiara Bentivogli e Lucia Scillitani (2002) *Internazionalizzazione dei Mercati, New Economy e Sviluppo Locale: Il Distretto Di Sassuolo Negli Anni '90,* ICE, Conferences and Seminars documentation, free available on http://www.ice.gov.it/editoria/rapporto/default.htm

Staefano Breschi, Maria Luisa Mancusi (1997) *Il modello di specializzazione tecnologica dell'Italia: un'analisi basata sui brevetti europei,* in Daniele Archibugi, Gianfranco Imperatori, *Economia globale e innovazione -La sfida dell'industria italiana,* Roma, Donzelli Editore, pp 239–69

CENSIS (2007) *Rapporto sulla Situazione Sociale del Paese,* Milano, FrancoAngeli

Giuliano Conti, Menghinello (1997) *L'internazionalizzazione produttiva dei sistemi locali,* in ICE, Rapporto sul Commercio Estero 1996, Roma

Marco Fortis (2005) *Il 'Made in Italy' nel 'nuovo mondo': Protagonisti, Sfide, Azioni,* Ministero Attività Produttive

Specializzazione sbagliata? I magnifici 7 del 'Made in Italy', Bollettino trimestrale Scambi con l'Estero, 2007, n. 4/2007, Ministero Commercio Internazionale

Roberto Grandinetti, Arnaldo Camuffo (2006) *A theoretical model of knowledge transfer and combination within Industrial Districts,* the paper was published at the 22nd IMP-conference in Milan, Italy in 2006

Emanuele Giovannetti, Karsten Neuhoff, Giancarlo Spagnolo (2003) *Agglomeration in the Internet: Does Space Still Matter? The MIX-IXP Case,* ICE, Conferences and Seminars documentation, free available on http://www.ice.gov.it/editoria/rapporto/default.htm

ICE (2007) *L'Italia nell'economia internazionale,* Rapporto 2006–7, Roma

ISTAT (2008) *Struttura e dimensione delle unità locali delle imprese 2005,* Roma, free available on http://www.istat.it/dati/dataset/20080319_00/

ISTAT (2008) *Statistiche sull'innovazione nelle imprese 2002-2004 (CIS4),* Roma, free available on http://www.istat.it/dati/catalogo/20080227_00/

The Maastricht Economic and social Research and training centre on Innovation and Technology (UNU-MERIT) with the support of the Joint Research Centre (Institute for the Protection and Security of the Citizen) of the European Commission (2008) *EUROPEAN INNOVATION SCOREBOARD 2007,* free available on http://www.proinno-europe.eu/admin/uploaded_documents/European_Innovation_ Scoreboard_2007.pdf

The Maastricht Economic Research Institute on Innovation and Technology (MERIT) and the Joint Research Centre (Institute for the Protection and Security of the Citizen) of the European Commission (2007) *European Innovation Scoreboard 2006*, free available on http://www.proinno-europe.eu/doc/EIS2006_final.pdf

Stefano Menghinello (2002) *Dimensione locale e competitività sui mercati internazionali: il contributo dei sistemi locali di piccola e media impresa alle esportazioni nazionali*, Roma, ISTAT

Stefano Menghinello, Pasquale Papa (2007) *Globalizzazione dei mercati e modelli di comportamento delle imprese nei settori del 'Made in Italy' tradizionale*, in ICE, *L'Italia nell'economia internazionale*, Rapporto 2006–7, Roma

OHIM (2007, 2006, 2005) *Statistics of Community Designs*, Alicante

Roberto Schiattarella (2003) *Analisi di sistema e delocalizzazione internazionale. Uno studio per il settore del "Made in Italy"*, ICE, Conferences and Seminars documentation, free available on http://www.ice.gov.it/editoria/rapporto/default. htm

Giuseppe Tattara (2001) *L'efficienza dei distretti industriali: una ricerca condotta dal servizio studi della banca d'Italia*, in Economia e Società regionale – 4, 2001

UIC/BANCA D'ITALIA I2007) *La Bilancia dei pagamenti della tecnologia 2006*, Roma, free available on http://uif.bancaditalia.it/UICFEWebroot/ DocServlet?id=new/it/stat/pubbl/bil-tecn/download.htm

WIPO (2007,2006, 2005) *Gazette of International Marks*, published by the International Bureau of the World Intellectual Property Organization Statistical Supplement, Geneva

Notes

[1] N. 4/2007 Quarterly report on Foreign Trade issued by the Italian Ministry of International Trade.

[2] The industrial district is a complex phenomenon that involves and integrates the economic and the social environment and therefore is substantially different from other productive contexts as clusters that are basically characterized by an high territorial concentration of SMEs.

[3] Patents but also technical data, formulae, standards, technical information, specifications, processes, methods, code books, raw materials.

[4] In Italy the article 98 of IP code provides for specific protection of secret information inclusive of know-how.

[5] The relevant skills are logistics, design, monitoring strategic phases of production.

[6] BPT presents data on disembodied technology transactions adopting OECD and IMF standards. The OECD standards require the gathering of these data in four items: trade in technics (*acquisition/ disposal of patents, royalties for patents, know-how, acquisition/disposal of invention*), transactions involving trade marks, designs, patterns (*licence fees and acquisition/disposal of trade marks, designs, patterns*), services with a technical content (technical assistance related to disposal and royalties, sending technicians and experts, human resources training, engineering and technical studies), industrial R&D performed abroad/financed from abroad, other settlements for technology. The IMF standards distinguish flows concerning acquisition/disposal of patents, know-how, inventions, trade marks, models and designs (*acquisition/disposal of 'non-produced non-financial' assets*), from flows concerning royalties and licence fees and other business services (R&D services and architectural, engineering, other technical services).

[7] BTP data reveal that these technological transactions are not bound to intra-group transactions.

[8] Branches of economic activities of BTP here considered are: food and wines, textile–clothing and leather and shoes, fashion, furniture, metal products, agriculture and industrial machinery, other industrial products.

[9] Data referring to 2007 are provisional and may change in volume within next six months owing to the data communication time from Chambers of Commerce to the National Patent Office.

[10] To have certain data on innovative behaviours on the part of enterprises there would be the need to match enterprises data (ASIA) with data on IPR applications; UIBM is carrying out initiatives to be able to provide this service within two years.

[11] 9.300 in 2005 and 10.121 in 2007.

[12] 50.464 in 2005 and 55.094 in 2007.

[13] 2.137 in 2005 and 2538 in 2007.

[14] 1.018 in 2005 and 1.437 in 2007 with an average of eight designs for each application.

[15] 4.897 in 2005 and 7.135 in 2007.

[16] 10.398 in 2005 and 10.863 in 2007.

[17] 4.199 in 2005 and 4.197 in 2006.

[18] 122.004 in 2005 and 128357 in 2006.

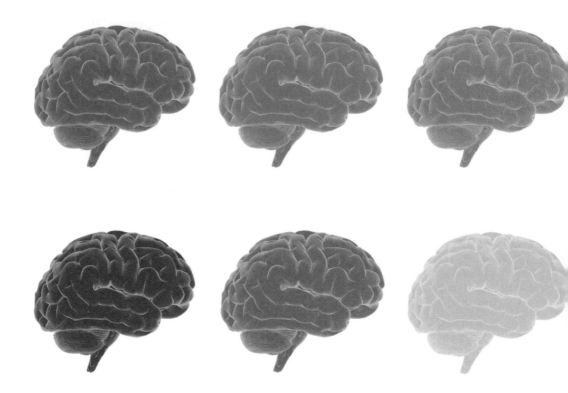

no grey matter

MewburnEllis

LLP

PATENTS • TRADEMARKS • DESIGNS • COPYRIGHT

IP fit for purpose

Use your commercial nous in selecting which IP rights to use, suggests Stephen Carter at Mewburn Ellis.

white elephant *n. 1. A rare, expensive possession that is a financial burden to maintain. 2. Something of dubious or limited value.*

Intellectual property protection can be costly. Not having IP protection can be more costly. The 'trick' in any IP strategy, but especially for a small, growing business with limited resources, is to keep your commercial wits about you and to closely match your IP strategy to your business goals. By spending wisely you can avoid your IP rights rapidly becoming a white elephant.

Imitation – flattering but is it good business?

They say that imitation is the sincerest form of flattery. It is also often the cheapest way for a new competitor to enter the market and, while competition might generally be considered a good thing, this form of (arguably unfair) competition is almost certainly not good for the original innovator whose efforts the imitator benefits from for free. IP rights are the mechanism that exists to legally prevent this imitation and can be particularly important for small and rapidly growing businesses that must look to outside sources for funds to support their growth, as adequate IP protection is more often than not a prerequisite for such investments.

So, IP protection can be crucial to the success of a business. But it is expensive. The question is how to spend your money to the greatest advantage. Put another way, where should the focus be?

Cornerstones

Rather than automatically taking an expansive approach and protecting all your ideas (a sure-fire way of busting the budget), you need to identify the cornerstone (from a commercial perspective) of what you are going to be offering. You will get most value out of your IP by protecting an idea that underlies everything else.

This is not always easy. Often it involves taking a conscious decision to leave aspects of your development unprotected. But taking these decisions at the outset will almost always be better for the business in the long run.

Make life difficult for competitors

Consider also what features of your development a competitor could best use to provide them with a 'springboard' into the marketplace. If you can prevent them from taking too many shortcuts in their own creative process then you can maximize the period of time in which you have exclusivity in the marketplace.

Revenue streams

It is also important to marry your IP protection up with your (potential) revenue streams – investors in particular will be looking for this. Sometimes it will pay to focus your protection more specifically on one or two particular revenue streams, rather than seeking very broad protection that may be harder and more expensive to obtain with little or no added benefit.

When going through this process, keep in mind that IP rights can play a varied role in the overall commercial strategy of a business. The traditional role that people tend to think of is the offensive one: actively using your intellectual property to exclude others, preserving a market for you or those authorized by you to exploit exclusively. Another role is use of an IP right itself to generate revenue, either through licensing or selling it. Also very relevant, particularly for growing businesses, is the role that IP rights, and more generally a good intellectual property strategy, play in attracting investors. In my experience in the technology sector, while investors are generally attracted to good science rather than good patents, the absence of an appropriate strategy for protecting the good science can often be a deal-breaker. An IP portfolio can also have a defensive role to play. It can deter competitors from enforcing their rights against you (for fear of retaliation) and any dispute might be settled by way of a cross-licence.

Which rights?

Having decided what to protect, thought needs to be given to how best to protect it. In fact, this can be an iterative process because the 'how' will affect the cost, so may inform to some extent the 'what'.

Some intellectual property rights come into existence automatically. One example is copyright. Stronger, 'registered' IP rights, including patents, registered trade marks and registered designs, need to be actively sought.

In some cases, the best protection may be afforded by keeping your ideas secret, if you can realistically achieve this – the protection is in effect perpetual (think of Heinz' secret recipe for its baked bean sauce) but the downside is that if the cat gets out of the bag then it may be too late to obtain any other form of protection. And of course, in many cases, the commercialization of an idea necessarily means telling the world all about it, in which case registered rights such as patents will be at the forefront of any IP strategy.

Often, you will choose a combination of the available rights. Patent key features but rely on trade secrets for the black box in the middle. Use design rights to protect the outward appearance of something where that has significance and trade marks to protect your name and logo.

Registered rights

Patents protect technical innovations. They provide protection for the technical concepts embodied in a product and/or in the processes for manufacturing the product so they can provide protection that is broader than the specific product or products that have been developed. Patents are infringed by a competitor's product that employs the technical innovation covered by the patent (as defined by the patent's claims), irrespective of whether or not the products look alike.

A trade mark is something (eg, a word or sign) that enables customers to identify goods or services as coming from a particular source. Marks can be very valuable and important if properly developed by advertising, promotion and correct use on quality products or services. Thus, it is vitally important for the mark's repute and the producer's repute to protect the mark. A *trade mark registration* generally gives the proprietor the right to stop others from using confusingly similar marks in relation to similar goods or services. In some circumstances the owner of a registered mark can even stop others from using a mark for goods or services that are not similar to those for which it is registered.

Registered designs give protection for the appearance of a product. A registered design will be infringed by a competitor's product that has the same or a closely similar appearance (whether it is 'technically' the same or not). So, registered designs provide useful protection where the appearance or look of a product is important to the end user and therefore adds value to the product.

Home or away?

Registered IP rights are territorial rights, ie they are limited to the specific territories in which you seek protection. The more territories you choose to cover, the more applications are needed and the higher the costs. Typical strategies include seeking protection in key (large or strategically important) markets and, where they are well defined, countries where competitors operate (eg, manufacture).

Systems exist that enable you to avoid the 'big bang' approach of seeking protection in all territories of interest at one time, allowing you to postpone the associated costs without harming the available protection. There are also some regional registrations (in particular Community Registered Designs and Trade Marks, and European Patents) that provide cost-effective routes to obtaining protection in multiple countries within the region.

For all of these registered IP rights it is possible to file a single application in one country to start with and to later file applications covering the other countries of interest that claim 'priority' from the first filed application. The priority claiming applications are treated as if they had been filed on the same day as the first filed application.

Time your run

For patent and registered design protection it is very important that the first applications are filed before the invention or design you are seeking to protect has been disclosed publicly. This is because the question of whether you will be granted protection is, in most countries, judged against what was in the public domain at the filing date of the application, including any disclosures you have made yourself.

It is also important to appreciate that in most countries registered IP rights are granted on a first come, first served basis. So, particularly if you are in a competitive field, it can be important to file an application sooner rather than later. On the other hand, the sooner you file an application the sooner you are committed to the potentially high costs of following the application through, and this factor may mean delay is appropriate in some cases.

Don't switch off

Once you are attuned to the commercial applications of whether or not you should seek protection in the first place, guard against letting yourself switch to automatic. It is all too easy to follow the same patterns over and over.

Instead, stop yourself at every decision point. Is an application appropriate? Can you drop it? Or do you need to take more protection? Always take the time to evaluate whether the protection you are paying for still makes commercial sense... or are you just creating a white elephant for your business?

A final word... watch your back

In all of this it must not be forgotten that your competitors may well have their own IP rights. It is important to be aware of the impact that rights of others could have: at worst, halting your activities completely. Prudent businesses will have in place strategies for dealing with this.

Such strategies might include watching the IP filing activity of known competitors. This may allow a business to work around a competitor's patents or other rights and/or to consider whether it might be vulnerable to attack. Watching a competitor's IP filing activity can also provide useful intelligence for its development work. And, as already inferred above, sometimes the best defence can be possession of your own portfolio of intellectual property rights.

About the author

Stephen Carter is a partner in Mewburn Ellis LLP, one of Europe's premier IP firms, with over 60 patent and trade mark attorneys and technical specialists, covering the full range of intellectual property issues: patents in all technology areas, trade marks, designs, industrial copyright and related matters.

Stephen has a degree and MPhil (Masters) in mechanical engineering from the University of Bath. He joined Mewburn Ellis in 1994 and became a Chartered Patent Attorney and European Patent Attorney in 1998. He worked for a law firm from 2000 to 2004, gaining experience in IP litigation and due diligence work for corporate transactions and IPOs, before rejoining Mewburn Ellis as partner in 2004. Stephen's work is mainly in the engineering and software fields. Further details: Mewburn Ellis LLP, York House, 23 Kingsway, London WC2B 6HP, Tel: 020 7240 4405, e-mail: Stephen.carter@mewburn.com, www.mewburn.com.

LOVEN
PATENTS & TRADEMARKS

Protecting
Innovation . . .

Advancing
Business
Potential . . .

West Central Runcorn Road   **t:** +44 (0)1522 801111   **e:** enquiries@loven.co.uk
Lincoln   LN6 3QP   **f:** +44 (0)1522 870505   **w:** www.loven.co.uk

Using IPR to improve your competitive position

Keith Loven of Loven & Co discusses how intellectual property can make economic sense for smaller companies.

Major companies know the importance of Intellectual Property Rights (IPR) to the growth of the business, but small to medium companies often take the view that IPR is only for the big boys: 'Patents are too expensive and if we are copied, we could never afford the cost of going to court.' This chapter will show that this is too short-sighted a view and that, handled correctly, IPR can add value to your business.

What's the point of IPR?

Let's go back to basics. The main argument for the law providing IPR is to encourage creativity. No one wants to invest time and money in developing new products unless there is some commercial advantage in doing so. If your competitors are just going to copy everything new that you bring out, then it is difficult to justify the cost of developing new products. The same is true of other forms of innovation, from product styling, through new brochures to new brands. So the law provides rights to innovators to prevent others immediately benefiting unfairly from that innovation. This is done in different ways – monopoly rights in inventions and designs and trade marks by formal registration procedures, and anti-copying rights provided automatically by copyright/design right.

Monopoly rights are subject to formal examination of originality, and can (if handled correctly) be used to control not merely identical copies, but also things that are similar to the protected invention, design or brand. Automatic anti-copying rights do not require any positive action to acquire, but can only be used to stop direct copying, not, say, the accidental arrival at the same thing. Both forms of rights require legal action to enforce, but while action in the courts is undeniably costly – a straightforward patent infringement action could well involve expenditure of over £100,000 if pursued to judgement – it must be borne in mind that this cuts both ways. The infringer is taking a considerable financial risk, and so long as neither party makes the expensive mistake of taking the matter personally (as inventors sometimes do, when they feel their 'baby' has been stolen), there is a strong incentive for both parties to make a sensible commercial arrangement to settle the dispute.

So, handled sensibly, IPR should be considered as an important type of commercial tool. But what can – and should – be protected, and how can it be done without breaking the bank?

Getting protection

Many people who come to our weekly IPR 'clinic' assume that they need a patent, but often without really knowing why. There is a general assumption that as soon as their idea is released to the world, it will be snapped up by voracious major companies, probably from the Far East. This is, unfortunately, based more on an optimistic idea of the value of their idea than on reality. In truth, it takes a lot of hard work to turn an idea into a money-earning product. Businesses might take an interest in a very successful product, but they are hardly likely to copy an unproven one.

So why should one seek protection? What protection is needed, and when? There are two main reasons why you might need protection. 1) If you want to approach a company to try to interest them in your idea, then without protection it is just an idea, and is free for anyone to use. Only if you have at least the potential to stop them copying, and perhaps more importantly the potential for them to stop their competition copying if they take up the idea, will they be likely to talk a deal with you. 2) If you are going to be selling the product yourself, having protection may enable you to deter competitors if the product is successful – if you are having the product made for you, the competitor could be your manufacturer.

What protection you need depends on what you have. You will need professional advice here – that means consulting a patent attorney, who will have the necessary knowledge of technology and the relevant law. It is very important to seek advice at the earliest possible stage, and in many cities free patent clinics are available to new enquirers. If your idea relates to the way something works, you may need to get a patent, however if it relates to the appearance, you may be advised to consider design registration. There are, however, rules covering what can and cannot be patented – you can only protect what is new, and not obvious to a skilled person. Don't assume that your idea is new just because you cannot buy one in your local DIY supermarket, for example. It may have been proposed in a published patent specification years ago, but never marketed because the market was not ready and, if it was, then it cannot now be patented.

It is a good idea to do some background searching before you start spending money on a patent application. There are experts who do nothing else but patent searching, and clearly the ideal would be to commission one such expert to investigate for you, but if you are prepared to spend some time yourself using the internet, you should be able to get some idea of what has gone before without having to spend.

The 'esp@cenet'[1] website gives access to millions of patent specifications, and permits you to search through them using a variety of criteria. You can, for example, search on key words (remembering that what you call your invention may not be the same as what others might call it, especially when translating from another language). Or you could use the very powerful patent classification key, although this requires some skill to get the best results. Such searching can never prove that your idea is new – if you find nothing, it may not mean that there is nothing there, simply that you haven't found it yet – but it can certainly show that it isn't new if you find something identical. In any event, it will give you a good feel for what others have tried to do to solve the same problem, say.

Remember that, so long as the particular combination of elements making up your invention is new, and that some form of argument can be put forward that it is not the obvious solution to the problem, say, then a patent application may well be useful, because at the least it creates uncertainty for your competitors. Uncertainty is not a good starting point for investment in new products by your competitors.

Timing can be critical. If you are going to seek a patent, it is vital to keep details of your idea confidential until you have applied for a patent (that does not mean, by the way, that you cannot tell your patent attorney about it – they are bound by strict professional rules guaranteeing confidentiality. I have been asked on a surprising number of occasions by over-eager inventors 'How do I know you won't just take my idea and make your fortune with it?'!) The problem is that, once you have filed a patent application at the Intellectual Property Office, a very inflexible clock starts ticking.

You only have 12 months from filing your basic application within which to file supplementary applications adding in details about developments to the invention that may have occurred since the first application was filed. During the same 12-month period you must take action to initiate any corresponding foreign patent applications. So once you have started the clock, you need to move forward as quickly as possible towards exploiting your invention, either by having a marketable product, or by securing a licence agreement with a company that can produce and sell the product.

In practice this means that you should have a clear map of how you will move forward with the idea from the concept stage through to marketing. How long will it take to develop from concept to working prototype, and from prototype to marketable product? Each of these stages might throw up problems that require significant changes, and in some cases further invention, and it is better if you can include the changes in the patent application – you won't be able to add them after the 12-month period has elapsed. So don't rush into filing your application too soon – the better prepared you are, the less likely you are to waste money in the long term.

What if it simply isn't patentable?

Other forms of protection may well be available, even if it is clear that you could not get a patent. While these might not stop the most determined copier, they will put obstacles in their way, which could at least slow their progress, giving time for your product to be established in the marketplace. A registered design might only cover the appearance of the product, but this might at least mean that the competitor will have to spend money on their own design instead of using yours, especially because defining the scope of protection afforded by a registered design is something that can keep patent lawyers profitably amused for many hours!

Finally, don't overlook the importance of branding. If your product is first on the market, you have the opportunity to develop a strong brand to associate with it. If that brand belongs to you (which means in practice being the proprietor of a registered trade mark), then even if the product cannot be protected in other ways, that association is a further obstacle to your competitor directly benefiting from your innovation.

To sum up, plan your innovation and its protection carefully. Seek early advice, but don't rush into a patent application because you fear that the world is just waiting for your invention. It took the likes of Dyson many years of hard work to become an overnight success that other companies wanted to copy!

About the author

Keith Loven is patent and trade mark attorney whose firm, LOVEN, based in Lincoln, has a spread of clients from SMEs and individuals to larger corporations in the UK and overseas. Keith has a degree in chemical engineering, but handles a wide range of technologies, as well as a growing trade mark practice. LOVEN aims to provide a personal service, understanding the client's business and seeking strategic business solutions for the client. Further details: Tel: 01522 801111; e-mail keith.loven@loven. co.uk. www.loven.co.uk.

Note

[1] http://gb.espacenet.com

Stimulating innovation through knowledge transfer

CARBON CO₂NNECTIONS

- Unique links with UK Higher Education sector

- Partnerships involving more than 60 commercial organisations

- Over 370 expressions of interest in first 12 months

- Over 100 full applications from 30% of UK universities

- 27 innovative carbon-saving projects funded

- 1 hard-working innovation network

For more information check
www.carbon-connections.org
or call 01603 591366

reducing carbon   developing technology   changing behaviour   **funding innovation**

Knowledge Transfer for a Low Carbon Economy

The UK's university sector has world leading experts, many of whom have the knowledge that could make them the next wave of successful entrepreneurs and allow them to tap into the world's biggest market opportunity in low carbon. So what are the universities doing to encourage enterprise in their academics?

"The knowledge driven economy"

In the 1998 white paper, "Building the Knowledge Driven Economy" the government set out its plans to reverse the trend of decline of the UK economy relative to the US economy and those of other European countries. At the heart of this white paper were measures aimed to promote the identification and development of new ideas and knowledge, the development of workplace skills and the acquisition of business skills by would-be entrepreneurs.

The 2001 white paper, "Excellence and Opportunity – a science and innovation policy for the 21st century", paved the way for streams of funding aimed at promoting links between universities, government research institutions, the National Health Service and the private (industry) sector. Following the ongoing support for successful schemes as a result of the 2001 paper, including the highly significant HEIF (Higher Education Innovation Fund) scheme, the spending review of 2004 (Science & innovation investment framework 2004-2014) spelt out the government's long-term commitment to providing funding and additional incentives to promote interactions between universities and industry. This review was a direct response to the government commissioned "Lambert Review of Business-university Collaboration", which provided an analysis of the requirements of industry and universities in forging improved links.

Commercial interactions between universities and industry typically involve one or more of the following:

- Licensing (or sale) of university intellectual property to industry
- Transfer of intellectual property and know-how through contract research and consultancy
- Formation of new ventures – start up and spinout companies and joint ventures

The activities described above, in combination with the transfer of skills, know-how and intellectual property to other non-commercial organisations are now commonly referred to under the heading of Knowledge Transfer.

Knowledge Transfer has been encouraged by government as part of long-term economic strategy and as a result universities have continued to receive funding to support these activities.

The recent Sainsbury Review of science and innovation policies records significant progress against the recommendations of the Lambert Review and confirms that capacity and infrastructure within universities for their Knowledge Transfer activities has continued to improve. However, this recent Review makes further recommendations including improving early-stage (venture-capital) funding and specifically pre-venture capital "proof-of-concept" funds.

In recent years much has been written on the relative importance of different aspects of Knowledge Transfer and the case has been made that licensing as opposed to company formation is the more natural and straightforward activity for UK universities. Furthermore, commentators have made the case that too much emphasis has been placed on the formation of spinout companies in the UK and that their relatively high failure rate is an inevitable consequence of their academic origin.

The Low-Carbon Economy

A UK government report of 2007 ("Moving to a global low carbon economy: implementing the Stern Review") highlighted the significance of behaviour change and technology development in tackling climate change. Specifically the report refers to the three key elements of the earlier Stern Report, which recommend action in the areas of carbon trading, technology development and behavioural change. Two of the elements were as follows:

"Encouraging innovation in low-carbon technologies – through policies that address separately the market failures associated with innovation and bring forward low-carbon technologies in a timely and cost-effective way."

"Removing barriers to action, as there are many other opportunities to reduce emissions that are unlikely to be taken up without policies to encourage long-term behaviour change, and to overcome other barriers that may prevent or deter individuals and businesses from taking cost-effective action to reduce their emissions, particularly on energy efficiency."

In the first recommendation, there is an obvious role for Knowledge (and specifically Technology) Transfer as described above but it is also the case that the research expertise, findings and in some cases intellectual property arising from universities can also be applied to the second recommendation.

Responding to the challenges of climate change and the Knowledge Transfer opportunities therein, in 2006 the Carbon Connections Programme was set up by a partnership of English universities led by the University of East Anglia, based in Norwich.

Carbon Connections was initially funded by the Higher Education Innovation Fund and the OSI. Its purpose was to apply university expertise, generated through academic research, to the problem of climate change. In broad terms, the funding is applied at the proof-of-concept end of the spectrum but it goes beyond the recommendations of the Sainsbury Review by removing the absolute emphasis on technology. This approach is in recognition of the significant role that behavioural change can have (at an individual and institutional level) to greenhouse gas emissions reduction.

The Carbon Connections Programme works by:

- Appropriate application of early stage funding
- Developing partnerships
- The application of alternative investment/funding models – such as funding for licensing ventures and royalty-based arrangements on new technologies
- Investment in behavioural change projects and applications of social science

Through its actions, the Programme aims to:

- Address the issue of market failures in innovation through proof-of-concept work
- Remove the emphasis on spinout companies as the only route to obtain investment in technology
- Improve speed to market of low-carbon technologies
- Stimulate behavioural change that generates revenues (or savings) in addition to carbon reduction
- Provide a better understanding of the carbon-saving potential and likelihood of uptake of new technologies

Case Study: Visible Energy

Interactive monitoring of energy usage

Project Summary: Examining the changes in energy behaviour patterns of households when provided with immediate visual and quantitative feedback.

Partnership:

- University of East Anglia, 5** rated School of Environmental Sciences
- SYS Consulting Ltd. (SYSCo), ICT experts specialising in data mining and pattern recognition
- Green Energy Options (GEO), who developed the Home Energy Hub system

Aims

To create a greater depth of understanding of behavioural analysis that will complement current energy monitoring and smart metering trials. An expected reduced carbon footprint for those households recruited. A feasibility report using the Home Energy Hub's data to recognise types of appliance in use.

Inspiration

Energy in buildings is invisible and very easy to ignore. Enabling people to see their energy usage is a primary tool in helping them become more energy efficient. Monitoring customer interaction with real-time energy will facilitate a long-term shift towards more sustainable energy use.

Innovation

Smart energy monitors provide consumers with easily accessible information on gross electricity consumption on a simple portable display. Green Energy Options (GEO) has developed the Home Energy Hub, whose key design concept is to engage people by making the product attractive, appealing, and eye-catching. The  information it portrays is striking, fascinating and captivating and will hold people's attention. The full system can monitor up to 100 sensors per household and includes a colour touch screen to be used in the main living area. The Home Energy Hub also measures oil or gas boiler usage and is web enabled so that information can be downloaded to GEO.

The project itself is innovative because for the first time it applies behavioural and change management to the implementation of technology in meeting policy objectives.

Development
210 homes will trial the hub, 140 of these with feedback display. The project will monitor whether providing people with more detailed information generates greater and more lasting changes. The project also addresses intelligent metering because an added feature of the equipment is a feedback/control element which has the ability to automatically switch appliances off based on 'normal' usage.

The expected outcomes are direct savings by changing energy use behaviours and reducing energy wastage. Potential carbon savings are between 5% and 20% from changing behaviours and a similar number for reducing wastage.

If the project achieves 5% penetration in 5 years (approximately 1 million homes) and assumes a 20% reduction per home at an average of 5 tonnes CO_2 emissions per home, this equates to 1m tonnes CO_2. The Home Energy Hub calculates the savings, which will be collected over the internet and used to estimate the total savings.

Summary
It is accepted wisdom that economic growth can be stimulated through the application of knowledge and the stimulation of innovation and enterprise. This is also entirely true for low-carbon economic growth with the additional driver of the need for timely development of new technologies and the stimulation of behavioural change.

It has been argued that the purpose of supporting Knowledge Transfer should not be simply for the possible financial gain to the institution involved; rather for broader economic growth. This is clearly evident for a low-carbon future where commercial drivers alone will not guarantee the uptake of new technologies. A clear role exists for innovators, private sector enterprises, large and small and government in appropriate use of policy and funding.

6

Technology projects

Innovation Nation –
A View from the Trenches

Innovation in the global economy

The UK has always excelled in coming up with bright ideas. It has been good at exploring them too; despite legendary cases where inventors went overseas for lack of interest at home. Half of the planet's most successful inventions have been accredited to inspired individuals or dedicated teams working in the UK.

The world is hungrier than ever for new ideas, but UK innovation is now badly in need of a boost. In today's highly competitive global economy, strong and dynamic businesses are built on innovation – the act of creating commercial advantage by finding new ways of doing things. The acquisition and use of knowledge is central to this new economy, therefore helping businesses to access and exploit knowledge must be a cornerstone of any innovation support activity.

There is concern that the productivity gap between Europe and the US is growing. This has led to renewed impetus at European, central, regional and local government levels where strategies and plans are being put in place for innovation to close the gap. The Lisbon Agenda of March 2000 agreed to make the EU "the most competitive and dynamic knowledge-driven economy by 2010". Although some progress has been made on innovating Europe's economy, there is growing concern that the ambitious targets set will not be reached.

Innovaro's 2005/06 Innovation Leaders assessment of the world's top 1,000 companies confirmed that leaders deliver significant and sustained growth through high impact innovation. New products, services and processes are all pushing the boundaries, exceeding customer expectations and capitalising on new knowledge and technology. They share common traits of:

- having a strong strategic focus
- possessing an excellent understanding of both their marketplace and customers
- clearly understanding their core capabilities and their partners and having a desire to work together to deliver innovative products
- utilising simple but effective processes to conceive, develop and launch new products and
- culture, roles and responsibilities which all support innovation.

These aspects are not seen as unique by leaders - rather they are seen as basic and essential to the way that the companies operate.

Innovation – a complex entity

Innovation is increasingly being recognised as a complex and multidimensional subject. It can best be understood by considering two dimensions – what will change and how novel is the change. Change can occur:

- to an organisation's product or service offering – product/service innovation
- in the way products and services are created and delivered – process innovation
- at the company level – organisational innovation.

The first two bullets can be termed 'technical' innovation, with organisational innovation being considered 'non technical'. But there are interdependencies and complementarities between the two that need to be recognised when innovation solutions are proposed. Innovation that encompasses two or more of the above at the same time is known as strategic or transformational innovation.

Degree of novelty is the extent to which change is experienced. At one end of the spectrum this could be incremental – the improved exploitation of existing products or services. At the other end radical innovation is seen as that which sweeps away much of a company's existing investment in skills, technology, product techniques or plant and equipment.

Successful innovation therefore requires a blend of **resources** (e.g. human, financial, equipment), **knowledge** (e.g. skills and expertise), and innovation management **capability** (e.g. strategy and foresight). The last is crucial for innovation performance since management capability gives added value by astute use of innovation assets.

These challenging dynamics further complicate the landscape of business innovation in the UK. In the past two decades there has been a fundamental shift in the size of British companies. Large corporations with centralised R&D facilities have been superseded by small and medium-sized enterprises much better suited for an age where reliable order books have been replaced by evolving opportunities that need swift, creative responses.

This cultural change in itself has created skills challenges for entrepreneurs. Many of today's SME owner managers have not had the benefit of exposure to the innovative culture of large corporates and the inherent training and skills needed to develop an innovative culture from scratch in a small company.

So, how do organisations start to innovate, given the importance of cultural aspects in the innovation process? One way is through assistance and intervention provided by an organisation specialising in the provision of innovation support activity to businesses, one that understands the management and delivery of innovation support programmes both locally and nationally.

A New Approach

The innovation attrition rate, especially for SMEs is high. They encounter a wide range of barriers when seeking to innovate, often comprising a combination of factors and circumstances. Observations based on empirical evidence gathered from work in this area confirm that barriers may be internal – culture, practices, ideas and custom and/or external – gaps in technical know-how, skills and capabilities. External barriers exposed to 'quick fix' initiatives respond well; internal barriers require more intensive interventions and support to overcome.

Work carried out on the subject of innovation support has shown that many SME companies can benefit from a support programme which:

- Initially provides training and skills development in the fundamentals of Innovation and Creativity management, taking a top-down approach and effecting a cultural change with the company
- Follows by the provision of an ongoing programme of mentoring by experienced innovation practitioners for top management and selected 'innovation champions' within the company.

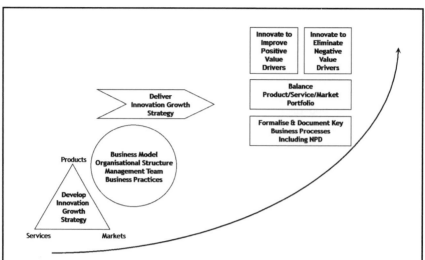

Figure 1. A holistic approach needs to be taken in an innovation growth strategy, encompassing technical and non-technical aspects. A formalised and successful strategy will balance innovation in differing areas of the business to deliver business benefit over time.

It is clear that the UK government recognises the need to accelerate the pace of change in UK businesses if we are to compete with US and European rivals.

The publication of Lord Sainsbury's review of government science and innovation policy "The Race to the Top" and the ensuing White Paper "Innovation Nation" have shown a renewed appetite for change and improvement, notably in the areas of public procurement, innovation funding and the provision of specialist assistance to small business. Whilst these policies and recommendations are well founded at the Macro level, the 'devil' will clearly be in the 'detail' of how national and particularly regional government implement these as actions.

So, far greater emphasis needs to be placed on training and subsequent mentoring of SME's in innovation management. Equally it is clear that government budgets will not stretch to the provision of such activity to all companies and it can only help those who would help themselves. It is down to the committed early adopter innovative SME's to make the most of recent changes in government innovation support policy.

Ged Barlow
Ged Barlow is Managing Director of C-Tech Innovation (**www.ctechinnovation.com**), an independent research and technology development company with more than 40 years experience in providing research and development services to companies, universities and government bodies. Their activities range from research to commercialisation of innovative new products and multi-disciplinary consultancy. Based near Chester in North West England, the company's world-wide customer base ranges from small start-up companies to large multi-nationals.

IP commercialization

Manage intellectual property as a commercial asset, says Billy Harkin, Chief Executive of QucomHaps, a specialist communications infrastructure business.

Most CEOs in *most* companies just do not have a clue when it comes to IPR. This is not a statement made flippantly. It is a proposal that CEOs of companies that hold any IPR portfolio should fundamentally review their company's current approach to the management/neglect of such assets; and plan for how they can be commercially managed to best bottom-line effect. Perhaps seeing the word 'intellectual' before the word 'property' is just too intimidating or off-putting for some. Too academic perhaps. But for whatever reason IPR asset management is given a very low priority, if any.

Imagine the scene if you will. A new CEO of an SME or a plc has reviewed the books and the asset register of the business now under their leadership. They then go for a fact-finding 'walkabout' in the company. Happening upon the Legal and Admin department they meet the head of this department who duly confirms that the various assets identified within the company books do indeed represent an accurate current status picture. The four asset classes listed are property (land and buildings), cash, equipment and (beneficial) trading contracts. The company has no bonds or gilts.

'All of our classes of assets are being strategically managed, as well as being well-managed within our daily activities under the declared Operational Plan, boss,' says the department head. 'Well done, carry on the good work,' says the new boss.

'Oh, one thing boss, we also own a number of patents, trade marks and design rights and I'd very much appreciate an increase in budget if possible, just to let me keep up with the various ongoing filings and renewals, etc.' The boss replies, 'No promises at this stage, but I'll definitely have the finance department see if there's anything they can accommodate for you,' as he heads for the door to continue the 'walkabout'.

IP is an 'asset class'

The above scenario is so common as to be the norm, all over the world and in almost every industry. Very few companies truly understand and treat their IP as being an *asset class*. Nor do they manage it strategically and then practically, day-by-day.

A wake-up call then for those CEOs and company boards that are still asleep in this key business area: intellectual property *is* an asset class! It can and should be viewed in much the same way as that other property asset class, the land and buildings one. The intellectual property portfolio can similarly be bought, sold, rented, or used for many business purposes.

This 'asset class' needs to be managed

Scenario continued: On reflection the boss stops at the door and asks, 'By the way, who's in charge of managing this particular asset class, the IPR assets, you know, setting the vision, the strategies to play out that vision, and then driving a practical execution plan towards realizing maximum value?'

'Well, er, no one is actually, boss. There's no vision or plan or anything like that. I just make sure that all the filings and the renewals get done. I've got a budget for that. And whenever anyone sends us any litigation notices, challenging any of our patents for example, then I just get one of the lawyers to look at those challenges, on a case-by-case basis.'

The boss raises both the stakes and the blood pressure. 'Really? Ok, so we do at least have an itemized list of all these various IPR assets. And our name does at least appear as the owners on the Property Register, or whatever they call it, at the Patent Office. And hopefully we do at least know how much money we've spent to date, and we spend ongoing presumably, having acquired ownership of these assets and then maintaining them.'

The department head nods positively. 'Excellent!' continues the boss. 'The only problem is that we have no clear coherent plan for what the hell to do with these assets, so we mostly just concentrate on owning them and occasionally defending some of them from attack, which is a bit like someone buying, say, a hotel asset and then constantly checking that they still own it, hiring very expensive security guards to defend it occasionally, but otherwise not bothering to try and get any paying customers to come to it! This is nuts!'

Who's responsible for managing the IPR asset class?

Our irate CEO continues: 'Who's responsible for this insane dereliction of duty? Our IPR portfolio represents key company assets. Maybe *the* key company assets! Who's responsible? I want to know, because I aim to fire them.'

'I'm afraid no one is, boss. No one is in charge and so there's no one to have their assets kicked! I'm afraid it's over to you, as the new CEO you're responsible, boss! As is the entire board of our company, to my mind. I've been telling them that for years, but no one's ever been interested in listening before. Too busy, I was always told.'

Adding salt to the wound the department head continues: 'And boss, it's not called the Patent Office any more either, because it covers an awful lot more than just patents. It's called the Intellectual Property Office these days!' The bruised CEO continues the walkabout, struck with the realization that someone will have to be put in charge of commercially managing these assets, and quick!

Acquiring units of the IPR asset class

IPR assets can be created in-house, purchased, or licensed-in from owners. The amount of assets that end up under ownership or control must not be some ad-hoc outcome. It usually is! The activities must be strategically planned and then organized to achieve the declared targets.

Registering ownership of units of the IPR asset class

Perhaps the legal fraternity has cornered the market on this one thus far – positioning pretty much everything to do with IPR as being a legal matter, concentrating on registration, renewals and defence. Understandable enough really, in the absence of any competition that would have more correctly positioned IPR as being a commercial matter. IPR are *not* a legal matter. They are first and foremost a commercial matter, pure and simple, and they must be managed as such.

Defending the ownership of the IPR asset class

Individual units of IPR, or even entire portfolios of IPR, can come under legal and PR attack.

Legal attacks, defence strategies and activities in such cases are often well publicized, but only in superficial overview. This legal activity of defending IPR is an expert area and is therefore best lead-advised by suitable legal experts.

PR attacks on IPR assets are becoming more common, and are typically lower cost to launch than are legal attacks. These attacking strategies aim not so much to have an IPR ownership dismissed or overturned, but more towards attempting to negatively position in the minds of people a particular company's product or service offerings, or a company's total value. PR attacks can in most but not all cases be counteracted by an effective PR response.

Trading the IPR asset class

'IPR commercialization' is, as the name might suggest, a commercial activity. IP assets that are owned or controlled can be 'commercialized' (that is *traded*) in a variety of ways. In general the amount of money that can be realized is directly related to how much value is first added to the assets, before they are traded.

From the bottom up the typical option routes are: the assets can be licensed under various terms of rights. They can be sold outright, as just 'paper' assets. Or they can be packaged along with prototypes and demonstrators, of lesser or greater sophistication – and then licensed or sold, at a higher value. Or one can elect to establish an entirely new company into which the assets can be licensed or sold – and which can then develop and grow itself as a business that offers products and/or services, before ultimately failing, achieving a trade sale, or an IPO at value, or simply carry on trading profitably – depending on how badly or well the new business is resourced and managed.

Increasingly, various philosophies are emerging on how to appoint 'valuations to IP assets'. I am a simple soul in that regard, believing that they are worth simply whatever anyone is willing to pay for them at any given time! Meantime, grand accounting schemes on the subject abound, as do attempts to apportion value of various IPR assets long before any hard value can really be measured. To my mind only when the usual 'trading outputs' of commercialized IPR assets can be measured can any meaningful valuation be achieved, ie measuring in hard monetary terms royalty streams, IP asset sales, profits arising from associated products and services being directly sold, and any capital gains gained, from new commercial entities that were given IPR.

Adding as much value to IP assets as one can afford to, before trading them – in whatever form one elects to trade them – follows exactly the same commercial rationale as applies when one is adding value to any other class of assets, before selling them on at the maximum achievable profit – in cases where profit maximization is a declared primary strategic objective.

Economic effect of the IPR asset class

At a microeconomic level, effective strategic planning and commercial management of IPR portfolios can dramatically improve the bottom-line performance of companies. When a land and buildings asset manager is commonly put in charge of, and held accountable for, maximizing the returns from that particular class of property assets, then isn't it high time that CEOs applied the same business sense to their IPR assets?

At a macroeconomic level, effective strategic planning, public policies and support for the creation, development and commercialization of IPR assets can be socially and economically transformative – offering a major competitive edge to the countries and regions that get it right.

About the author

Billy Harkin is the CEO and founder of QucomHaps Limited – a specialist communications infrastructure business that has developed and integrated IPR assets to enable delivery of radio coverage services. QucomHaps today has 200 full-time staff and has subsidiaries in Malaysia, Indonesia and the Czech Republic, where the group wholly owns an aircraft factory and a public international airport.

Billy has been creating IPR and managing IPR portfolios for himself and for others, in both the public and the private sectors in various countries, for over 25 years. For four of those years, he was Head of Technology Transfer at Glasgow University, where he recruited, trained and led a team that commercialized the IPR assets of the university. Successes included Kymata Ltd, the fastest growth university spin-out company in terms of market value and number of employees hired. Within two years Kymata grew to a value of $1 billion and employed 540 staff. With a change in the technology market, it was successfully sold to Alcatel. Ten other spin-out launches and a selection of licence deals followed.

Billy is a regular guest speaker at IPR commercialization conferences around the world and has presented in the United States, South Africa, France, Ireland, Japan and throughout the UK. Contact: Billy Harkin via his PA at admin@qucomhaps.com.

Innovation into business

There are eight different ways to fund the commercialization of innovation, say Dr Jelena Angelis and Don McLaverty at Oxford Innovation.

The development of innovative products and services, and the development of new businesses based upon innovative products and services, usually requires a significant amount of money. It is therefore essential to establish how these developments are to be funded before starting a project or a new business. There are many different sources of funding and choosing the right one can be crucial for long-term success.

The right choice is often a balance between several factors such as the ability of the innovator (whether an individual or company) to accept financial risk, the control it has of the product, the level of control the company is willing to accept, and the speed required to get the product into the market. The *right* choice is therefore often very dependent on the *specific* needs of the innovator.

Eight different funding options have been identified that can be relevant for the commercialization of innovative products, services, processes and businesses. Table 6.2.1 shows a generalized 'funding roadmap' for selecting the right funding option(s).

The major sources of funding are:

1. *Internal funding* – this can include the reinvestment of funds generated from company profits and the injection of private savings from company owners, inventors, their relatives and friends.
2. *Client funded development* – typically involves selling an idea for development to an established company that obtains priority exploitation rights in exchange for providing development funds and practical support.

What exactly is the Intellectual Assets Centre?

The IA Centre exists: "to assist Scottish businesses to maximise the economic potential of their intellectual assets".

Funded by the Scottish Government, the Centre is the first of its kind in Europe and is a trailblazer in the field of intangible asset management.

The underlying aim of the IA Centre is to develop the market by encouraging the eventual emergence of a strong private sector demand and supply for IA services.

So why are IA seen as so important to Scottish businesses?

IA and IP have critical roles as the drivers of innovation, business strategy and corporate value in the knowledge economy. Although intangible, they are frequently extremely valuable and can include: brands, goodwill, know-how, trade-secrets, technical information and contracts, as well as IP. In modern economies, they create more competitive advantage than land, labour, or even capital.

IA need to be nurtured and managed as they are business qualities that have the potential for wealth generation and can help businesses survive and grow. The identification, protection and effective exploitation of IA informs business strategy, opens business opportunities, and can suggest and control alternative income streams.

Whilst often associated with technological innovation and high technology businesses, the reality is that IA affect all sectors, sizes and types of organisation. Improved products, new products and services of all types, new markets, new production techniques, improved supply and distribution channels all involve the ownership, control and management of IA.

In brief, IA:
- are frequently extremely valuable – they are often worth more than tangible assets;
- are intangible – and hence can be lie unrecognised;
- are recordable and communicable – once recognised;
- are protectable or safeguardable – by Statute law or other laws such as the law of contract;
- define, control and add corporate value – they are real commercial strengths; and
- support business growth – they inform business strategy and create opportunities.

Furthermore, ignorance of their own IA or that of others can leave organisations exposed to litigation and conflict and mean that they miss competitor and technological intelligence.

What then are the business benefits of effective IA management?

Good IA management can open up a number of different opportunities and significantly enhance the prospects of an organisation, irrespective of its size, maturity, constitution or sector. As such, the benefits of effective IA management to an existing or start-up company are manifold.

Among other benefits it has been demonstrated that effective IA management can:-
- maintain and control competitive advantage;
- inform strategic planning;
- maintain and create corporate value;
- suggest alternative business models;
- identify and control additional income streams;
- present new product development opportunities;
- lead to new sectoral or geographic markets;
- assist in raising finance;
- help resist and deter competition;
- provide competitor and technological intelligence;
- avoid litigation and conflict;
- assist in the generation and control of business relationships and strategic alliances; and
- act as a deterrent to hostile predators or assist in resisting take-overs.

For early stage companies, the IA may be the only readily identified source of the future income; the ownership, control and management of the IA and the clear communication of such can significantly increase investor confidence, particularly when private or public sector organisations are providing seed corn finance. IA therefore help to underpin early phases of commercialisation.

Larger organisations are more likely to address these issues than are SMEs (with perhaps the possible exception of some young hi-tech companies). However, even in these companies, the full potential of the IA is frequently not recognised, resulting in under-valuation and ensuing difficulties in raising investment.

So what can the IA Centre do to help?

The IA Centre acts as a catalytic and evangelising body that has set out to develop a high profile as a 'Centre of Excellence' in intellectual assets (IA) issues relating to business and economic development. Its aim is to be seen as a resource that complements and adds value to the current and future activities of both public and private sector intermediaries; it seeks to be the 'place to go' for impartial advice on IA management.

The IA Centre:

o Raises Awareness & Understanding of IA, their value, identification, protection, management and exploitation for business benefit

o Demonstrates how IA impact upon the development of strategy, products processes, services, markets and supply and distribution channels

The IA Centre delivers through:

o IA focused events, training sessions, seminars, tailored one-to-one advice, and information provision

o Tools which answer the questions about IA, why they are important to all organisations; how to identify, assess and to record IA; how to manage IA; and ultimately how to extract additional value from IA

The aims of the IA Centre are to:

o Guide, Direct and Signpost Scottish organisations to suppliers of IA management products and services

o Encourage the development of a strong private-sector-led supply of IA management products and services

o Develop Scotland's international profile as a leading exponent of IA management and exploitation

The Centre works with companies and organisations across Scotland regardless of size, sector or status and offers a free advice, guidance and one-to-one service tailored to the companies' individual needs. In addition there is an ongoing programme of sector-specific initiatives which aim to deliver a bespoke service to identified sectors ranging from software to education and from digital media to renewable energy.

Running in parallel with this client focussed activity, the IA Centre runs a series of masterclasses for those working in the 'supply side' of IA Management. These masterclasses bring the very best of European and international thinking to Scotland in order to help those working in the field to develop their skills, knowledge and expertise. Those working in the legal, accountancy, consultancy fields, along with academics and tertiary educationalists are amongst those who participate in these events and use this international perspective to develop their own working practices.

Further details about the Intellectual Assets Centre can be found at our web site **www.ia-centre.org.uk** – if you would like to find out how we can help *your* business – either as a client or as a supplier – simply log on … and get in touch.

Table 6.2.1 Suitability of funding in difference situations – Roadmap

Funding Option	Size of Business			Risk/Reward Profile			Comments
	Micro (<10)	Small (11 - 50)	Medium (51 – 250)	Low Risk/Reward	Medium Risk/Reward	High Risk/Reward	
Internal Funding	○	●	◐	◐	○	○	Good source for established companies that are in profit
Client-Funded Development	○	◐	●	●	◐	○	Only suitable when aims of business and client coincide
Grants & Credits	○	○	○	○	○	○	
The Carbon Trust	○	○	○	○	○	○	Some funding for low carbon technologies
Collaborative R&D Award	○	○	○	●	○	◐	Bi-annual competitions in priority areas
EU Framework Programme	●	○	◐	●	○	○	For collaborative R&D with European partners
Grant for R&D	◐	◐	○	●	◐	◐	Highest awards for smaller firms and 'research' projects
KTP	○	◐	◐	○	◐	◐	Excellent route to transfer knowledge from a university
Shell STEP	◐	◐	◐	◐	◐	○	Supports summer projects for undergraduates
Tax Credits	○	◐	◐	◐	◐	◐	SME Scheme can provide funding even with losses.
Bank Loans	○	◐	◐	◐	○	●	DTI's SFLGS supports small firms that lack security
Business Angels	◐	○	●	○	◐	◐	Business angel networks provide access to investors
Venture Capital	○	◐	◐	◐	◐	○	Some funds have regional or technology focus
Corporate Venturing	◐	○	○	●	◐	◐	Bioscience and ICT sector companies are most active
Public Offering	●	○	◐	◐	◐	○	Long term goal for most new high growth businesses

Suitability Rating   ● Unlikely   ○ Possible   ◐ Good

3. *Grants and credits* – for innovative technology-based ideas, it is possible to attract grants and/or tax credits towards the costs of R&D. Sometimes it is necessary to collaborate with other organizations.
4. *Bank loans* – bank loans and overdrafts are traditional sources of business funding. Unfortunately, the cost can be high, and banks usually require loans to be secured against saleable assets.
5. *Business angels* – business angels are normally wealthy individuals who are prepared to invest equity in businesses with good growth prospects. Tax relief is available to investors.
6. *Venture capital* – there are numerous funds that make equity investments in companies with good growth potential. However, many don't consider small investments due to the cost of 'due diligence'.
7. *Corporate venturing* – typically involves large companies that have the finance to make investments in growing businesses. Often they focus on businesses that are symbiotic with mainstream activities.
8. *Public offering* – involves raising equity finance on a stock market and allowing the public trading of shares. It is important for companies that are unable to support expansion from business cash flow.

From the perspective of the typical individual innovator or start-up entrepreneur, business angel finance, combined with one or more of the other options, is often the most appropriate solution for their needs. Oxford Innovation operates three business angel networks that introduce our members to innovators and entrepreneurs seeking to commercialize novel technology or science. The British Business Angels Association website lists other business angel networks; see http://www.bbaa.org.uk.

Entrepreneurs who are seeking to commercialize their technology often have similar questions to ask when they are preparing for fundraising: What is the business angel network fundraising process? What do prospective investors ask entrepreneurs? What questions should the innovator ask the funder or business angel? Tables 6.2.2 and 6.2.3 and checklists in this chapter seek to address these common questions.

Commercializing technology into a business requires funding. It is good practice for innovators or entrepreneurs seeking funding to:

■ Start seeking your funding as soon as possible, because fundraising always takes longer that you think.
■ Prepare well in advance for due diligence (auditing) of your proposition by the investor – technical references, financial information, business plan and patents. This will both add to the credibility of your proposal and speed up the fundraising process.
■ If you are seeking to raise funds by selling equity or a share in your new business, be prepared to negotiate on share price, investment terms, warranties – you will strike a better deal if you have thought through what is really important to you.
■ If possible secure customer testimonials, customer interest in purchasing the products resulting from your technology and, if available, actual sales. Customer

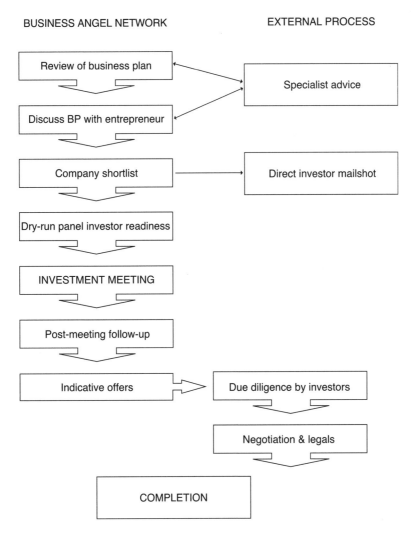

BUSINESS ANGEL NETWORK   EXTERNAL PROCESS

Figure 6.2.1 What is the Business Angel Network fundraising process?

validation significantly strengthens the innovator's prospects of securing funding for their proposition and hence building a successful business.

About the authors

Dr Jelena Angelis is a consultant with Oxford Innovation Ltd focusing on the topics of innovation, technology transfer and support to SMEs, especially in the area of R&D partnerships and alliances between small businesses and large corporations.

Don McLaverty has substantial experience in all aspects of business growth in corporations such as BOC, Intel and Granada Group as well as several early

Table 6.2.2. What are the typical questions that entrepreneurs are asked by prospective investors?

1.	What type of business experience does the management team have?
2.	Can the team accomplish the job outlined in the business plan?
3.	How does your company and product fit into the industry?
4.	What are the current market trends?
5.	What are the key success factors in your industry?
6.	How did you determine total industry sales and its growth rate?
7.	Why does this business have high growth potential?
8.	Why will this business succeed?
9.	What is the expected lifecycle of the product?
10.	How do advances in technology affect your product and business?
11.	What is the product liability?
12.	What makes this business and product unique?
13.	Does the product meet a specific (or perceived) customer need?
14.	Is the purchaser the end user of the product?
15.	How do you compete on price, performance, service and warranties?
16.	If you plan to take market share, how will you do it?
17.	What are the critical elements of your marketing plan?
18.	Is this primarily a retail or industrial marketing strategy?
19.	How large is the customer base?
20.	What is the usual lag between initial contact and the actual sale?
21.	What is the capacity of your facility?
22.	Who are your suppliers and how long have they been in business?
23.	How many employees do you have?
24.	What are your capital requirements over the next five years?
25.	Do you lease or own the property/facilities?
26.	Will the expansion require relocation?
27.	Who owns the patent?
28.	What licensing arrangements have been made with the patent holder?
29.	Does anyone else have licensing arrangement?

Table 6.2.3. What questions should the innovator ask the funder or business angel?

1.	What business angel investing experience do they have?
2.	What experience do they have in the market concerned?
3.	Why do they want to invest in the opportunity?
4.	How much capital is available?
5.	Does the business angel co-invest with others?
6.	How long is the business angel prepared to wait until exit?
7.	How extensive is the business angel's due diligence process?

stage technology businesses. He is currently part of the Innovation Advisory Service South East, a leading exponent and facilitator of Open Innovation and has overall responsibility for Oxford Innovation's business angel investment networks: Oxford Investment Opportunity Network (OION), Thames Valley Investment Network (TVIN) and Oxford Early Investments (OEI).

Oxford Innovation provides services to entrepreneurs, growing innovative companies, and to government bodies that promote enterprise. The company operates 13 innovation centres that provide flexible office and laboratory space to over 350 technology, knowledge-based and creative companies. It also manages three highly successful investment networks that link investors with entrepreneurs seeking funding from £20,000 to £2 million: OION (Oxford Investment Opportunity Network http:// www.oion.co.uk), TVIN (Thames Valley Investment Network http://www.tvin.co.uk) and OEI (Oxford Early Investments http://www.oxei.co.uk). During the last five years, the investment networks have helped over 90 companies raise £19.5 million. For further information: www.oxin.co.uk or e-mail enquiries@oxin.co.uk.

Research projects with universities

Input from a university can take a company to the next level, but you have to get the relationship right first, says Ian Wilkinson, Head of Invest Northern Ireland's Technical Advisory Unit.

Companies use a variety of means to differentiate their products from the competition. These range from clever marketing ploys to added functionality. An increasingly popular approach is to employ the services of an expert, often from a university or college, to assist in integrating new or state-of-the-art technologies within the product.

Myths, and indeed many anecdotes, abound as to how beneficial or disastrous this approach can be. Often success is down to the company doing its homework properly, so that it is fully aware of the university's skills, and what it can offer. As with any service provider there can be difficulties, but by following some basic guidelines, companies can benefit from the great opportunities presented by being able to tap into the knowledge contained within university departments and associated centres of expertise.

Project issues

Having worked with a large number of small companies over the last 17 years, many of whom used academia to assist with product development, I've concluded that a certain amount of planning is necessary to ensure maximum benefit is achieved from any such collaboration. The following is not an exhaustive checklist, but rather issues that should be considered before signing contracts or agreeing to terms of reference (ToR):

- *Selecting the right people*. Use your own knowledge, get references and look at the person's previous work – was it commercialized?
- *IP ownership*. The first thing to be discussed should be intellectual property (IP) and who will own any that is developed. The university may own IP associated with the project, which may need to be licensed or be subject to some form of agreement. A Non-Disclosure Agreement (NDA) should be used to protect any IP that the company may own.
- *Terms of reference*. Try to develop the ToR as much as possible before meeting the university staff. Consider carefully what you want them to do and what you don't want them to do! Their input should be focused less on 'what' and more on 'how'. Be very aware that universities are highly motivated by research projects and may wish to scale up the project. Resist this, unless it fits with your plans, timescale and budget.
- *Timescales*. Ensure that timescales are well defined as some university or college departments may operate to academic term times.
- *Expectations*. Make sure your expectations and theirs are aligned as closely as possible.
- *Progress meetings*. Regular meetings, or a feedback mechanism, should be established to ensure the project's progress can be monitored and that appropriate action can be taken if it goes off track.
- *Financial support*. There are various R&D support mechanisms available to companies in Northern Ireland, including some national programmes such as Smart and KTP (Knowledge Transfer Partnership). A recent addition is the Innovation Voucher initiative, which offers funding at up to 100 per cent to small enterprises using publically funded knowledge providers to assist them with R&D and innovation type projects (see text box for more details).
- *Focus on deliverables*. Your company needs to remain focused on what it wants out of the project. Payment should be clearly linked to the deliverables expected.
- *Communication*. During the whole project it's crucial that there are effective lines of communication between both parties.

Risks

There are risks associated with any type of research and development project, whether using in-house expertise or employing outside experts. University involvement carries its own particular set of risks, but as with everything, forewarned is forearmed. Here are some of the issues to be aware of:

- *Further from the market than planned*. This can happen if the project is not effectively managed. I have seen examples where the university, having been excited by some of the research findings, began to explore more complex technologies resulting in a delay and loss of rapport between the two sides.

■ *Non-commercial focus of academia.* Universities are highly motivated by research work. Where this is well controlled, it can be of great benefit to private enterprise. Where it is not, the focus of the project can quickly shift to research papers, collaborative research and total loss of commercial focus.

■ *Other priorities.* The main role of universities is to educate students. A secondary role is to be recognized for important research and attain any IP associated with the projects. It's important to ensure that the university will give sufficient priority to the R&D project and that ownership of any IP developed is assigned to the company.

■ *Costs can be higher.* This relates to both the consultancy costs for university staff and the resulting product costs. Consultancy daily rates vary greatly. Universities inexperienced in working with industry may apply totally unrealistic rates or quote too many project days. So it's important to be aware of what typical costs are. (With some very specialist research it may be difficult to get such comparisons.) On the product cost side, it's important that 'design for manufacture' is addressed. In some cases the research body will not have this experience, so you need to keep product costs competitive.

■ *Turnaround times.* It's crucial to agree timescales and to specify the deliverables in a Gantt chart or similar project plan. Some university departments have a reduced staff level over four summer months, so it's important to check that your project won't be adversely affected by this.

Benefits

Despite the potential risks, things must be kept in perspective. The benefits from employing the right people from the right research department can be enormous and can take your company's product to the next level, differentiating it from the competition. Integrating appropriate state-of-the-art technology into a product can have as positive an effect on its marketability as developing a new product from an R&D project.

TruCorp

TruCorp is an emerging company with the specific mission to research and develop systems for medical skills training and competency assessment. The company is a spin-out from the Department of Anaesthetics at Queen's University, Belfast. TruCorp has developed a range of products, but a common feature of them all is the AirSim airway. It is a faithful reproduction of the human airway anatomy and as such is invaluable as a training aid to help health professionals develop airway management skills.

The construction and material used in the product produces a human-like tactile feedback during use and the airway behaves like a human airway when being manipulated. These features combine to give the user positive feedback during and after correct placement of an airway device.

The initial design project to develop this human replica airway and all subsequent tooling to manufacture it were managed and created by the Northern Ireland Technology Centre (NITC) at Queen's University, Belfast. This collaborative link with the NITC's expertise in design and materials led to the successful launch of TruCorp's globally distributed product range.

TruCorp continues to work closely with NITC, which provides a powerful technical resource for TruCorp's research and design.

Innovation Vouchers

Northern Ireland's Small Enterprise sector has an extremely valuable role to play in the development of our knowledge-based economy. Small companies can adapt quickly to market changes so they are often in an ideal position to exploit new ideas.

The objective of the Innovation Voucher is to build links between public sector knowledge providers and small businesses on the island of Ireland. This will create a cultural shift in the small business community's approach to innovation.

How does it work?

Small Northern Ireland-based companies, wishing to solve a business problem or avail of an opportunity, can apply for an Innovation Voucher worth up to approximately £4,000. The voucher can be exchanged for advice and expertise from accredited knowledge providers. The project must require an innovative solution, provide additional value for the company and have ongoing benefits.

What can small companies gain?

The company can concentrate on running the business while knowledge providers devise a solution that could take the business to the next level. The voucher also opens the door to knowledge providers, building links between the company and researchers that could yield further benefits in the future.

Who can apply?

All registered small Northern Ireland companies are eligible to apply for an Innovation Voucher, except for those in the transport and agricultural sectors, in line with State Aid guidelines.

Who are the knowledge providers?

Companies can approach any university, college, institute of technology or publicly funded research organization on the island of Ireland, provided they have agreed to participate in the Innovation Voucher initiative.

Can companies pool their vouchers?

Yes. A company is free to join with other small businesses also in receipt of an Innovation Voucher to work with a knowledge provider in solving an issue of common concern, up to a maximum of 10 companies. To find out more about the Innovation Voucher scheme visit: www.investni.com, e-mail: tau@investni.com or tel: Kieran McGuinness on 028 9069 8818.

About the author

Ian Wilkinson, a chartered mechanical engineer, is the Head of Invest Northern Ireland's Technical Advisory Unit. The unit, comprising scientists, engineers and intellectual property specialists, offers advice to Northern Ireland manufacturers on a range of technology and product/process development issues including professional, low-cost routes to compliance with legislation, eg CE marking. Ian has a breadth of product development experience gained over 25 years working in both industry – defence and aerospace – and more recently in regional development agencies.

The risks in technology IP

If your invention amounts to a radical breakthrough in technology, there are some specific issues to consider, says Sue Scott at Abel & Imray.

Introduction

Managing a company is all about managing risk, and satisfactory management of the intellectual property (IP) in a company requires a full understanding of the risks inherent in the particular project. Where an invention is made that amounts to a radical breakthrough in technology, it is particularly important to ensure that the IP risks are fully understood, and that your IP strategy reflects these risks. This chapter deals with some aspects of patent strategy and patent risk management in the form of a 10-point plan for dealing with patentable breakthrough inventions.

The 10-point plan

1. First, select your winner

It is always difficult to spot which inventions are going to be commercially successful, and this is particularly true when the invention is a radical breakthrough. A good example is the hovercraft. Invented by Christopher Cockrell in the 1950s, the first working embodiment of this invention was a Nescafé coffee tin and a hairdryer. The commercial people who decided to back this device bouncing along their corridor were far-sighted; the dividing line between the visionary image of the future and a mad inventor's crackpot idea is very thin. Tom Watson, the CEO of IBM in 1943, came down on the wrong side of that line when he said: 'I think there is a world market for about five computers.'

There are no magic ways of avoiding being the next Tom Watson, but do remember that patents have a 20-year horizon, so even if you think the market is not yet ready for your amazing breakthrough, it might be worth filing a patent application as an insurance.

2. Decide whether to patent

If you have a breakthrough invention, your very first decision is whether to patent (in which case details of your invention will be published), or to try to maintain secrecy. Obviously secrecy is often not an option, as the nature of the invention will become apparent as soon as the invention is put on the market. You cannot keep a dual cyclone vacuum cleaner (James Dyson's famous invention) secret once you have sold it. However, some inventions can be kept secret. Famously, the recipe for Coca-Cola, first invented in the 1880s, remains a secret today. The main advantage of patenting is obvious: patents potentially enable you to keep competitors out of the market, or to limit their presence in a controlled fashion. There are really only two downsides of patenting. The first is cost (and as anyone reading this book will doubtless already know, patents are very costly), while the second (which, in fact, is often an upside) is that patenting inevitably leads to publication of the details of your invention.

There are two advantages of keeping an invention secret: one is that this is very cheap – it costs you no money; and the second is that in some cases you may be able to keep your competitors in the dark for ever. There are, however, two big risks: once secrecy is lost, it is lost for ever; and, crucially, a competitor might make the same invention independently, and may obtain a patent. If this does happen you may, depending on the circumstances, have some rights to carry on doing what you were previously doing in secret. However, such rights are of very doubtful scope and value, and are likely to be completely inadequate for your needs.

So, keeping an invention secret can be very risky and can have massive implications for your own freedom to use your own invention, a topic that is dealt with below.

3. Make sure you know who the true inventor of your invention was, and ensure that the ownership rights properly belong to you

If there is any doubt about the ownership, sort it out *now*. *Never* say, 'It will be OK, we can sort it out later.' You can be absolutely sure that once an important invention is making money, any lack of certainty regarding ownership of the intellectual property rights will come back to haunt you. Fudging inventorship or ownership is one of the biggest risks you can take.

4. Make sure that your patents are high quality

There are occasions when the actual quality of a patent is not very important. In the electronics industries, companies typically file large numbers of patents. Electronic devices typically contain many hundreds of different parts, and it is unusual for any single patent to be of overriding importance. Companies cross-license large numbers of patents without too much consideration of the relative values of each. The quality of an individual patent may not matter greatly.

However, the quality of your patents covering a breakthrough invention is going to be absolutely crucial. Potential competitors are bound to investigate your patents, and will go to great lengths to try to avoid them or knock them out. The better the quality of your patents, the more likely you are to be able to maintain your control of the technology. The patent covering a breakthrough invention is not the one where you wish to compromise on quality just to save a little on the cost. You need to put effort and money into making sure that your patent is as well drafted and as well supported by technical information, including where appropriate experimental data, as possible.

5. Take good patent filing decisions

You will need to decide in which countries you want patent protection. Remember that patents are all about *keeping others out* of the market. Therefore, you need to consider where your competitors or potential licensees might wish to operate. Other things to consider include how easy it is to enforce patents in a particular country, and how easy it is to get patents covering particular subject matter in a particular country. For example, many countries (including those in Europe) do not allow certain kinds of computer software-related inventions or medical methods to be patented.

Finally, cost is going to be a major issue. It is important to keep your commercial objectives in mind, to remember that patents have a 20-year horizon, and to make sure that your cost projections are realistic.

6. In due course, investigate your freedom to operate...

If you are proposing to put your own invention on the market, you will need to consider whether you are likely to infringe any patents owned by third parties. Failure to address this issue could lead to complete failure of your project or even your company. Kodak was taken completely out of the market in instant cameras during the 1980s when it infringed patents owned by Polaroid, and was ordered by a US court to pay damages of almost US$500 million.

It is impossible to stress too strongly that possession of your own patent does *not* give you the right to use your own invention commercially. It only gives you the right to *stop other people* using your invention. Even if you have a patent, you could infringe a patent owned by a third party. Failure to understand this can lead to huge problems.

7. ...in conjunction with deciding on licensing vs in-house exploitation

Broadly, companies have the choice of either selling a new product themselves, or licensing the product to another company better able to access the relevant market (or a combination of both).

There are pros and cons to both approaches. Investing in your own company can involve a very high level of risk, with a big investment of funds being necessary and with a relatively high risk of failure, but can also (sometimes) deliver a correspondingly high level of reward. Licensing tends to involve a lower level of risk, but is unlikely to deliver the highest levels of reward.

If you wish to license, the possession of strong patents becomes not just desirable, but essential. After all, if a manufacturing company loses a patent, it loses its exclusivity, and may therefore lose market share and see price erosion. However, it can still continue to sell its product. If a licensor loses a patent, it almost always loses all its revenues. There may be some value in secret know-how, but almost always where a breakthrough invention is involved, if there is no patent, there will be no licence. Make sure that you factor your patent strategy into your commercial strategy to reduce risk.

8. When further inventions come along, consider building a patent portfolio...

An important element of risk management in the patent context is the building of a portfolio containing a number of different patent families. A patent for a breakthrough invention is likely to be the subject of a single, strong, broad, patent family. This patent family may be extremely valuable. However, it is not unusual for the real commercial value of a breakthrough technology only to be realized following the making of further inventions addressing practical problems hindering implementation of the original invention. If these inventions are not made for several years, the remaining life of the patent for your original invention might be quite short, and obtaining patents on later inventions might be essential.

Additional patents might also be useful because: i) your original patent may be rejected by a patent office, and you may need the back-up provided by other patents; ii) the existence of many patents makes it more difficult for a competitor to clear the ground: knocking out one patent might be possible, but it might be much more difficult to knock out all the patents in a portfolio; and iii) your patent may prevent others from obtaining their own patents and impinging on your commercial freedom (although this effect can also be obtained simply by publishing details of your invention).

Whatever your particular reason for adding an additional patent to a portfolio, or deciding to retain a particular patent in the years following filing, building a well-controlled portfolio will reduce your exposure to risk, provided you have proper long-term planning and finance in place.

9. ...and then, regularly, review and manage your portfolio

As anyone who has ever managed a patent portfolio will know, costs increase dramatically with time. Adding a new invention to the portfolio is initially relatively inexpensive. However, the cost of extending patent protection for that invention to all the countries you might wish to file in, can be extremely high. If you keep adding new inventions to your portfolio, without abandoning patents and applications that no longer serve your strategic objectives, your costs can rapidly spiral out of control. For this reason you must make sure that you review your portfolio regularly. A formal review process, with sensible allocation and delegation of tasks and decisions, will be necessary in all but the smallest companies.

10. Finally, deal with infringers

If you or your licensee are successfully selling a breakthrough product, chances are that sooner or later you will be faced by infringers in the marketplace. You will then need to decide whether you can live with the situation, and take no action; whether it would be best to approach the competitor in a constructive fashion, possibly with the offer of a licence; or whether you should approach the competitor aggressively, with the intention of litigating to keep them out of the market if this should prove necessary.

No one should ever underestimate the disruption that patent litigation can cause to a company. Quite apart from the expense, which can be huge (particularly in the United States and also to a slightly lesser extent in the UK), the disruption caused to the business as the litigation eats up valuable management time needs to be taken fully into account when deciding whether to litigate. Sharing the market through licensing may often be the best option and, in most situations, litigation should be a last resort.

About the author

Abel & Imray is a leading firm of patent and trade mark attorneys handling all aspects of intellectual property. Clients range from multinationals to small companies, operating in all areas of technology. Sue Scott works as a consultant in the London office, handling a wide range of patent and agreement work. Prior to joining Abel & Imray in 2002, Sue was Head of Patents at BTG, the leading technology transfer group, and Deputy Head of Patents at BP. She has acted as an adviser on patents to the UK government, and has a deep knowledge of patents and their management. Further details: www.patentable.co.uk.

Software inventions

Hans Hutter at Nederlandsch Octrooibureau discusses the scope for patenting software programs and IT solutions in Europe.

Suppose you are a manager of a firm offering all kinds of IT solutions for many different problems. You wish to be sure that your innovations are protected and not copied by your competitors. What can you do? You know that your software program is protected by copyright but that the protection offered by copyright is limited. Moreover, you may have heard that patents may provide you with a broader protection than copyright but that it would be difficult if not impossible to patent software in Europe. If so, then the first message should be that this statement is incorrect: 'Software inventions can be protected by patents in Europe provided they solve a technical problem.'

    This chapter explains when a software invention can be patented in Europe. The rules in other countries as to when a software invention can be patented are different. However, for the purpose of this article you may keep the following second message in mind too: 'If a software invention can be patented in Europe, most probably it will be patentable in other countries, like the United States and Japan, too.'

General rules for patents in Europe

The European Patent Convention specifies four basic requirements to be fulfilled by a patentable invention: there should be an invention, and if so, such an invention should be new, include an inventive step and should be industrially applicable.[1] In the field of software innovations, the last requirement of 'industrial applicability' is not an issue. So, here, I will only deal with the other three requirements.

Invention

For an innovation to be an 'invention' in the context of the European Patent Convention, the innovation should have 'technical character'. The European Patent Convention does not define what this is but it provides a list of subjects that are *not* considered to be inventions:

■ discoveries, scientific theories and mathematical methods;
■ aesthetic creations;
■ schemes, rules and methods for performing mental acts, playing games or doing business, and programs for computers;
■ presentations of information.

These subjects share a substantial lack of technical character, ie they essentially relate to ideas only.

Of course, the presence of 'programs for computers' in this list has been the great problem for all innovators in the field of software. However, the European Patent Convention also specifies that the subjects above, including programs for computers, are only excluded from patentability 'as such'. Case law has now clarified this in the form of the following third message:

> *patents cannot be granted for computer program listings and/or source code but software innovations when claimed in the form of an apparatus with a processor running such software or a method operated by such an apparatus can be patentable provided they are new and involve a technical inventive step.*

In the latter case the patent may also claim the computer program itself. The latter form of protection may be essential to producers of software since it provides protection not only on the level of distributing software via data carriers like CD ROMs but also via the internet.

An example clarifying this is as follows.[2] When somebody develops a computer program for estimating sales activities of a product at a sales outlet and the patent application only claims a mathematical and statistical method to evaluate data gathered from the business environment, such a claim will be rejected because of being a non-invention, ie it is a method of doing business only. However, if the claims of the same patent application are directed to a computer running a program performing such a method, such claims will be regarded to relate to an 'invention'. This is, however, not the same as saying that these claims are patentable: such claims will be first assessed as to novelty and inventive step.

Novelty and inventive step

So, basically, when you, as a business manager, feel that your company has made an important software invention that you wish to protect, you have to consult a good

European patent attorney who knows how to draft proper claims that will not be rejected because they do not claim an 'invention'.

Then, you (or your inventor) should take the time to discuss the items of novelty and inventive step with your patent attorney. I have provided some guidelines as to how such a discussion can be carried out, in the form of a flow chart, shown in Figure 6.5.1.

Flow chart

The flow chart shows a chain of questions to be answered. It may be used once one has defined the essential idea of the invention in the form of a legal claim. Such a legal claim has to be appended to the patent application and can be defined by your patent attorney after having discussed the invention with you or the inventor.

Below, I will use the example of an invention relating to a computer program used by an airplane to control its wings and engines in a new way such that when landing at an airport, the airplane does not follow the usual descending path, with the effect that its engines are substantially less nuisance to people living in houses near the airport.

Step 1

Steps 1 and 2 relate to the question of whether the invention is new in view of the prior art. To that effect, in step 1, one compares the content of the claim with the prior art. This step assumes that such prior art is known so that this comparison can be made. At the time of filing a patent application, the 'real' nearest prior art may not be known to the inventor. Then, one uses the nearest prior art available.

Step 2

In step 2, one establishes if a contribution to the prior art could be found. This step assumes that one uses the contribution approach, in the sense that one looks at the whole content of the claim and not just to features that are new in view of the prior art. So, like in the example of the airplane, there is a contribution over the prior art and one continuous with step 3.

When no contribution to the prior art can be established, the analysed claim lacks novelty and the claim will be rejected, as indicated in block 7.

Step 3

In steps 3, 5 and 6 one tries to find out whether the invention has made a technical contribution to the prior art. Since the European Patent Office does not provide a definition of 'technical', one has to make some practical tests shown to be supported by case law of the European Patent Office.

In step 3 one has to answer the question of whether the contribution is related to controlling a process in the natural world. In the example of the airplane, one could say that the novelty is only in a new mathematical equation used by a processor onboard the airplane to control its wings and engines. However, the real contribution over the

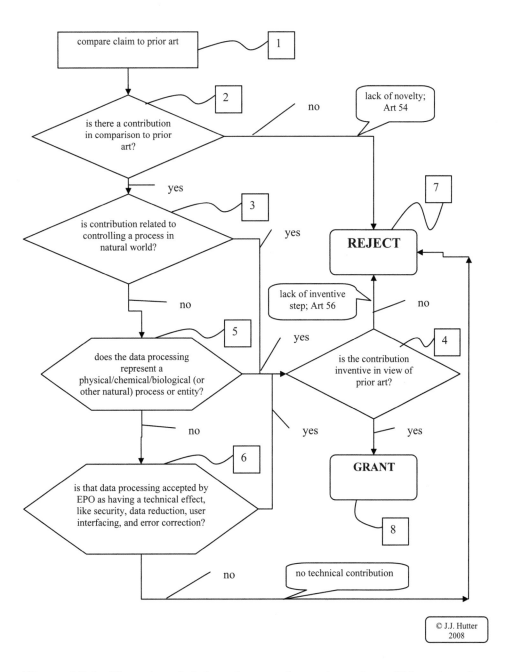

Figure 6.5.1 Flow chart defining when a software invention will be rejected or granted by the European Patent Office

prior art is a new way of controlling the wings and engines of the airplane using that equation. This is an example of controlling a process in the natural world. So, one continues with step 4.

Step 4

In step 4, one has to answer the question of whether the contribution over the prior art includes an inventive step. The approach most commonly used by the European Patent Office to establish the existence of an inventive step is the problem–solution approach. Briefly stated, the question to be answered is whether a person skilled in the art (who knows the prior art) would arrive at the claimed invention without any inventive effort. If not, the claimed invention will be inventive and a patent will be granted, as shown in block 8. If yes, the claim will be rejected, as shown in block 7.

In the example of the airplane, there is a fair chance the European Patent Office will conclude that the claimed invention is inventive because there is a clear advantageous technical effect: noise reduction for people living near the airport.

Step 5

If it is established in step 3 that the contribution to the prior art is not relating to controlling a process in the natural world, the conclusion should be that the claim deals with a mere form of data processing. If so, one does not go from step 3 to step 4 but to step 5. In step 5, one has to answer the following question: does the data in the data processing as claimed represent a natural process, like a physical, chemical, or biological process or other process in nature? Note that this question differs substantially from the question in step 3 (even though it may not seem so at first sight) where the question relates to *controlling* a natural process. Here, examples are: the data relates to weather conditions or to congestion in telecom networks. Other examples are calculating a DNA profile (bio-informatics) or the physical constitution of geophysical layers.

If the answer to the question in step 5 is positive, the contribution will be considered to be 'technical' and one can continue with step 4. Then, one only has to find out whether the contribution to the prior art is inventive in view of the prior art.

Step 6

However, if the answer to the question in step 5 is negative one has to continue with step 6. Step 6 is, as I see it, a final stage of 'rescue' of the patent claim. Step 6 is a check whether the contribution to the prior art relates to a form of data processing that is clearly accepted by the EPO as being 'technical' because the *effect* of the claimed invention is accepted as being 'technical'. Areas in which data processing is accepted as being 'technical' in this regard are:

■ improving confidentiality of data via encryption of data (no matter what the content of the data is, ie the data may, for example, be financial or physical);
■ improving data transmission or processing in a processor by encoding of data;

- reduction of the amount of data without (substantially) losing data content by compression of data;
- reduction of errors in received data by using error correction codes (eg, checksums);
- proving the authenticity of data by using digital signatures;
- improving user interfaces, eg in the way data are presented on a monitor and the way a user can input data to a computer.

If the check in step 6 is positive, one can go to step 4 again where one has to assess inventive step. If, however, the check is negative, one has to conclude that the invention as claimed relates to a non-technical contribution to the prior art.

The above example about the computer program for estimating sales activities of a product at a sales outlet may further clarify this. In that case, one may direct claims to a computer system that uses a mathematical and statistical method to evaluate data gathered from the business environment. Such claims will be regarded as an 'invention' within the meaning of the European Patent Convention. However, the real contribution to the prior art will be seen in the implementation of a new algorithm only, ie all questions in steps 3, 5 and 6 will be answered negatively. Therefore, such a claim will be rejected because of lack of a technical contribution.[3]

Deciding whether or not to file a patent application

Following the checks using the flow chart will give you important information as to whether or not to file a patent application for your software invention. However, another important check is whether or not you will ever be able to prove that a competitor infringes your patent. If the effect of the claimed invention is clearly visible from the outside of the computer system, as may be the case in the example of the airplane, the proof may not be too difficult. However, if the invention is well hidden, for instance because it relates to a new calculation used in an encryption method, the proof may be difficult. Then, one may decide not to apply for a patent. However, if you are going to use the invention yourself, it may still be wise to patent it to protect your own future products. Moreover, in many European countries, a judge may nowadays grant a request for some kind of 'discovery' of the technology used by a competitor. My advice is to discuss these things in detail with your patent attorney before filing any patent application.

About the author

Hans Hutter is managing partner of Nederlandsch Octrooibureau at the Hague office. He is a Dutch and European patent attorney and his areas of practice include semiconductor technology, lithography machines, LCD devices, software, telecommunication, optical discs and smart cards.

Hans joined Nederlandsch Octrooibureau in 1991. He started his patent career with the Netherlands Industrial Property Office in 1988. Before that, he studied electrical engineering at the University of Twente. He worked as a teacher in computer science at the University of Twente and holds a PhD from Eindhoven University of

Technology in the history of science and technology (1988). Further detail:, www. octrooibureau.nl, e-mail: hutter@octrooibureau.nl, tel: + 31 70 33 12 505.

Notes

[1] For a thorough summary of Case Law of the Boards of Appeal of the European Patent Office, see case T 0154/04.
[2] Cf. T 0154/04.
[3] Cf. T 0154/04.

Oppositions and appeals

Patents are often speculative in nature and their true commercial value is only established post-grant, as Peter Bawden at Bawden & Associates explains.

Patenting can be divided into three key phases:

1. invention identification, scoping and patent application drafting;
2. asset development through securing grant by patent offices around the world;
3. post-grant activities, generally the establishment of the valid scope of protection and its enforcement.

The patent, once granted, is a commercial asset whose scope is defined by its claims and it needs to be managed as such. Underlying these phases is the essential ingredient that what is claimed in the patent must be:

a. new;
b. inventive;
c. supported by the general description; and
d. sufficiently well described to allow a skilled person to repeat the invention.

An invention and the associated patent application initially are, inevitably, ill-defined, speculative to a degree and based on incomplete information. A major challenge for the draftsperson is to prepare a patent document that satisfies criteria a) to d) above, reflects the uncertainties and above all captures the commercial requirements.

Patent systems understand these difficulties and allow applicants/inventors to augment their application during the first year of its life and to amend claims to

Achieving success through nanomaterials

Technology providers include
- Harman Technology Ltd
- Intertek MSG
- Johnson Matthey
- Lubrizol Advanced Materials
- MacDermid Autotype
- Maelstrom APT Ltd
- Smith & Nephew TSG
- The University of Liverpool
- Intrinsiq Materials Ltd
- Hosokawa Micron
- MacDermid Autotype Ltd
- Imerys

NanoCentral is driving the safe, beneficial and profitable commercialisation of nanomaterials.

We are an alliance of organisations capable of providing you access to a broad range of leading edge technologies, equipment and services. NanoCentral uniquely provides existing and potential manufacturers or users of nanomaterials single point access to an integrated and comprehensive set of nano-related capabilities that encompass:

- A coherent service spanning Synthesis; Dispersion, Functionalisation & Formulation and Applications Development
- Technical expertise and broad commercial experience
- Connections within the nanomaterial supply chain
- Access to targeted SHE advice

If you are a business aiming to capitalise on the huge commercial benefits that nanomaterials can bring to products, or a provider with a specialist technology offering, NanoCentral is here to help.

NanoCentral®

To take the first steps towards making the right connections call Dr. Steve Devine on 01642 442 464, or Dr. Dan Gooding on 01223 437 067 or visit our website
www.nanocentral.eu

overcome difficulties during the whole life. The opportunities to amend vary from country to country but a guiding rule is that prior to grant one cannot amend to encompass something not disclosed in the original application and, additionally, after grant, one cannot broaden one's scope of protection.

During the asset development phase the manner in which the invention is claimed is first determined by the applicant and knowledge of the industry, which is, inevitably, incomplete. The claims are assessed by patent offices around the world based on the information that is available to the searcher and examiner. Again this is incomplete. For example, the applicant and the patent examiner may be unaware that a third party has been practising the invention before the date of the patent in question and the invention may be in a publication of which neither the applicant nor the patent examiner was aware.

During the development stage 2, patentability is determined between the applicant and the patent office with little, if any, opportunity for third parties to question the arguments and evidence provided in support of patentability. The patent systems around the world have recognized this situation and provide the opportunity to challenge the validity of a granted patent whose claims may threaten a current or planned business activity. The mechanisms provided by the patent systems vary considerably, which has time and cost implications for the parties and should be taken into account in commercial decisions concerning offensive or defensive global patent enforcement.

This chapter is concerned with oppositions that are one means of contesting patent validity. Opposition is not available under all patent systems (for example, not in the United States or Japan) although alternate means of contesting validity are available. The strategic and tactical thinking reviewed in relation to oppositions applies equally to other patent systems but not all (notably costs issues in the United States).

Oppositions

The basis

An opposition filed in the patent office that has granted the patent must be filed within a limited term following the date of the grant of the patent. An opposition to the grant of a European patent may be filed within nine months of the date of grant; in Germany it must be filed within three months. The decision to oppose should be a *commercial* decision based on an assessment of the opposition case, timing and associated costs. An opposition is initiated by paying the appropriate fee, filing a statement and evidence supporting the grounds of opposition. Typically the grounds are that the patent does not satisfy one or more of the criteria a) to d) set out earlier.

The onus to prove these issues is on the opponent and grounds a) and b) must be based on information that was made available to the public before the relevant date. The opponent therefore needs to establish:

■ what was made available;
■ that it was made available to the public;
■ that it was made available before the relevant date.

Written information, commercial activities and oral communication can all be applied provided these criteria can be established. Good corporate record keeping is therefore essential.

After filing, the patentee is given an opportunity to respond, which can be simply counterarguments or counterarguments combined with claim amendments. Although the claims may be amended they cannot be broadened in scope. The patent office will then assume the management of the case and may offer the parties the opportunity to file further observations, it may issue a decision, or it must appoint Oral Proceedings if they have been requested by the parties.

Any decision may be appealed by any party that is adversely affected by the decision. Accordingly, if a patent is maintained in amended form both parties can be adversely affected and it is possible that both parties may appeal. As with the initial opposition, the decision to appeal should be based on a commercial assessment of the situation resulting from the outcome of the opposition.

Timing

If an opposition and an appeal are allowed to take their normal course, each stage can take up to three years. Accordingly it is not unusual that the final decision on the valid scope of a European patent is not obtained until six or seven years after patent grant. Given that examination can take three to four years from the filing of a patent application there can be a lengthy period of uncertainty for patent holders and potential infringers, which can provide various strategic and tactical opportunities for patentees and opponents to optimize their position.

Implications

Oppositions take place after the patent has been granted and the patentee therefore has the right to enforce the patent despite the opposition. Patents granted through the European patent system are national patent rights effective in those countries where the owner wishes to have the protection. The patentee may therefore initiate an action for the infringement of the patent in one or more territories despite parallel opposition in the European Patent Office.

An infringement action is filed in the national court of the country in question and the court will decide if it will allow the action to proceed in parallel with the opposition or will stay the action until the opposition is resolved. An infringer can therefore use an opposition to try to protect its position against litigation. However, increasingly courts will proceed with the action because they consider the time involved in an opposition and any subsequent appeal can significantly disadvantage a patentee.

Infringement actions generally proceed faster than oppositions and in order to protect one's business against an adverse decision while the opposition or any appeal is pending it may be prudent, wherever permitted, to counterclaim in an infringement action for the revocation of the national patent despite the existence of the opposition. However, not all countries, and Germany is a notable exception, will permit a revocation action against the German arm of a European patent that is being opposed.

If someone is accused of infringement or is sued for infringement under a national patent derived from a European patent that is under opposition, they may join the opposition even though the opposition period has expired. If, however, the opposition period has expired without any oppositions being filed, any challenges to the validity of a patent must be made in the national court or courts.

There are a variety of options open to a patentee and a potential defendant or opponent in situations where there are patent enforcement or infringement risk concerns, and all the factors should be considered in depth to enable the most favourable action to be taken. The principal factors consist of the business at risk, timing, costs, likelihood of success and determination the preferred litigation forum.

An opposition can be used to create uncertainty on the validity of a patent, perhaps deterring the patent holder from filing an infringement action, and here the opponent may wish to prolong the opposition to achieve as long a period of uncertainty as possible. On the other hand, an opposition may be filed to initiate settlement and licence discussions, in which case the opponent may wish to rapidly demonstrate the strength of their case. Another scenario is that an opposition may be filed in order to demonstrate to customers that their interests are being looked after.

If a quick decision demonstrating the invalidity of the patent is required, it may be better to file a national revocation action in counties such as the UK, Germany and the Netherlands where such actions proceed much more quickly than oppositions in the European Patent Office. National revocation actions are, however, generally more expensive than oppositions. If a national revocation action is under consideration it is important to determine from historical decisions which court, or court within a country, provides the best prospects of success.

As far as a patentee is concerned, the options are more limited unless the patentee is aware of infringement and is contemplating an infringement action. In this instance it may be desirable to rapidly file an action in the court of choice to ensure that any actions take place in that court rather than in the court preferred by the defendant. If on the other hand a patent is contested, this may be an indication that the patent is of concern to the opponent and an investigation of their activities may be useful to understand why the opposition has been filed. This, in turn, may raise the possibility of an infringement action and consideration of the factors previously discussed.

Amendment of claims

Patentees may amend their claims during oppositions and appeals, and in some national revocation proceedings. An opposition can therefore be a battle between the patentee and the opponent in which the opponent is attempting to secure revocation of the entire patent and, as a secondary but equally important consideration, to force the patentee to limit the claims in a way that establishes freedom for the opponent's activities. An opponent therefore needs to ensure that the attack is against the aspect of the claims that impacts their interest. An opposition that results in the maintenance of the patent with stronger claims that still impact the opponent's activities is counterproductive. When considering whether to file an opposition it is therefore important to consider the amendment opportunities that may be available to the patentee and to structure the opposition in a way that pushes the patentee to amend in a way that removes the threats posed by the patent.

Similarly, a patentee who has been opposed needs to understand why the opposition was filed so that if a claim amendment is required they can try to amend in a manner that retains the value of the patenting.

Costs

The costs of an opposition will vary according to the complexity of the case. Many of the arguments in an opposition are of a technical nature and may require experimental data to support the opposition. In planning it should therefore be recognized that technical resources will be required. The costs are made up of internal technical and legal activities, legal representation, patent office fees, plus any travel and accommodation that may be required in the development and progress of the case.

Appeals

In all legal systems a first instance decision can be appealed and most systems provide an opportunity for further appeal. Whereas there is continuity between examination and opposition in the European Patent Office with the pre-grant examiner generally being a member of the opposition board, the Boards of Appeal are totally distinct from the Opposition Division.

The Boards of Appeal review cases *de Novo* on behalf of parties who have been adversely affected by an earlier decision either in the Examination Division or in the Opposition Division. The course of an appeal in an opposition is similar to that of an opposition, and the factors to consider – business at risk, timing, resource requirements and costs – can be much the same as in an opposition. Appeals typically take from two to three years for a decision. An appeal therefore provides the parties with the opportunity to employ the same tactical considerations as were discussed in relation to oppositions.

Although national courts are not bound by the decisions of the Boards of Appeal of the European Patent Office, they will take them into account and it is unlikely that a national court will find a patent to be invalid on grounds that the Board of Appeal has considered and found the invention as claimed to be patentable.

The European Patent Systems provides an Enlarged Board of Appeal as the highest authority. However, until December 2007 the Enlarged Board of Appeal could be invoked only upon the request of a Board of Appeal. A patentee or an opponent could not appeal from a decision of a Board of Appeal and so their decisions were final. Since December 2007, under a modification of the European Patent Convention (known as EPC 2000), it is now possible for a patentee, applicant or an opponent to appeal to the Enlarged Board of Appeal. It is, however, anticipated that only appeals relating to legal or procedural issues will be accepted by the Enlarged Board. This remains to be seen.

This chapter gives a brief insight into the post-grant issues that can surround patenting and establishing its true value. It shows that in a world where nothing is clear cut there are ways and means whereby one can try to optimize one's position and that the opportunity to secure value requires a fully informed and professional organization that can bring together the relevant commercial, technical and legal issues.

About the author

Bawden and Associates provides management consultancy advice to corporate management and provides professional services on global intellectual property issues including patents, trade marks and copyright as well as technology transfer, licensing and the protection of confidential information. Particular expertise lies in the strategic approach to the identification and development of intellectual property, to generate assets and use of real commercial value. Peter Bawden is the owner and is a Chartered Patent Agent and European Patent Attorney, as is his partner Stephen Geary. Peter previously held overall management responsibility for the global IP activities of Exxon Chemical Company and Stephen held senior positions in ICI and Unilever. The company's activities include the development and exploitation of IP portfolios around the world, offensive and defensive patent office and court activities and the coordination of contentious issues such as oppositions and litigation in Europe, the Americas and Asia. Peter may be contacted on +44 (0)1582 466702 or by e-mail: pb@bawden.co.uk. Bawden and Associates website: www.bawden.co.uk.

7

Market innovation

Brand-based innovation

Brands have proved themselves to be the most effective and efficient source of innovation, says Rita Clifton, Chairman of Interbrand.

I must confess that when I hear from companies that one of their core values is 'innovation', my instinct is to imagine guilt until innocence is proven. This is because 'innovation' has become one of Those Words in businesses and organizations of all kinds. Rather like the terms 'customer focus', 'openness and transparency' and 'value', 'innovation' tends to be over-used, ill-appreciated and under-delivered. There are a number of factors that conspire to make this the case.

Over the years, numerous surveys and correlation studies have consistently demonstrated the value and importance of 'innovation' to the most successful enterprises. There is little need to argue the theoretical case any more. The real issue is pinning down what is really meant by the term – and how, under all the day-to-day operating and financial pressures, organizations can really sustain the levels of innovation that are required to succeed in every market today and in the future, in both benign and difficult market conditions.

What is innovation?

It is interesting to look at a range of definitions of innovation from marketing text-books: 'innovation is changing the value and satisfaction obtained from resources by the consumer'; 'an innovation is an application of ideas and knowledge to meet successfully a current or future market need'; and, most succinctly, 'invention is a new product, innovation is a new benefit'. The last definition is also telling in that it distinguishes invention from innovation – something that many organizations find difficult. Producing new 'stuff', particularly in the area of technology, is certainly the most visible and high-profile part. However, there is always a danger that the energy that goes into inventing new products is not focused enough to give the best return on investment – nor to ensure the best minimization of risk. A past president of Coca-Cola went so far as to say 'New products are a lazy man's marketing.'

The most effective and efficient innovation is brand-based innovation. It is not hard to demonstrate that the brand is the most important and sustainable corporate asset. And indeed, it is usually the most productive asset to sweat. If you start with the brand, and so with the key insights about your customers and customer relationships, it gives a clear and disciplined platform for innovation across the *total brand experience*; this includes service innovation, retail/3-D and the online experience, and in process as well as product areas. Brand-based innovation will give longer, deeper and more potentially sustainable competitive advantage than a reliance on product inventions alone, particularly in most of today's markets where long-term product differences are becoming less consumer noticeable. You have to think about stitching in a branded advantage to every contact point with your customers if you are going to gain, retain and build the strongest customer relationships and so create sustainable brand value.

Strong brands, old or new, have three critical characteristics: clarity, consistency and leadership. That means being *clear* about what the brand stands for, about its values, its purpose and its future direction. It means being clear about how your brand is different not only from today's competitors, but also, in today's blurring and converging markets, potential competitors in the future too. Being *consistent* is about living and communicating those clear values, both inside and outside the organization; increasingly, a brand's people are the major part of the brand experience. But the most important characteristic correlating to long-term sustainable value is *leadership*. This is not necessarily about size and financial muscle, nor indeed about who runs the company. It is about 'setting the agenda' and standards in a market, and this can apply as much to traditional brand leaders as to challenger brands. Above all, leadership demands great innovation, across all areas of operation.

Who's doing it well?

A good place to start for inspiring examples is amongst the world's most valuable brands. Coca-Cola is in the pole position it is today not just because it has refreshed and innovated in the product over time. Clearly, Diet Coke, Caffeine-free Coke and Coke with lemon and vitamins have been important initiatives and 'new news' to retain interest over time, but it was also brand-based thinking about putting Coke's refreshing qualities 'within an arm's reach of desire' that inspired innovation in distribution and merchandising through vending machines. Innovative advertising and marketing communication, including global and local sponsorship, have ensured that the brand stays fresh and current to its young, demanding and otherwise fickle target audiences.

IBM, now number three in the world brand league table, may have been kicked into more innovative behaviour by the original product challenge of Apple, but it has made up for it since by innovating and extending the brand around consultancy and e-business. Again, it started not with the question ,'How can we make more and different boxes', but rather, 'How can we use our technology, authority and expertise to create more value for our customers?' As far as Apple is concerned, the fact that the brand is about humanizing technology and thinking differently has propelled it not only into new product areas like iPod and iPhone, but also into retailing in a different way – by having Apple stores that look and feel as though hotel designers and people who love what they do were involved in their creation, rather than conventional store fits.

Possibly the most intriguing brand in the top 10 is Intel. Clearly, it has helped that Intel is driven by, and lives for, innovation, as it says in its literature, and that it invented the world's first microprocessor. However, what really propelled Intel into its valuable position today was innovation in customer targeting and marketing thinking. Communicating directly with computer buyers, rather than just IT professionals, created real market 'pull', while the Intel Inside cooperative marketing programme ensured that Intel moved from being a technical ingredient to being the ultimate 'cuckoo in the nest' ingredient brand.

Samsung also stands out amongst the top 100 brands as one of the most effective turnarounds and growth stories over the past 10 years. Again, this is not only down to its technical innovation around the digital platform, but also particularly due to its decision to build a premium brand, rather than pursue the low price and commodity, OEM road to perdition. Having made this decision, process innovation came in the form of measuring its people's performance by their contribution to building the value of the Samsung brand as an asset, rather than just being measured by straight financials. It has paid off many times over.

Starbucks has been another strong performer over time, despite some more recent struggles on home turf. The innovation in Starbucks is absolutely about the total brand experience. Not only has Starbucks recognized the value of the 'total coffee experience', in all its varieties, it has also recognized the opportunity for the brand to be about the 'third place' for its customers to hang out between home and an office. This has then given it the energy and licence to 'accessorize' the third space with music and books – and to have allowed the distribution 'innovation' for Paul McCartney and a new album. A coffee house innovating as a book seller and music retailer as well.

Probably the most dramatic growth story of the past few years has been Google, as one of the 'new paradigm' global brands to tap into a global online community, rather than the traditional way of buying up the world physically, geography by geography. What is fascinating here is Google's innate culture of innovation, and its clear drive to 'organize the world's information'. It has recognized that its people need to be able to spend free 'brain time' to achieve the levels of innovation it needs – and allocates 10 per cent of its people's time to their own personal projects. This free thinking has yielded Google mail and Google WiFi.

In the UK, Tesco is probably the best example of a company using brand-based innovation around its customers' 'life needs' to create a constant stream of relevant products, services and marketing initiatives. Its approach to innovation epitomizes the original meaning of the word, derived from the Latin word *innovare*, meaning 'to renew'. Tesco's brand focus on winning lifetime customer loyalty forces a constant state of renewal and growth, and this is championed by the CEO and management team. *Fortune* magazine had an interesting perspective on this when it described the companies that succeed in innovating as having 'mastered the art of maintaining continuity while fostering a state of perpetual renewal'.

The word 'renewal' also implies a 'whole company' approach to innovation, and this is still a challenge for so many organizations. While speeches made by CEOs might feature the innovation word, too often innovation is still believed to be the province of the R&D and marketing departments. This leads us into the first point of the last section, which is about the lessons we can draw for more effective and efficient innovation in the future.

So what?

An innovative culture has to come from the top

This may seem an over-used point, but the CEO must be seen as the CBO – Chief Brand Officer. The customer focus this brings forces innovation on to everyone's agenda, and encourages people to see the brand as an inspiring – and efficient – central organizing principle for all areas of innovation.

On a parochial note, it would certainly help encourage more innovation from the top if we had a rather more positive media climate in the UK. It is a sad but true observation that some UK CEOs are nervous about championing high-profile, unusual innovation in case they are criticized in an increasingly cynical national press. Yet innovation is so critical to the future success and wealth creation in the UK that business leaders must show courage and leadership in taking this on.

You need truly cross-functional and integrated thinking to get the best results

To avoid the 'invention-only/not my department' trap, it is critical to include people from across any organization (and absolutely including the finance team) – and to make some type of innovation a measured (and rewarded) part of everyone's roles. It is also critical that this type of working is continuous practice rather than a one-off, and using the brand is a constant source of energy and competitive perspective.

You need true customer obsession

This does not mean commissioning more and more reams of market research; it is just as much to do with looking at macro-trends, behavioural observation and powerful listening to consumers. There are also many and varied participative techniques for getting customer participation in co-creating the future they would like.

Recognize that innovation comes from product, service, 3-D experience or process, and can be breakthrough or incremental.

Above all, use the brand

The brand is not only the major wealth creator in any business; it is also a springboard, a rallying point, and a testing filter for new ideas. Innovation based on the brand is the most cost-efficient and effective innovation you will have.

About the author

Rita Clifton is Chairman of Interbrand in London. Prior to this, she was Executive Planning Director at Saatchi & Saatchi. Rita has authored and edited various books on brands, marketing and communications, including The Future of Brands *and* The Economist *book,* Brands & Branding. *She is in demand as a speaker at conferences and in the media around the world. Her other roles are as Chairman of Populus, the opinion pollster to* The Times, *as a non-executive director of DSG international, and as a trustee of WWF (Worldwide Fund for Nature).*

Create customers before you create products

Take your innovation to your customers as soon as you can, says Peter White, founder of YTKO, Cambridge, and get them to set price, performance and profit expectations.

Innovation needs marketing to turn inventions into revenues. 'The business enterprise has two – and only two – basic functions: marketing and innovation. Marketing and innovation produce results; all the rest are costs.' So said business guru Peter Drucker. But that was in 1953, and many companies are still not putting the two together and getting the rewards they deserve.

Taking the time to do a value proposition, at the earliest possible stage in development, not only shows you what the real worth of your innovation is, but also indicates how – and to whom – the concept should be marketed, and customers' eagerness to buy and implement. A value proposition attempts to demonstrate quantified benefits to prospective users; benefits they will receive through the implementation of your offering. You can kick-start the whole, essential, business development process by working with customers to meet – or better, exceed – their needs and wants. You prove that your offering has value in their situation.

A value proposition isn't simply a sum showing how many times faster, or cheaper, your offering is. It takes into account how much your solution costs to buy, implement and maintain, and then details what the savings or advantages are. Value propositions work best when you're selling business-to-business. If you're in the consumer marketplace, then you'll need good market research to give you a clear idea of the value your customers will put on intangibles such as status and fashion – even on innovation itself.

Let's be specific: the four steps here should be enough for any company, large or small, to determine whether its newest concept will sell, or sit on the shelf:

1. Start off by describing what the prospect could improve: productivity, efficiency, revenues, safety, time to market; what they can reduce: costs, staff turnover; and what they might create: satisfaction, position, new services – by buying from you.
2. Then project how much this improvement would be worth in terms of cash, reduced timescales or provide a percentage/range. You'll need to have done your homework on what typical costs of people, materials and machinery are. But of course you are talking to the market regularly, and you're not doing your innovation in a vacuum, are you?
3. Now you'll be able to talk to your prospective users about what they'll be able to do differently. Here you can create a scenario of a wonderful, innovative future.
4. At this time, any interested customer will ask you straight out: what will it cost me? Don't tell them. Get them to agree on what the saving really could be, or the extra productivity. Be specific, but keep it experimental and informal. Ask them what proportion of that likely saving they'd be prepared to pay. Sticking to talking value lets you set the agenda, enables you and the customer to jointly agree the value, and makes the customer set the price.

Now, if you can't make it for what they'll pay, this way you'll have saved yourself development headaches, and the pain of trying to sell an unwanted product. It means going back to the drawing board, but now you're well informed, and have a clear cost goal.

At the very least communicating your outline value proposition, and showing how you arrived at the worth of your solution, will create curiosity in the mind of clients. They will want to know if it really will apply in their own situation, and will work with you to help develop the best solution. Then do it all over again. And again. You can never have too much customer information.

Shouting about innovation still doesn't get you the sales. You must demonstrate the inherent value to the customer that should be integral to your offering. If that value is not obvious, or not specific, or not sufficient to make the customer buy, then you should work together with those customers to find where the value lies. Just because it's innovative doesn't make it saleable.

All of this is common sense. Like much of marketing, it's obvious and sensible. Yet very few of the many SMEs we see discuss the customer's needs and processes. 'We send our business development manager out three times a week to talk to prospective customers,' said one founder. 'We're building a terrific database.' Perhaps to those possible purchasers, the new product would indeed be suitable, but a 'must-have'? At no time had had they talked about value, or about the return on investment the customer would expect in order to justify a purchase.

Companies get overly secretive. 'If we talk to the market now, then our competitors will pick up what we're doing and we'll lose our edge.' We riposted: 'If you reckon your competition is so good they can catch up with your R & D in a few weeks, are you really innovating?'

Let's agree, then, that every innovative company needs to engage with the customer at the earliest opportunity. A market is not just a single buyer, though. Even within the customer there are different roles and different value judgements: you must assess and then address.

A buyer determines needs, assesses suppliers, orders and pays for and takes delivery of a product or service. The value proposition to the buyer often focuses on speed of delivery, quality of service, maintenance levels, service level agreements and overall quality delivery. The user motivation is different. They want to do their job better. These are people who looking for an outcome. It may be doing a job that they haven't previously been able to do before, or simply performing that job better, or removing obstacles in their way. These are the group focused on the performance, and the value proposition for the user needs to reflect these outcomes.

This is early-stage marketing. It sits neatly alongside your early-stage innovation, and informs those concepts and creativity. It ensures there's no ivory tower of invention, and provides a reality – and profitability – check, so you know you've got a business to back your innovation. And it adds new resources to your innovation team: customers. They're the people who daily struggle with the problems you're looking to solve, and who will tell you exactly the value of what you're working on. They'll do that for free, and then pay you money when you can prove your concept to them. Get engaged.

About the author

Peter White is the founder of YTKO, the European economic and enterprise development organization. Peter describes his company's work as 'creating customers for science and technology'.

Peter works closely with scientists and technologists to create sustainable market-driven enterprises. He is a leading practitioner of proof of commercial concept, using innovative processes to develop and accelerate market engagement and revenues for early-stage science. His innovation and enterprise expertise spans bioscience, where he is Director of the Yorkshire Enterprise Fellowships, the largest pre-incubation project in Europe, in healthcare and in ICT. He sits on the European Commission's Sector Innovation Panel for biotechnology, and is a non-executive director of three technology companies including one developing a high-performance optical processor, for which he holds three patents.

He is an honorary alumnus of the Theseus Management Institute, France, an editorial board member of the International Journal of Innovation and Regional Development, *and board member of the Yorkshire Concept Fund. Further details: Peter White, YTKO, St John's Innovation Centre, Cambridge CB4 0WS, website:www. ytko.com.*

What can you do with a trade mark?

Simon Bentley at Abel & Imray discusses how to use trade marks to capture the value in your innovation.

The simplest and most effective way to capture the value in the mark you have chosen to market your innovation under is to register it. Although it is possible in the UK to acquire some rights solely through use, our legal system generally favours the first person to register a mark, rather than the first person to use the mark. It is therefore advisable to register, if possible, any trade mark you wish to use and monopolize.

Registration of a trade mark allows action to be taken against third parties for infringement. Without a registration of the trade mark it might prove difficult, if not impossible, to prevent such unauthorized third party use. It is also likely to prove more expensive to take legal action without a registration because the onus is then on the owner of the right to substantiate its existence.

Also, by not registering a trade mark, it might be open to a third party to apply to register a similar or identical mark in respect of similar or identical goods. Even if you have been using your brand before the date on which the third party applies to register the later mark, the registered rights could restrict your future commercial activities and in particular your ability to expand into new markets (whether new geographical markets in the UK or new products/services). In the worst case, you may have to cease use of your mark.

Although it is advisable to register a brand, it may also be possible to take action against others for 'passing off' if they are using a brand, trading style, 'get-up' (ie the look or shape of a product or its packaging) or, for example, a house colour. In the past, the owners of the JIF lemons brand have successfully prevented competitors selling lemon juice in lemon-shaped containers, and BP has prevented use of the colour green as applied to the fascia of petrol stations.

What marks to protect

Choosing a mark is essentially a commercial decision. Many companies prefer marks that allude to the characteristics of their goods and services, such as Kleenex for tissues and Juicy Fruit for chewing gum. On the other hand, there are other companies that prefer newly coined brands or more 'off the wall' brands with little or no relation to the goods or services, such as Kodak for photographic film and Elephant for car insurance, on the basis that they are more memorable. Of course, it is often much easier to obtain registration of trade marks that are not at all descriptive of the goods and services of interest, or characteristics thereof. Whatever mark you choose, you should carry out a search to try to ensure that you do not unwittingly infringe someone else's rights.

It is also important to realize that you may be using several brands – the main mark, a sub-brand, an inventive and distinctive strap-line or logo. The public may even recognize the shape of the product's packaging as a trade mark of your business. Also, a product or service may be provided under an umbrella brand, for example, in the form of a family brand, the name of the company, or the name of a product range. Consider, by way of example, the trade mark rights embodied by a bottle of Glenfiddich whisky.

Figure 7.3.1 Glenfiddich

William Grant (the brand-owners) has sought to protect independently the word marks, device marks, logos, 3-D marks and other elements that combine together to embody the Glenfiddich brand. Examples are shown in the following figure. While some elements have changed over time, as the brand has evolved, the collection of rights provides a valuable and robust IP portfolio that captures and protects the value in the brand.

Figure 7.3.2 The Glenfiddich brand. Images reproduced with the kind permission of William Grant & Sons Ltd

It will be seen that, ideally, registration of all of the brands and brand indicators should be sought, although trade mark attorneys can advise on how best to maximize your protection at the lowest cost. It should also be remembered that some of the appearance of a product (or its packaging or 'get-up') or website, etc may also be protected by the law of copyright and/or the law of passing off.

Some brands are priceless

Once a mark is registered (or indeed once a mark has been applied for) it becomes an object of property. Indeed, for many companies (eg clothing designers), the main mark is the most valuable object of property. When the Donna Karan business was sold, it was rumoured that much if not most of the value was attributable to the trade mark. It would of course be trite to suggest that registration alone is responsible for the value, but it does help to crystallize that value and does so in a way that facilitates its commercial exploitation in a number of ways:

∎ *Sale of the mark* – during due diligence, potential purchasers devote significant time and effort to establish what intellectual property rights a potential acquisition enjoys and what, if any, conflicts might arise with third parties. Anyone who has watched the BBC's *Dragons' Den* television programme will know what store potential investors put on the proper protection of the IP in innovations and the value of exclusivity. Registered marks can therefore be fundamental to the calculation of value of an innovation or business.

■ *Licensing* – it may be practically impossible for an innovator to bring a product to market without the assistance of a manufacturer. Having a registered mark facilitates the process of licensing a brand and can ensure that you stay in control of its use. Similarly, a registered mark makes franchising much more attractive to potential franchisees because of the relative security that it offers. In the event that franchisees start to misuse a mark, it can also help to bring them back into line.

■ *Collateral* – many companies can raise finance by offering their intellectual property rights as collateral against loans. Again, it is no surprise that banks and other financial institutions prefer to deal in the 'hard currency' of registered trade marks rather than brands without any statutory protection.

Don't lose the value in your marks

It is important that marks retain the ability to differentiate goods or services of one trader from those of another. Although in itself a sign of business success, when a mark becomes the generic name for the type of product, it is in danger of being lost forever. Many famous marks including Aspirin, Escalator and Linoleum have been lost because they become the industry standard term for the product. To avoid this happening, trade marks should never be used as nouns (eg, 'You'll never need another [mark] again'). Instead, they should be used as adjectives ('Our new [mark] widget will revolutionize the market!'). You should also try to educate your customers, retailers and the press as to the correct use of your mark.

You should also advertise your claims to enjoy rights in a trade mark by using distinctive font and bold characteristics to distinguish the mark. It is also advisable to use the ^{TM} symbol or, when, and only when, a mark is registered, the ® symbol.

Registered marks must be used after a certain time has elapsed since registration – in the UK, this is five years – or they can be lost. It is also important to check that the form of the mark that you are currently using is close enough to the mark as registered. Finally, you need to ensure that your registrations are renewed – they expire after 10 years in the UK. For this purpose, it is important that you record any changes in address so that you receive reminders from the UK IPO or your trade mark attorney.

About the author

Abel & Imray is a leading firm of patent and trade mark attorneys handling all aspects of intellectual property. Clients range from multinationals to small companies, operating in all areas of commerce. Simon Bentley (Partner) is an experienced trade mark attorney of the firm and advises on both contentious and non-contentious issues. Simon has lectured to fellow professionals on matters concerning European trade mark law and is actively involved in the Institute of Trade Mark Attorneys (ITMA), having been elected to the Council of ITMA in 2007.

8

Business models

Business models for effective innovation

Challenge the rules of the game and identify all potential lines of revenue before you decide how to approach the market, says Julian Wheatland at Consensus Community.

One of the most common mistakes made by organizations (both large and small) attempting to launch a new business, is focusing solely on the first business model that occurs to them. In reality, there are many different ways to approach the market and many different positions to occupy in the supply chain; selecting the right one can have a significant affect on value creation and can be the difference between success and failure.

How to approach the opportunity

Starting with the assumption that a market opportunity has been identified, the challenge is to consider how to address the market and organize the business to take advantage of it. The opportunity may have arisen from evolving customer demand, the discovery of an exciting new technology, a strategic review, or a focused product development programme; the origin is unimportant. The essential first building block of a new business is the identification of a clear, validated, quantified addressable market and the capability to deliver a solution.

Let us assume that we have an exciting new technology to make a better widget. That's nice in as far as it goes, but what we really want to know is, *how are we going to make money from it?* The naive assumption that customers will pay more for it, or buy more of it, because it's 'better' than the competition, is inadequate. An opportunity exists to create value by innovating the business model itself – maybe our widget is just the catalyst rather than the entire solution!

When Apple launched the iPod (a very clever, better widget) it achieved moderate market success through effective design. It achieved market dominance only when it had turned the entire music industry global supply chain on its head, by providing easy lawful access to music online and an innovative approach to the retail experience (using techniques largely learnt from Amazon).

So, before designing the new business model, the very first step should be to *identify all of the potential different lines of revenue that could be generated.* This means thinking clearly about what product and service offerings can be provided.

For example, the 'razor and razorblades' business model is now well established across many sectors for locking customers into a product and making the bulk of the profit on spares and replacement parts:

■ In the men's grooming market, Gillette makes almost no margin on razor handles, but the replacement blade market generates handsome profits.
■ Hewlett Packard makes most of its profit from replacement ink cartridges rather than its printers.
■ GE Aviation makes little profit from aircraft engines but does very nicely from its global spares and maintenance business.

Another service offering that has often changed the shape of industries is the bundling of financial services. Not only do well-tailored finance plans assist in the sale of the core product, but they also represent significant additional revenue lines in their own right:

■ dfs, the furniture retailer, offers interest-free credit with nothing to pay for four years to encourage consumers to purchase more expensive items than they might otherwise have bought.
■ As part of an effort to capture a larger share of the after-sales service opportunities on the back of its core products, GE created a US$20 billion revenue stream in its commercial finance arm – which generates 50 per cent higher profits than the manufacturing business.
■ Dixons, the electronics retailer, makes a significant share of its revenue (and an even larger share of its profits) from the sale of insurance services on the back of its core hardware products.

Successful entrepreneurs look at markets and challenge the status quo; serial entrepreneurs often have a process for challenging industry assumptions. Many opportunities for business model innovation occur in markets that are mature and established – and ready for a shake-up!

Richard Branson, far from just spreading his Virgin brand around indiscriminately, has developed a track record for changing the rules of the game. For example, it was

Five steps to business model innovation

1. Challenge industry assumptions – force yourself to think of different ways of doing things.
2. Identify multiple lines of revenue.
3. Identify other products and services that can be bundled with the core proposition.
4. Experiment with different combinations to identify where significant value may be hidden.
5. Having identified the entire universe of things you potentially could do, select what you will do very carefully.

only when he launched Virgin Upper Class that premium airline travel became a door-to-door experience rather than airport-to-airport. Tata in India challenged the assumption that mobile telephone services had to be paid for. It launched a service that gives free mobile minutes in return for customers viewing advertisements.

Some questions to challenge the business model

There are four main areas of the business to focus on in order to challenge initial thoughts and ideas about how to structure the business model and how to make money:

1. customer identification;
2. product sourcing;
3. service offerings;
4. distribution channels.

1. Customer identification

Who are our customers?

The starting assumption of this chapter was that you have identified a market opportunity and have the means to deliver a solution; the challenge is to consider who your customers will be and where you will sit in the supply chain.

Ask yourself: Could you move backwards in the supply chain to be a provider of licences or patents by focusing just on development activities? Should you be a provider of components to OEMs? Or should you move forward along the supply chain into direct retailing?

2. Product sourcing

Should we manufacture ourselves?

If you have the technology and have the product, the simplest business model is to plan to manufacture it yourself. However, unless you have a background in manufacturing, or production requires very specialist plant and equipment, in-house manufacture may not be the best route. Establishing an in-house manufacturing capability requires a significant amount of additional skills and capabilities within the organization. It also substantially increases the capital required.

Ask yourself: Is this where you can create most value? Is manufacturing an area where you have, or wish to build, core competence?

Should we outsource manufacturing?

By outsourcing manufacturing to a third party you can reduce the complexity and capital requirements of the new business. In fact, it may be possible to source production in the developing world, thereby significantly reducing costs, although, of course, careful attention must be paid to patent protection issues.

Ask yourself: Is there a good reason for not outsourcing? Can you produce the goods as cheaply and efficiently in-house as a third party could?

Should we license or sell the IP?

Another business model that can be very lucrative, while at the same time avoiding major operating risks, is to license, or even sell, the IP. This model leaves manufacturing and marketing to third parties with particular expertise in these areas; it also significantly reduces the capital investment required. For example, ARM Holdings of the UK has built the leading mobile chip design business on a 'design to licence' business model.

Ask yourself: Where do your key strengths/capabilities lie? Could your market share be higher by providing technology to several manufacturers, rather than competing with them?

3. Service offerings

Can we offer a maintenance/repair service?

As has been discussed earlier, many businesses are structured on the basis of there being more value in the after-sales service than in the sale of the original product. This could be the supply of replacement parts using the 'razor and razorblades' model (like Mont Blanc pens) or a locked-in routine maintenance like Rolls Royce aircraft engines. Tom Tom, the European satellite navigation provider, makes a good margin on its hardware but a much better one on its map updates service.

Ask yourself: Are there after-sales product or service offerings that could extend the relationship between you and your customers?

Can we offer a finance package?

On capital equipment, more and more companies are bundling finance/lease packages with their products. Car manufacturers like Ford make as much margin on their finance products as on their cars, and medical equipment is now routinely leased in order to provide an easy means of periodic upgrade.

Ask yourself: Would an integrated finance package make your customers buying decision easier? Could you partner with a bank and take a share of their revenue?

Could we provide the entire business process?

Why just provide a new technology to your customers? Why not operate it for them as well? Many new technologies, while improving the efficiency of a business process, also provide the means and/or a rationale to outsource it entirely. Payroll processing is now routinely outsourced by SMEs, enabled by modern data communications and software systems.

Ask yourself: Can an economy of scale be created by providing a service to multiple customers? Is substantial capital investment required to implement the new technology? Is this a non-core business process for your customers?

4. Distribution channels

Can we re-engineer the supply chain?

Don't accept the prevailing wisdom of your industry that there is only one means of getting your product to customers. Successful entrepreneurs often achieve success from the way they shake up their industry, rather than just the products that they launch.

Ask yourself: Can you dis-intermediate elements of the supply chain that aren't adding much value? Can you go directly to your ultimate customers and cut out the middle men?

Can we use virtual distribution?

More and more goods are being sold over the internet, thereby cutting out physical retailers; and now more and more goods are being distributed over the internet too. The music industry is an obvious example, but similarly computer games and software are being installed without ever having taken a physical form. Nowadays it's possible to take delivery of a whole host of products over the internet including stamps, books and airline tickets. Who knows what will be next… will we be able to print our own cash?

Ask yourself: Does your product ever really *need* to have a physical presence prior to distribution? Can you re-engineer your offering to avoid physical manifestation?

Case example – Nestlé

Nestlé is one of the best examples of how to tackle a distribution problem and get directly to consumers in the face of the increasing power of retailers.

Nestlé partnered with equipment manufacturers to create an in-home espresso coffee 'system'. Having bought one of their machines, consumers then have to buy Nespresso capsules direct over the internet. Nestlé makes lower margins on the machines, but each capsule costs a stunning 23p – for a single cup at home. The business has had a compound growth rate of 30 per cent over the last five years!

About the author

Julian Wheatland is Chief Executive of Consensus Community and a director of Edengene Ltd. Consensus is a leading UK investor in growing technology companies, with a particular emphasis on the environment and homeland security; investee companies can utilize the Consensus international platform to assist their global expansion. Edengene is an innovation, strategy and change consultancy, specializing in helping some of Europe's largest companies transform their ability to achieve consistent, sustainable growth.

Telephone: 020 7355 7777, e-mail: j.wheatland@cbg.uk.com.

Innovation platforms

Innovative enterprises can go wrong in all sorts of ways, says Lesley Anne Rubenstein, Chief Executive of the Thames Innovation Centre, so be realistic in finding a business incubator that is more than an address.

Business incubators are a well-known tool for helping companies to start up businesses. This industry started up in the United States in the 1980s, in Israel and Europe in the 1990s, and in the South East region of the UK (funded by SEEDA), in the 2000s. At their most basic, they are serviced office buildings sharing a reception, meeting rooms, common office equipment and offering telephone-answering and a mail service. This helps a start-up to look more successful than it is, without having to pay for rooms that would be empty most of the time. Doctors and lawyers have been doing this for years – it's a classic way of sharing overheads. For all intents and purposes, this type of operation could just as well be a 'Regus' office suite and has the same amount of value-add. For some savvy start-ups that are well-financed, have a strong management team and a competitive edge, and have possibly been round the block a few times, this is all they need.

More often than not, however, start-ups are not savvy. They do not have a sound business plan (some of them don't even possess a business plan); look like deer caught in the headlamps when asked for a copy of their management accounts; are not clear on their unique selling points; think that they don't have competition; and believe that the 'sky's the limit' when it comes to the size of their target market. (I'd bet any money those of you who are professionals in the industry are nodding your heads and smiling knowingly by this point – we've all met such entrepreneurs).

The better business incubators and innovation centres offer much more than a real estate proposition. They take into account that for start-ups and micros, business

The Thames Innovation Centre

the right place for you, the right place for your company

The Thames Innovation Centre offers a wide range of **modern, stylish workspaces for hi-tech, creative and science based companies.**

With close links to London, Europe and the M25 motorway, the Thames Innovation Centre is ideally located for start-ups and established companies looking for a new UK base.

Whether it's our stylish reception area, the stunning Atrium or even our powerful IT infrastructure, when you bring your business to the Thames Innovation Centre you'll have all you need to run an efficient and productive operation.

In addition to its creative and vibrant atmosphere and extensive **business support programs,** the Thames Innovation Centre is **an eco-building that leads the way in sustainable commercial development.**

...the freedom to innovate

www.thamesinnovationcentre.com

tel : +44 (0)20 8320 1000   e-mail : info@thamesinnovationcentre.com support must go hand-in-hand with the space offering. Indeed, the space rented out is considered to be just one of the value-added services on offer. A good innovation centre may offer events, networking opportunities, training workshops, one-to-one business support, etc. Some will even help their tenant companies get 'investment-ready' and help them to raise funds – public (eg, R&D grants) and private (angel, seed, venture capital) – as well as bank loans.

Ultimately, it's the screening process that massively increases incubator rates of success. The process should include receipt of a business plan (or a promise to attend business plan workshops and work with the centre on a business plan), a three-month rental deposit (really bad sign if they can't afford this), a credit check (which won't help if it's a start-up), Google (if nothing comes up for the founders and/or the business, that may turn on warning signals) and, where possible, references. Most importantly, don't forget to use your antennae. Money laundering businesses may have excellent credit ratings, but if it quacks like a duck, walks like a duck...

Depending on the region the innovation centre is in, one should set entrance criteria that make sense. If the centre is in Cambridge or Oxford, or on a research-led university campus, it might make sense to concentrate on technology-led companies. If one is in a rural area, without local centres of excellence or corporations and/or technology clusters, using those criteria would probably not make sense. This needs to be managed carefully as having too stringent criteria can lead to the centre's ultimate failure and being too flexible can sometimes defeat the purpose for which the centre was built. On the other hand, when an innovation centre does choose certain sectors that fit with the strengths of the region, it can create a win–win situation if the strengths of the region are represented either on the board, or on the advisory board, and the tenants have access to this expertise. It can create investment opportunities, supplier contracts, product definition, access to finance, etc.

I believe the main help an incubator/innovation centre offers is the screening process in the first place, the asking of 'difficult questions' that make the founders stop and think, such as:

- How do you measure your costs?
- What do you include in your direct costs?
- How will you protect your know-how/IP?
- What's to stop someone bypassing the patent? Reverse engineering?
- Where do you want to be in five years time? In 10 years time?
- How are you planning to get there?
- How are you motivating your staff? Getting them to work as a team? Increase performance?
- How are they linked to the bottom line?

In spite of all of the above, innovative enterprises will still often fail, and below are the typical reasons why.

Reasons for failure

Management team

Especially for technology start-ups, new enterprises often fail due to the fact that the inventor/founder manages the company, without having the requisite business acumen to do so or the nous to realize that they should be the CTO and not the CEO.

Founders

Partnerships can go sour (spouses, friends, family). Divorce of one of the founders, leading to financial stress on that partner, and psychological upset; illness or death of a key founder (especially in the first two years of start-up) can have a devastating impact.

A problem that needs solving (market pull, not push)

Inventors often invent products that don't actually solve a problem that needs solving and then try to convince the market that there is a need for the solution, often at a cost that is a non-starter. BBC's popular *Dragons' Den* provides lots of examples of this. To be honest, this is a sub-set of the management team not being savvy or doing its homework at the outset. The best way around this is to work with a potential client/ clients and to ask them to alpha and beta test the product, getting them to help/input into the product definition.

Technology

All too often, products are either over-engineered to death and late to market with functions that most of the end users wouldn't use, or they aren't debugged enough in the local market before being commercialized. An illustrious example of this occurred when rapid prototypers entered the market in the early 1990s. Two main types of technologies led to six companies all coming out with their products at the same time. One of these was an Israeli company that shipped out its product to several clients in various parts of the United States, only to find that soon after problems arose and technical service teams had to be flown out to the clients for several days and sometimes weeks, working remotely, to solve the problems. The prohibitive costs of flights, hotels, shipping parts and time away of the employees almost caused the company to go into administration.

Patents and freedom to operate

Having a patent doesn't necessarily mean one has the freedom to operate if the patent is thought to infringe other patents. Should a large company decide that the start-up is infringing its patent and the court rules that the start-up cannot operate until the outcome of the case is determined, a start-up could fold during the process if it doesn't have the finances to fight the case.

Finance

Rule of thumb – entrepreneurs take at least twice as long to get to market as they think they will and need twice as much funding as their worst case scenario. Hence typically entrepreneurs raise around 25 per cent of the funding they actually require and cause too many funding rounds due to their naiveté – this then leads to first round investors and founders becoming so diluted that they sometimes lose incentive.

If all else fails, blame the incubator

When it all does go pear-shaped, a company may look to shed responsibility and point the finger. This is unfortunate but some start-ups will blame the incubator for not doing more for them. Sometimes there's truth in this when the incubator crosses the line and gets too heavily involved and takes over the management. Ultimately, it's up to the company to make it work – use the incubator and milk it for all its worth and is willing to nourish, but don't lose sight of the fact that the company needs to be independent from day one and is responsible for its success or failure. No one else can assume that responsibility. The worst thing a client can do is let the incubator take over. That is the beginning of the end in 99 per cent of cases.

In short: the better incubators and innovation centres are not just buildings, they are business support centres. A start-up or SME would be well advised to use their services as they would stand a better chance of survival and growth – but don't rely on them to do the work for you.

About the author

Born in Britain, Lesley Anne Rubenstein has spent most of her life in Israel, receiving her Masters in medical sciences at Ben Gurion University of the Negev (BGU) in Beer-Sheva, Israel, and her Masters in management from the joint programme of Boston University and BGU. Prior to her academic studies, Lesley served in the Israel Air Force as an electronics technician. She was one of the first women to serve in this role.

Together with a steering committee, she established the Initiative Center of the Negev (now known as Maayan Ventures PLC), a high-tech business incubator for start-up companies, in 1989, in Beer-Sheva. She managed it for 14 years, and took it from being a not-for-profit organization into that of a privately owned for-profit company, raising $2.24 million to do so. She arrived back in Britain in January 2004 to take on the post of the first Hub Director for the Canterbury Enterprise Hub, one of SEEDA's (South East England Development Agency) hubs, located at, and supported by, the University of Kent. She joined the Thames Innovation Centre Ltd in November 2006. Further details: www.thamesinnovationcentre.com.

Find the right channels to market

It is incredibly easy to fall into the trap of assuming that the traditional supply channel for a given product or service is the one that should be followed, says James Sweet, Commercial Director at C4Ci.

This chapter discusses the importance of choosing the most appropriate supply channel when bringing new products, processes or services to market.

So, you have invented or innovated, you have tested, tweaked and improved the concept, you may have had peers pick and poke at your idea, probably spent a fair sum of money and now finally you are sure that you have a product that works, that is needed and that there is a demand for. While this is a good start, remember it is merely part of the journey towards your product becoming a success in the marketplace. The reality is that your product will only be successful if those who want it can get it at a price they are willing to pay and in a manner they are prepared to receive it, on a consistent and predictable basis, time after time. This is why you need to give careful consideration to the selection of your supply channel – without which the best product in the world will fail to achieve the success it deserves.

We live in changing times ...

So what exactly is changing and how should the innovator respond?

First, ignore for the time being what you assume to be the traditional route. I would reference two great books that expand on this actuality, *The World is Flat* by Thomas

L Friedman and the *Long Tail* by Chris Anderson. It is incredibly easy to fall into the trap of assuming or accepting that the traditional supply channel for a given product or service is the one that should be followed; don't completely rule it out but be sure to investigate other options as real alternatives. Indeed, not using the conventional channels may ultimately prove to be an innovation in itself, allowing conventional products or services to be delivered in a new way. In addition, assess and define your target market; what it is being influenced by now or likely to be in the future, and understand how the market is viewed by its customers.

Finally, establish all the principal parameters and in particular the 'deal breakers', and clearly understand what might be demanded of you throughout the process in terms of service, corporate social responsibility, and similar big picture issues, including:

■ environmental – energy use, sustainability and the climate change agenda;
■ waste disposal – packaging and material disposal/collection;
■ regulatory conformance – third-party accreditation;
■ health and safety;
■ citizenship.

Once this initial analysis is complete it is necessary to evaluate the responsibility chain that exists in getting the innovation through the chosen channel. Is your business expected to handle or contribute to the above in any way? What costs, penalties or exclusions may be imposed upon you for non-conformance? Can your competitors tick these boxes? Do you have any unique advantages that can be leveraged? And lastly, will the supply channel partner(s) that you pick support and *complement* you with regard to these issues? They should apply equally to their business too.

Tip 1

Acknowledge, that the rulebook is changing and that there are drivers beyond simply 'make it and ship it' that have an impact on your offering. Find a complementary partner.

'Start with the end in mind' *Seven Habits of Highly Effective People* by Stephen Covey: research and more research:

■ Who and how does each constituent in the process, from manufacture to responsibility for disposal, interact with the product?
■ Understand that your customer may not be the company that you invoice directly and that you may be able to provide a service further up the supply chain that improves the flow of product through the remainder of the channel, thereby changing the service needs (value add) thereafter – and possibly even changing the channel itself. Always try to define what the ultimate customer needs and work backwards from that end point. The more real value you can add the more you can charge!
■ What is your offering – does it come as a package or can it be segmented and delivered through different channels? It is vitally important to assess the impact

it has from manufacture through to disposal. Concentrate upon what you are intending to deliver and what the target customer wants or needs to receive and, most importantly, *how it needs to be received.* From our experience at C4Ci, it is amazing to see how clients will forgo the bows and ribbons when you tell them how much they cost! Start by giving the customers what they need and then charge for any benefit that has a real added value to the clients. The principles surrounding Six Sigma are a great place to start – engage the target customer and in the nicest possible way, interrogate what he or she does with it when it is received.

Tip 2

Adopt cradle to grave thinking and clearly understand where the value and important interactions exist in the supply chain and what can be done early in the supply chain to add value later.

'Know your friends but know your customers better' *Customer, Competition, Peers and Agents.*

■ More (or less) sophistication? There is far greater understanding of supply channel as a result of industries bringing in supply channel experts or managers from other industries. These individuals have a broader perspective and do not carry the baggage that others may have who have only ever seen one channel. One word of caution however: they may often not see or appreciate the nuances, quirks and relationships of a particular industry, so factor in some existing market experience also.
■ Within your industry, who sets the benchmark – who has got it right?
■ Who appears to be driving innovation end to end?
■ What supply channel(s) do your competitors use?
■ How effective are these channels and what challenges do your competitors face?
■ Are any of your competitors innovating in the supply chain and have they been successful?
■ If the customer demands exclusive rights or their own branding , assess very carefully.

Tip 3

Know how your industry works intimately and research how other industries operate. Keep an open mind to alternative ideas.

Tip 4

Fully assess whether the supply route or channel partner you pick can expand with you, or whether they preclude other opportunities elsewhere.

Tip 5

Agents – check out the legal and financial implications of removing them from the channel at a later stage.

Tip 6

Exclusivity and third-party branding are a high price to pay if the opportunity is bigger than these particular customers can realize for you – so don't give this away too quickly or at all.

Getting it there – not as easy as you might think:

■ Identify with whom and how you are going to provide the delivery in full, on time, to specification, to the final customer.
■ Would the innovation benefit from' bundling' with complementary products to improve transport efficiency or would this be too complicated?
■ Some key elements that influence steps in the supply chain:
  – export markets: import duties, trade tariffs;
  – waste handling and restitution: what it arrives in or on;
  – product handling, eg container unloading, physical location and suitability of premises, expertise;
  – health and safety;
  – JIT delivery;
  – stock holding safety-net back-up: in case of emergency or force majeure;
  – inventory management, product tracking, bar coding;
  – environmental;
  – bundling of complementary products;
  – payment terms between partners in the channel.

Tip 7

Fully analyse the options available for movement of innovative products along the supply chain. Write the alternatives down, and evaluate the advantages and dis-advantages of each.

Tip 8

Constantly test the whole process with simple questions. Can I deliver and service it myself? Do I want to? Do I have the expertise? What do my chosen partners bring? What will they cost? What will the cost be of not having them? What *value* do they bring?

Tip 9

Leave difficult and skilled service functions to trusted experts and consultants – don't stray too far away from your comfort zone or expertise.

Looking to the future:

■ What are the future influences or drivers that may be imposed upon each constituent in the supply chain from outside sources (government procurement, technology, location, legislation, competition law)?

- Is the supply channel partner or structure robust enough to see you through the products evolution or is it an expedient for entry?
- How will you manage transition from latter to former when the time comes?
- What impact could internet trading have and could you use it to your advantage?
- Is your place of manufacture appropriate to your target marketplace?

Tip 10

Where or how do you see your product developing? Try to ensure that you are selecting a supply channel that will evolve with you and the market.

Summary

There are arguments for short supply chains (quicker, simpler, less potential for price escalation, fewer people to get it wrong, etc) and for longer supply chains (more specialist expertise, greater sales networking, less responsibility on any one party, etc). Make your decision by constant reference to what the customer needs, how it needs to be received, whether you can provide it, and if not who else you need to help. Every constituent that interacts with your product must add a value that either you cannot or do not want to do. If it doesn't, remove it!

Final tip

Innovation is born out of improving a product or service that already exists in the market; this comes as a result of knowing intimately the market and the current product offerings. Employing the same innovative creativity in terms of how the product gets to the customer will enable you to offer more than just an innovative product – it will become an innovative package, significantly increasing the value it had as a standalone entity.

References

Anderson, C (2007) *The Long Tail,* Random House Business Books, London
Covey, S R (1999) *The Seven Habits of Highly Effective People,* Simon and Schuster, London
Friedman, T L (2006) *The World is Flat,* Penguin, London

About the author

James Sweet is a director and founding shareholder of C4Ci (Consultants for Construction Innovation) a multidisciplinary consultancy practice specializing in bringing innovation to the construction industry. He has extensive commercial experience in the construction products industry, and is now responsible for business development within C4Ci across all markets. Tel: +44 (0)7798 676610; e-mail: james.sweet@c4ci.eu.

Licensing

In commercializing innovation, licensing can be a highly effective model, says Dominic Elsworth at Hargreaves Elsworth.

While few businesses stop to consider how the licensing of technology might bring new opportunities, most could in fact benefit from licensing technology.

So why license? The answer ought to be simple: to provide opportunities to earn money, whether licensing-out technology to others or licensing-in technology to gain access to it.

Licensing-in technology

There can be no getting away from the fact that research and development is expensive, in terms of facilities, technical staff and management time. Furthermore, years of research and development may not produce any marketable product. For many organizations resources must be devoted elsewhere. Nevertheless, every organization must look for new opportunities, be they to maintain a competitive edge in an area in a market sector in which the organization already operates, or to enter a new market sector where it simply does not have the relevant technical expertise. One answer is to allow others to bear the risk of research and development of the technology required, to seek them out, and enter into licence agreements with them to exploit the technology required.

The benefits of licensing are numerous. First, the uncertainty and expense of research and develop is avoided. Second, the licensed technology would typically be protected by some form of intellectual property right, giving the owner a monopoly in the technology of limited duration. The licensee gains the benefit of the monopoly.

Third, the licensee may well be able to negotiate this access to technology in return for the payment of a royalty on a sale. Hence, if the technology does not sell, there is little liability.

How do you find what you want to license?

A very cost-effective way to find out who has developed what technology is simply to conduct a patent search in the area of technology under consideration. Whether the technology is in use can quickly be established.

While awareness of intellectual property rights in many organizations is perhaps not what it might be, it is possible to raise awareness within even the smallest SME without great expense and devotion of management time. A regular search of patents and design registrations will soon build up a library of information on potential sources of technology (and also competitors). Another way to license-in technology is to talk to technology transfer offices of universities and other research institutions.

Common pitfalls for the licensee

■ Can the technology do what is promised of it, or is it actually going to need considerable resources to bring it to the stage of a saleable product? A prospective licensee ought to be able to assess and satisfy itself of this during the due diligence stage of negotiations.
■ Is the licensee going to be dependent on the licensor, for example for technical support? If so, what commitments can be obtained from the licensor to guarantee provision of such support?
■ What about further development of the technology? Might the licensor sell it to another party? At what price might it be available?
■ You are buying into someone else's monopoly. Does the monopoly exist? What will the position be if that monopoly is challenged?
■ Are you building your own business, or someone else's?
■ Might you be entering into an agreement that is in breach of competition laws?

All these issues can and should be addressed in a Licence Agreement.

Licensing technology out

The licensing-out of technology is an option open and useful to many more organizations than one might imagine. Yes, there are research organizations such as universities that have fantastic research facilities, but no capability beyond that in terms of bringing technology to the marketplace, and with no desire to develop such capabilities.

However, licensing technology can be used in many imaginative ways. For example, instead of seeking to build export markets and service them from a home base, why not seek out an organization in the target territory and license the technology to that organization for a particular territory or group of territories that the potential licensee can service? This strategy can allow a very wide market for technology to be built with little requirement for capital. It is also very useful where products are by their nature cheap to manufacture but expensive to transport (usually products that include a great deal of air). The licensor may well be able to supply certain key elements of the technology to the licensee.

One of the problems with licensing technology out is that the intellectual property right licensed may be of limited duration, for example 20 years for a patent. So, where the technology has a very long life potential, one may unwittingly give away markets. This can be protected against by the use of trade mark registrations and licensing the technology such that it must be marked with a particular trade mark. While a patent may expire after 20 years, a trade mark may be maintained indefinitely, as long as renewal fees are paid. The patent may expire, but the reputation built in the technology is associated with the trade mark. So, either the licensee will still need a licence, or if the licensor does not wish to continue with the agreement after expiration of the patent, the licensee may enter the market itself, or through another licensee, using the trade mark in which the reputation has been built.

In the same way that licensing may be used to develop overseas markets, the same principles may be applied to using licensing to develop markets for technology that has utility across a number of fields of use. The licensor's interests may lie in one particular field, but by licensing the technology to another party in a different field, a valuable income stream may be obtained.

Common pitfalls for the licensor

- What if the licensee does not devote sufficient resources or effort to the promotion of the licensed technology? Will it just sit on the shelf?
- Can the licensee deliver what it says?
- Is the licensee interested in a long-term relationship and open to licensing further developments of the technology, or is it just using licensing as a means of spring-boarding into a market?
- What happens when the Licence Agreement terminates?

Again, such issues can and should be addressed in a Licence Agreement.

The Licence Agreement

Both licensors and licensees may avoid difficulties by paying attention to the agreement that they reach. The negotiation of such agreements is often a very long-winded affair, but those negotiating the agreement should not lose sight of the fact that their business may depend on it, and while all parties may get on well at the time of entering the agreement, 10 years down the line the people involved may have changed completely.

For busy executives the two most important considerations should be: what do I want to happen and what do I not want to happen? Ultimately, to reach an agreement it is likely that compromise will have to be made on some points. However, don't make a compromise to do a deal if in fact it is a compromise too far. The result will be a dispute somewhere down the line.

About the author

Hargreaves Elsworth is a patent attorneys practice established in Newcastle upon Tyne in January 2002 by its founder, Dominic Elsworth, a registered patent agent, trade mark agent, European patent attorney and European trade mark attorney.

The ethos of the practice is to bring to its clients a service of the highest quality, tailored to specific business requirements, at a reasonable cost. The practice provides both UK and international clients with advice and support services in all areas of intellectual property law, and in particular patents, trade marks, designs and copyright, know-how, and technology transfer. Further details: www.heip.co.uk.

Competing globally

Peter Bawden at Bawden & Associates discusses how to manage time and costs in building a global IP position.

There is not a product that does not rely on creativity, and the success of many products around the world has relied on good intellectual property (IP) whether it is patent protection, trade mark registration, design protection or copyright. Equally, many products have floundered due to inadequate attention to the associated IP.

IP and its effective generation, protection, exploitation and management throughout the world are therefore often the life blood of an enterprise and a key corporate asset. One person's right is nonetheless another's restriction and the threat of competitive IP may present a looming spectre ready to erode business value.

Active management of opportunities in creating and developing an IP portfolio to support a business, and identifying, assessing and acting to minimize the risks presented by competitor IP is crucial. Whether the organization is a start-up, a small enterprise, an academic institution, a medium-size company or a large multinational, and whatever the industry, awareness of the criticality of IP has never been greater. Increased general awareness of the impact of IP on business, global trade and strong emerging competitive economies in Europe, Asia and the Americas have all heightened the importance of IP and its protection.

But, an appreciation of the importance of IP in generating value or avoiding value erosion due to the impact of competitive IP is only a starting point. There are activities such as research, development, marketing, manufacturing, sales, personnel and the other essential planks of a business that all require funding, attention and a strategic approach. Thus, heightened awareness or sensitivity to IP, how to manage and fund it, must be viewed in this broader business context.

The effect of not paying appropriate attention to IP may, however, be dramatic. Failure to secure optimum IP protection runs the risk of ineffective or incomplete protection for markets, enabling technology and next stage developments; unnecessary costs in maintaining ineffective rights; lost enforcement opportunities and competitor product encroachment; brand dilution and general erosion in what could have been a powerful business asset. Unless properly understood and managed effectively, competitor rights may similarly have a direct impact on business performance, through exclusion from a product or geographical market, payment of licence fees, threats to plant operation and sales, inferior products through the need to design around competitive IP, curtailment of freedom in research and development affecting next generation technology, and customer leverage on pricing. Failure to understand and manage IP effectively runs the risk of directly affecting business performance in the same way.

Effective management of IP is paramount in generating a global portfolio of real value in a timely manner and reducing serious risks to a business. This requires IP to be understood throughout an organization and viewed as a top-tier strategic priority, and for the approach to managing it to form a part of the cultural identity or make-up of the business. How can this be achieved?

The global portfolio development

IP may deliver value only through supporting the key objectives of the business. Viewed another way, the business objectives, medium and long term, define the goals for and so determine the IP strategy. In seeking to achieve this, key aspects of the technology supporting today's and future business must be adequately protected at the optimum time, and protection of pipeline developments secured through continued active management. The IP must be developed to protect not only one's own business and research and technology strategy but also those of competitors around the world. The identification of competitive threats at an early stage, coupled with effective

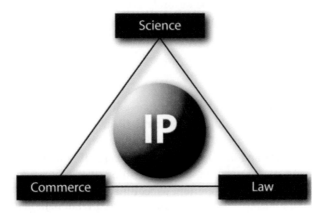

Figure 8.5.1   Integrated to create strategic value

planning and action to sweep the planned business and research path clean, is equally important. An awareness of the differing global legal systems, practices and law is also essential so as to be best able to utilize local circumstances to advantage. It is the integration of these factors that enhances the opportunity to create value through IP.

The nature of the portfolio

Business objectives may differ widely, depending on many factors including the nature of a business, its maturity, position in the global market, scale, financial health and the like. Unless these objectives are supported by appropriate scope of protection, filing strategy and ensuring resilience to attack in preparing and in developing a global patent position, full value will not be realized. As a business grows, the patent position upon which it is based ideally evolves in parallel to reflect the developing business position. This may be achieved through integration of the IP professionals with the developing business and the associated technology generation, and through informed portfolio development in the patent offices around the world to establish a robust relevant patent position, and follow-on filings. It should also reflect developing research, development and market opportunities while shadowing the evolving competitive business.

The IP position supports a business; it is therefore important to identify opportunities for IP protection afforded from the business point of view within the bounds of the legal framework, rather than decisions being lead by narrow legal considerations. This ensures the IP position grows with the business and supports the business objectives rather than developing a life of its own, as often seems to happen. IP portfolio management has more to do with shaping an IP position in an appropriate manner to protect the short- and long-term global business positions and how best to optimize the protection around the world rather than the mechanics of administration of the IP position.

For smaller enterprises, particularly at an early stage in their life, there may be one or a few key enabling technologies that underpin the business. Growth and indeed the viability of the company may be severely compromised by failure to adequately protect such key technologies, undermining the foundation of the company and the platform for future development.

Resource needs

Developing and implementing a global IP strategy involves management of a number of factors and ongoing stewardship to ensure the IP strategy maps to and evolves with the developing business position. Bringing together the right mix of skills, experience, resources, systems and management processes for IP allows the integration and effective harnessing of the professional capabilities of the IP practitioner with the business and its objectives. An important aspect includes nurturing an understanding of the effects of IP in business and technology leaders so that managing IP becomes a part of the fabric of an organization rather than an expensive or unwanted diversion.

The IP policy may vary according to the nature of an organization and its business. For example, technical leaders will have a different IP policy from technical followers. National organizations will have a different policy from international organizations.

Cost-effectiveness

Patenting is not cheap, but the required expenditure can be budgeted and controlled with effective management. Funds may be scarce in the early life of a company and unless IP is viewed in the same strategic sense as other matters, the IP position may be overlooked in favour of other funding priorities, potentially causing impairment of a cornerstone asset. Also, funding of an IP position in an early stage may represent proportionately a much higher investment than for a mature company and this may act to constrain IP activities. However, it is essential to ensure that the appropriate IP is put in place and fully protects the strategic interests.

The IP position of a technology company often plays a central role in determining whether funding may be provided by investors and is subject to scrutiny through due diligence. Adequate investment in adopting a strategic approach to offensive and defensive IP at the outset is therefore essential to the long-term health or survival of a new company, and also potentially to securing further investment. Understanding the cost implications of this activity and budgeting accordingly while understanding the implications of not adopting a strategic approach to IP form a key part of effective business management.

Costs can be managed by good decision making at key stages in the life of a patent, including an understanding of the cost implications of each decision. Typically decisions involve whether to file, where to file and where to maintain patents. These decisions should be based on the value of the business being protected, the scope of patent protection available and the costs involved. Systems such as the Patent Co-Operation Treaty and Regional Patent Systems such as European Patent Systems enable costs to be staged and managed in parallel with business portfolio development.

Identifying the opportunities

Opportunities for valuable IP protection can be missed, but the risk can be reduced by effective integration of IP activities with business and research programmes such that offensive and defensive decisions are informed and are taken at an optimum time. A delay in patent filing can lead to a lost opportunity and competitive problems, whereas a delay in understanding a competitive portfolio can result in the inability to use the results of expensive research and development. Linking research funding and IP development can be useful.

As candidate technologies for commercialization emerge, it is imperative that those technologies are assessed with a view to securing IP protection. A decision as to whether, and if so which, technologies to protect requires an awareness of the research strategy and business goals. It allows IP resources to be targeted to those options of potential interest and value to the business. While the research and development function may identify candidate technologies, the IP professional is best placed to identify opportunities for patenting those technologies and to develop and secure protection of optimum scope to match business needs. To ensure that opportunities are not overlooked, 'invention mining' may be used as a collaborative, ongoing process between the IP professional and the research and development function.

In assessing inventions and opportunities for useful patenting, an awareness of prior activity in the field is essential. This provides a window on the activities of competitors and how the patenting activity may best be shaped to have maximum impact. An organization needs to have the background information to properly assess and scope opportunities to develop IP of value and to provide a warning of possible competitive patent threats.

As the candidate technologies develop, it is essential to assess them against competitor patent rights. A study to determine risks of infringement is different from a study to assess patentability of new technology. An infringement study requires an assessment of the scope of protection covered by the competition in the global markets of interest, whereas a patentability study involves assessing the technical content of global publications of any sort against the new technology. By selecting the appropriate time for the infringement review, the technologies may be sufficiently developed and few in number to allow a meaningful comparison with the competitor patent position, yet still sufficiently early in the development process so as not to incur wasted effort and expense in running into third-party patent obstacles.

In addition, as patent law and practice in gaining and enforcing protection vary widely around the world, an appreciation of the markets allows the IP professional to advise as to opportunities that may arise in some markets or be denied in others. In shaping a patent portfolio in this way through close involvement with the business objectives, the value of the protection sought may be enhanced.

As candidate technologies are filtered, review of IP for discarded or lower priority options and pruning a portfolio accordingly provides a means of focusing IP expenditure on those areas of value. Fees must be paid to maintain IP through its lifetime and consideration should be given to retaining IP in areas that might be of interest to competitors, as leverage may provide opportunities for licence revenue or cross-licensing, or to prevent competitors utilizing similar technologies embodying the technical benefits derived from your research activities.

Summary

Through informed management, IP of value may be developed in an interactive and timely way. Integrated with science and the business interests, resources may be focused on those areas of genuine commercial interest, minimized in protecting areas of low interest, and employed in identifying risks at an appropriate time in the innovation process to avoid wasting funds in development areas fraught with difficulties.

About the author

Bawden & Associates provides management consultancy advice to corporate management and provides professional services on global intellectual property issues including patents, trade marks and copyright, as well as technology transfer, licensing and the protection of confidential information. Particular expertise lies in the strategic approach to the identification and development of intellectual property, to generate assets and use of real commercial value. Peter Bawden is the owner and is a chartered patent agent and European patent attorney, as is his partner Stephen Geary. Peter previously held overall management responsibility for the global IP activities of Exxon Chemical Company and Stephen held senior positions in ICI and Unilever. The company's activities include the development and exploitation of IP portfolios around the world, offensive and defensive patent office and court activities and the coordination of contentious issues such as oppositions and litigation in Europe, the Americas and Asia. Peter may be contacted on +44 (0)1582 466702 or by e-mail: pb@bawden.co.uk. Bawden & Associates website: www.bawden.co.uk.

Freedom to operate

Is your idea going to launch into a clear landscape, or is there a danger of infringing someone else's rights? William Bird, a European, British and Germanpatent attorney at Bird Goën & Co, reports.

FTO or 'freedom to operate' refers to determining whether a commercial action, such as licensing, testing or commercializing a product or process, can be done without infringing the valid intellectual property rights of others. Business transactions where FTO can be of importance include mergers, acquisitions, financing of new companies or projects, joint ventures, spin-offs, licensing, and buying or selling goods or services. Establishing FTO is becoming more difficult simply because patent application filings and issued patents have increased in recent years.

It can be important to have an FTO analysis to present to a potential investor when assessing a company's products and patent portfolio, eg in helping to reassure investors that the marketing of the intended products will not be challenged by third parties. Hence, an FTO analysis is often part of a due diligence evaluation.

Investment analysts are often as interested, or more interested, in a company that has FTO than one that has a patent portfolio able to control copying. Competition can mean a technology or price war – an injunction can mean a total stop. If a new company has FTO, then this can be a significant advantage that permits the company to move forward.

The FTO search and analysis

The aim of FTO analysis is product or process clearance, ie to proactively identify patents that might prevent, delay or hinder exploitation. This can reduce the risk of

later patent problems. However, the FTO search can never guarantee that there is a clear path to market products or implement processes: it is necessarily limited by the effectiveness of the search. Also, a patent application remains secret for 18 months after filing – hence not all of the potentially relevant applications can be searched at any one time.

Since IP rights are specific to different nations or geographical regions, an FTO analysis should include all countries or regions where the commercial action is to be carried out.

If a patent application or patent is found in a database that seems to relate to FTO, you can't immediately conclude that there is a problem. There are a variety of reasons why a patent right might not be relevant. That is, there are *defences* against patent infringement. These defences may vary in the likelihood of success, ie on how reliable they may be. For present purposes, the actual success rate of each defence is not so important – what matters is that there is a significant *chance of failure with any defence*. So, a freedom to operate analysis is essential if one is to reduce the business risk of patent infringement to acceptable levels.

It is easy to write down the steps of an FTO analysis:

1. search all known patent databases to determine those patents and patent applications that are relevant;
2. analyse each patent or patent application to determine if the intended product or process infringes any claim either directly, by equivalence, or in a contributory way;
3. if a claim is found that is infringed, determine whether that claim is valid;
4. if valid and infringed, take appropriate action (see later).

However, FTO analysis is easier said than done. An FTO can only be based safely on an accurate technical description of the product or process. This may not be available at the time the FTO analysis is to be performed. In fact, one object of the FTO analysis can be to define which product and/or process is the safest one to implement.

Analysis of this kind is likely to be expensive. For example, the cost of the search can vary a great deal. The UK Intellectual Property Office quotes about £1,500 to £3,000 plus VAT per item searched for most technologies. For searching certain areas of technology, eg an organic chemistry structural search, £3,000 to £6,000 plus VAT is quoted. A single search is often not enough – multiple search strategies, and possibly multiple searchers, databases, or searching facilities may be required. By performing an FTO analysis, the risk of infringement can be minimized (even if not eliminated) and, consequently, it can potentially save a significant amount of time and money later on. It has been reported that an FTO can cost between $20,000 to $100,000 to conduct. Compared to the legal costs for patent litigation, damage to a company's reputation and/or forced withdrawal of the technology from the marketplace, the cost of an FTO analysis can be relatively small.

All aspects of the product or process need to be considered and searched. When searching for patents, one uses keywords that hopefully catch all potentially relevant documents. By using such broad terms one usually gets a lot of 'noise' – patents that are clearly not relevant or are only marginally relevant. All these patents must be excluded by careful study. Highly relevant patents are typically analysed in separate non-infringement opinions. The prosecution file histories and prior art of record should be obtained and analysed. A patent attorney usually analyses the relevant patent rights and also assesses how the issued claims are to be construed and whether or not the issued claims might be invalid, for example by additional searching. A separate non-infringement analysis needs to be done for each independent claim in each patent. For such patents it is often useful to investigate whether the patent has survived an opposition or has been litigated. Patents that have survived a challenge are much more powerful. Also, during litigation, patent claims may be construed by a court. This may help in determining the claim scope. Both direct infringement and infringement by any relevant doctrine of equivalents as well as contributory infringement need to be considered.

Invalidity analysis typically involves first construing the claims, then reading the claims on the prior art to determine whether the claims are valid. Sometimes, questions of non-infringement and invalidity are inextricably intertwined. For instance, sometimes a patent claim can be reasonably interpreted in two different ways, for example a first broad interpretation that would render the claim invalid as failing to distinguish over the prior art, and a second narrow interpretation that preserves the claim's validity, but fails to read on the accused product.

Once generated, an FTO opinion has to be updated to cover changing business circumstances. For example, the product design changes may alter FTO. Moreover, new patents may issue, and new patent applications may be published. The business strategy may change, thereby rendering the analysis of an earlier opinion invalid.

What to do if there are blocking third-party rights

If there are valid and blocking patents of others, several options are available. A first option is to license-in the technology. The license may be limited to certain activities, in certain markets and for a specified period of time. The convenience of such an agreement will depend largely on the terms and conditions of the proposed licence. Despite the fact that the patent holder will probably require a lump sum and/or periodic royalty payments, it may be the simplest way of obtaining clearance. Sometimes a patent pool is available or a clearing house for patent rights. If a licence is refused a compulsory licence may be requested in some countries. If one wishes to investigate the legal position abroad, competent foreign patent counsel should be engaged to report separately on FTO in foreign countries.

A second option is cross-licensing. Cross-licensing requires a patent portfolio that is valuable to potential licensing partners. A third alternative is to attack the validity of the patent, eg in an opposition or nullity proceedings before a court. Such a procedure usually takes several years, is of uncertain outcome and is usually too slow to be in time for marketing. One can also consider filing for a declaration of non-infringement at a court.

A fourth alternative is to invent around the invention. This implies making changes to the product or process in order to avoid infringing on the third-party patents.

A more extreme solution is purchasing the patent or the patent owner's company. Buying the patent, buying out the patent owner or negotiating for a licence is often time-consuming and costly. In licensing, the most commonly reported problem is that licensing negotiations are overly complex. The time taken to negotiate a licence can be several months, often six months or more. The most common effect of difficulties in licence negotiations is that projects get changed. A particularly difficult problem occurs when licences for many valid patents need to be obtained from many different parties.

If a company does not have FTO, and is thus subject to one or more third-party patents, then the question becomes how to get access to third-party intellectual property without incurring heavy upfront fees or reducing profit by paying royalty fees. One solution is collaboration or some other type of sharing arrangement, where access to third-party intellectual property is part of the deal.

In the case of blocking process patents, it is possible to move the manufacturing offshore where blocking patents do not exist, until these patents have expired. However, many patent laws protect not only processes but also the direct product of such processes. So even though a process may be safely executed in a non-patent country, the import of the resulting product into a country where patent rights exist may still be patent infringement.

A few examples

Golden Rice is a well-known example. Potrykus succeeded in genetically enriching rice grains with beta-carotene, the precursor to vitamin A. However, an FTO survey uncovered 70 patents belonging to 32 different organizations. Let us imagine that 32 different licence agreements were then required to guarantee FTO and let us assume that we want a 90 per cent chance of having that freedom. This means that the probability of obtaining each licence must be about 99.7 per cent certain if the cumulative probability is not to drop below 90 per cent – ie we must be almost 100 per cent certain of obtaining each licence otherwise the project will fail. Looked at in this way, an FTO can change its direction from the searching of patent databases to a search for reliable and safe licensors.

In terms of numbers of licences, the Golden Rice case is a simple one compared to commercializing more ambitious projects, such as those in telecommunications. Determining essentiality of patents for a patent pool is just like an FTO analysis. As an example, the MPEG-LA patent pool – to license just a part of image processing involving the MPEG2 standard – includes more than 700 patents. Selection of these patents involved analysing over 8,000 patents. The determination was a laborious manual process entailing hundreds of hours of highly priced attorney time. If the patent pool did not exist, each company offering MPEG2 would have to perform the same FTO as was performed by MPEG-LA – and negotiate all the bilateral licences as well!

Three pharmaceutical companies, Cambridge Antibody Technology, Micromet AG and Enzon Pharmaceuticals announced in 2003 a non-exclusive cross-licence agreement. In the agreement, all three parties were said to obtain substantial FTO by authorizing each other to use some of their respective patented technology. Agreements of this kind have become more common in some sectors, as companies seek to ensure that their products, processes and services do not infringe on the patent rights of others. However, horizontal agreements between competitors may be subject to unfair competition law, especially if they pool patents and create a barrier to market entry.

Some practicalities of FTO analysis

As FTO is costly, it is necessary to prioritize which projects will be considered and also to determine the best time to execute the FTO.

Ideally, a company should have a clear idea of the product or process that is going to be implemented, but this is rarely the case. For some development projects a good time to execute the FTO would be at the start of the project, ie prior to a lot of investment. Conducting FTO early provides an opportunity to design-around if necessary. Also, by starting early, time is probably still available to explore other solutions if a design-around fails, eg challenging the validity of the patents, or obtaining licences.

However, starting early can also result in wasted time and effort, for example if the project is still too vague as to its likely outcome. Ideally, it is advisable to have a clear picture of what the product is likely to be. Therefore, one can invest a percentage, eg 40 per cent of the total R&D budget, or wait until 40 per cent of the forecast project time has elapsed, before requesting an FTO. This should result in a more accurate and realistic FTO.

FTO can also be a long-term project. An ideal situation is always to be ahead of any third-party patents, ie to have a history of product sales, patent filings and technical publications that prevent third parties from gaining a proprietary position over your own products and/or processes. It has been reported that on average about 35 per cent of a patent portfolio is designed to maintain FTO compared to about 47 per cent used to protect current products from imitation.

It's all about elbow room – capture a piece of technology turf and then hang on to it.

About the author

William E Bird is a founder partner of the IP law firm Bird Goën & Co. During the last 20 years he has worked as both a corporate and a private practice patent and trade mark attorney in Germany and Belgium. He has expertise in both common law and codified legal systems, in IP law, technology transfer, IP licensing and setting up of spin-off companies. He is a European, British and German patent and trade mark attorney, a tutor at CEIPI and a lecturer at the Vlerick School of Management. Further details: www.birdgoen.com.

Index of advertisers